Regulatory Bargaining and Public Law

In *Regulatory Bargaining and Public Law*, Professor Rossi explores the implications of a bargaining perspective for institutional governance and public law in deregulated industries such as electric power and telecommunications. Leading media accounts blame deregulated markets for failures in competitive restructuring policies. However, the author argues that governmental institutions, often influenced by private stakeholders, share blame for the defects in deregulated markets. The first part of the book explores the minimal role that judicial intervention played for much of the twentieth century in public utility industries and how deregulation presents new opportunities and challenges for public law. The second part of the book explores the role of public law in a deregulatory environment, focusing on the positive and negative incentives it creates for the behavior of private stakeholders and public institutions in a bargaining-focused political process. *Regulatory Bargaining and Public Law* presents a unified set of default rules to guide courts in the United States and elsewhere as they address the complex issues that will come before them in a deregulatory environment.

Jim Rossi is the Harry M. Walborsky Professor and Associate Dean for Research at Florida State University College of Law. He holds an LL.M. from Yale Law School, a J.D. from the University of Iowa College of Law, and a B.A. in economics from Arizona State University. He has served as a faculty member at the University of North Carolina School of Law, and he has been a visiting faculty member at the University of Texas Law School. A scholar in the fields of administrative and regulatory law, Professor Rossi's publications have appeared in *Virginia Law Review, Michigan Law Review, Duke Law Journal, Texas Law Review, Northwestern University Law Review, Vanderbilt Law Review*, and *Energy Law Journal*, among many other journals. He is co-author of the leading textbook on energy law, *Energy, Economics, and the Environment* (2000).

Regulatory Bargaining and Public Law

JIM ROSSI
Florida State University College of Law

CAMBRIDGE
UNIVERSITY PRESS

CAMBRIDGE UNIVERSITY PRESS
Cambridge, New York, Melbourne, Madrid, Cape Town, Singapore, São Paulo

Cambridge University Press
40 West 20th Street, New York, NY 10011-4211, USA

www.cambridge.org
Information on this title: www.cambridge.org/9780521838924

First published 2005

Printed in the United States of America

A catalog record for this publication is available from the British Library.

Library of Congress Cataloging in Publication Data

Rossi, Jim, 1965–
Regulatory bargaining and public law / Jim Rossi.
p. cm.
Includes bibliographical references and index.
ISBN 0-521-83892-4 (hardcover)
1. Public utilities – Law and legislation – United States. 2. Telecommunication – Law and legislation – United States. 3. Transportation – Law and legislation – United States.
4. Deregulation – United States. I. Title.

ISBN-13 978-0-521-83892-4 hardback
ISBN-10 0-521-83892-4 hardback

Contents

Preface

Theories of economic regulation modulate between optimism – associated with those who view regulators as benignly pursuing the public interest or other civic-minded goals – and pessimism – most commonly associated with the public choice school, which sees regulators as captured by the powerful private firms they are charged to regulate. These accounts of regulation focus mainly on regulation's substance, rather than the process by which it is enacted and its ability to promote stability in government policy for the operation of markets and the decisions of investors. Yet, whatever account is best in the abstract, regulatory law has failed utterly to examine the evolution of regulation and how it interacts with changes in technology, economic conditions, and political preferences. Examining regulation and regulatory law through the lens of bargaining sheds light on the institutional role courts can play, particularly given the new issues that arise in deregulated, or competitively restructured, markets.

Under the regime of natural monopoly regulation, predominant in the twentieth century, public and private interests converged in ways that were often (to the extent the public interest account of regulation is correct), but certainly not always (as public choice reminds us), welfare enhancing. Natural monopoly regulation, which represents a contract of sorts, was plagued with its own problems; however, it provided a relatively stable legal system for more than 50 years. The stability of cost-of-service rate making largely limited renegotiation to the firm-specific rate-making process, working to minimize the incentives for regulated firms to attempt to influence government ex ante (i.e., prior to the formulation of a public decision) outside the regulatory agency. Against this backdrop, traditional doctrines of regulatory law purported to protect investors and consumers. In fact, for most of the twentieth century, courts played a modest role in regulated industries. Courts engaged in judicial review of regulatory agency decisions, but by and large agency decisions were not upset by the judiciary, which routinely deferred to the expertise and political accountability of regulators. Regulators were largely seen as facilitating a convergence between private and public interests, particularly where they regulated only a handful of firms on an ongoing basis.

Deregulation has many benefits. It is often touted for its propensity to allow private and public interests to converge through price mechanisms. At the same time, many criticize deregulation for falling short of this goal. In an electric power market with price competition, for instance, firms may face strong pressures to abandon their traditional service obligations in favor of higher-paying (and hence, more profitable) customers, leading to a divergence between public and private interests in market decisions.

Less examined is how deregulation may present new tensions between public and private interests in the regulatory process and for public law. With deregulation, the firm-specific rate hearing is no longer the norm for the adoption and implementation of deregulatory policies, inviting a much less focused and less predictable type of private influence on the regulatory process. As regulators look to alternative mechanisms for the implementation of deregulatory policies, such as general legislation, rulemaking, and standard tariffs, government potentially shares some blame with private firms for any welfare-reducing divergence between private interests and the public interest. Just as the traditional regulatory process may have responded disproportionately to the strongest interest groups, the process by which deregulatory policies are formulated and implemented may invite policy makers to respond disproportionately to new interest groups, possibly leading to the enactment of economic policies that thwart, rather than enhance, the overall welfare effects of competition. For instance, given the dual-jurisdictional system for regulating electric power in the United States, firms have strategic ways to escape the jurisdiction of state or federal regulators, taking advantage of gaps or jurisdictional overlaps in regulatory enforcement. In contrast, cost-of-service regulation provided ways of coordinating these gaps between regulatory authorities and evaluated firm-specific conduct more carefully – backing this up with enforcement in the setting of the firm's rates – thus minimizing (but certainly not eliminating) the divergence between private and public interests.

In expanding the range and degree of potential divergence between public and private interests, deregulation challenges policy makers and courts to reevaluate many of the traditional public law doctrines that frame the process for defining and implementing the rules in competitive markets. This book sets out to advance this project. In contrast to the predominant accounts of public choice theory and public-interested regulation, the book draws on government relations bargaining as a mechanism for assessing regulatory law. Contract-based approaches to regulation analogize to a legalistic (judicially enforced) contract, drawing primarily on judicial authority to compensate or deter renegotiation by a regulatory agency. In contrast, this book embraces a broader understanding of the regulatory contract as a starting point for its method. Drawing on the literature from the law and economics of corporate governance and contracts, an "incomplete contracts" approach is presented in the institutional setting of economic regulation. This approach isolates incentives and welfare states associated with contract renegotiation. In contrast to legalistic contracts, which emphasize judicial enforcement of contracts, the government relations bargaining approach highlights the insurance implications of regulation and its renegotiation. This approach is supplemented with a comparative institutional analysis, which evaluates the institutional setting for governance of deregulated markets; it does not limit its analysis to the decisions of a single regulator but pays attention to alternative institutions, including courts, the legislature, and state versus federal regulation.

Using a case study of electric power deregulation to draw general lessons, the framework is applied to traditional doctrines of regulatory law, including customer service obligations, the takings clause as a constraint on regulators, the filed tariff doctrine as a mechanism for limiting ex post judicial enforcement, the dormant commerce clause and state action immunity from antitrust enforcement, and regulatory federalism. By isolating ex ante and ex post incentives and stressing the institutional context for renegotiation, the framework reveals weaknesses these traditional doctrines of regulatory law present in a deregulatory era and suggests ways courts might correct for them.

The title of the book – *Regulatory Bargaining and Public Law* – might seem oxymoronic. A bargaining approach implies that government regulation will be replaced with market-based ordering, especially as industries are deregulated, leaving public law irrelevant to the bargaining process. As is well known, though, deregulation is an extreme and somewhat idealized concept. In this sense, "deregulation" is a term that can be criticized on the same grounds as other commonly referenced media terms, such as "serious comic," or loaded political terms, such as "peace-keeping force." Yet, there is a point to simultaneously invoking bargaining in a deregulatory environment and regulatory concepts and theories. As even the most extreme market proponents are aware, deregulated markets rely heavily on regulation for implementation and oversight, especially where network facilities, such as electric power transmission lines, provide the primary means for market access for suppliers and customers. Further, as the book argues, regulatory bargaining entails much more than the negotiation of firm-specific regulation. Contractual relations abound in public law even where private firms are not an immediate party to anything approaching a legal contract. The government relations bargaining approach includes within its scope these relations, as well as more traditional regulatory contracts between the firm and the state. Public law retains relevance in framing these bargaining relations, even when markets are deregulated. Its role in this environment is the primary topic of inquiry within this book.

Acknowledgments

A scholarly book is not a short-term project. This one is several years in the making. Several individuals provided feedback to me along the way. Jim Chen, Dan Farber, Susan Rose-Ackerman, and Joseph Tomain provided extremely useful comments on a complete manuscript of the book. Bits and pieces of the manuscript have also benefited from conversations with and comments by numerous individuals – far too many to name here – but I am particularly grateful to Robert Ahdieh, Rob Atkinson, Amitai Aviram, Scott Baker, Steven Bank, Barbara Banoff, Fred Bosselman, Mary Burke, Joel Eisen, Larry Garvin, Mitu Gulati, Adam Hirsch, Bruce Johnsen, Jonathan Klick, Kimberly Krawiec, David Markell, Greg Mitchell, Susan Rose-Ackerman, J. B. Ruhl, Mark Seidenfeld, Jacqueline Weaver, Phil Weiser, and Ellen Yee. Scott Baker deserves particular credit for encouraging me to think more broadly about regulatory law as a type of incomplete contract during the year he and I were colleagues at the University of North Carolina. I am also grateful to participants at workshops and conferences at Duke Law School, Emory Law School, University of Florida–Levin College of Law, George Mason University Law School, Georgetown University Law Center, University of Houston Law Center, University of Indiana–Indianapolis School of Law, University of Iowa College of Law, Marshall-Wythe School of Law at the College of William & Mary, University of North Carolina School of Law, Pepperdine University Law School, University of Richmond School of Law, University of San Diego School of Law, University of Southern California Law Center, University of Texas Law School, and Washington & Lee University Law School, all of which provided useful input and criticism on individual chapters.

As a young energy attorney in Washington, D.C., in the early 1990s, I was fortunate to work with a number of lawyers who understood the significance of the changes facing public utility industries. Earle O'Donnell and Robert O'Neil deserve particular mention for educating me about energy issues, as well as the practice of regulatory law. I may have gone into academia thinking I would escape the highly specialized world of energy law, but that was impossible. For the past decade, the American Bar Association Section on Administrative Law and Regulatory Practice has served as my main professional bridge to regulatory law practice and governmental agencies. Although my involvement with the Section has focused primarily on administrative law issues, many individuals from the Section have given me advice about this project, and my scholarship more generally.

I would not have been able to complete this book without the institutional support of Florida State University College of Law. Dean Don Weidner has always provided generous support for faculty research, even against precarious and declining state-based support for it. The institutional environment within the law school at Florida State University has also been more nuturing and supportive than any young scholar could expect. My on-site colleagues have tested my analysis, making the concepts, applications, and writing in the manuscript better over many discussions. My students patiently endured some discussion of the ideas in this book. Greg Goelzhauser provided diligent and thorough research assistance as I was preparing chapters.

To all of these people, thank you.

My inquiry into bargaining and regulation began with a series of law review essays and articles on public utility law and deregulation. Chapter 4 draws from an article on the duty to serve originally published in *Vanderbilt Law Review* in 1998.[1] Chapter 5 takes seed from a book review published in *Texas Law Review* in 1998.[2] It also draws from an article on deregulatory takings published in *Virginia Law Review* in 2000 (coauthored with Susan Rose-Ackerman),[3] which was invited by the World Bank for a 1999 conference on infrastructure and investment in Rome, Italy. Chapter 6 owes much of its analysis to an article on the filed tariff doctrine published in *Vanderbilt Law Review* in 2003.[4] Portions of this

[1] Jim Rossi, *The Common Law "Duty to Serve" and Protection of Consumers in an Age of Competitive Retail Public Utility Restructuring*, 51 VANDERBILT LAW REVIEW 1233 (1998).

[2] Jim Rossi, *The Irony of Deregulatory Takings*, 77 TEXAS LAW REVIEW 297 (1998).

[3] Susan Rose-Ackerman & Jim Rossi, *Disentangling Deregulatory Takings*, 86 VIRGINIA LAW REVIEW 1435 (2000).

[4] Jim Rossi, *Lowering the Filed Tariff Shield: Judicial Enforcement for a Deregulatory Era*, 56 VANDERBILT LAW REVIEW 1591 (2003).

article were submitted as expert testimony on behalf of California public power interests in the PG&E bankruptcy, but this article was prepared in advance of my involvement in those proceedings. The framework idea and California example in Chapter 1 were laid out in a book review published in *Michigan Law Review* in 2002, and this review also inspired me to address the issues raised in Chapter 7 (although I also reject some of my earlier analysis in Chapter 8).[5] I am grateful to these journals for allowing me to test drive the ideas I more fully elaborate on in this book. Although these chapters draw on some of my earlier works and extend them in new directions, particularly within a bargaining framework, much of the chapters – as well as the rest of the book – consist of entirely new material.

Tallahassee, Florida (December 2004)

5 Jim Rossi, *The Electric Power Deregulation Fiasco: Looking to Regulatory Federalism to Promote a Balance Between Markets and the Provision of Public Goods*, 100 Michigan Law Review 1768 (2002).

1

The Scope of Regulatory Bargaining

Contracts and other bargains are fundamental to competitive markets. Deregulated electric power and telecommunications markets look to contract to define the relationships between private firms, as well as between private firms and customers. As Joseph Kearney and Thomas Merrill (1998) note in the leading legal treatment of the topic of deregulation: "The new paradigm seeks to subject to ordinary contractual relations all common carrier and public utility services that can be provided through multiple competing providers" (1363). With deregulation, contract will become the primary mechanism for ordering market transactions between private firms and their customers, largely displacing traditional regulatory doctrines that required firms to provide service to customers on predetermined terms and conditions.

Contract is also fundamental to theories of regulation and regulatory law.[1] As economists studying regulated industries with natural monopoly characteristics have long recognized, regulation bears structural similarity to a long-term bilateral contract (Goldberg, 1976; Joskow & Schmalensee, 1983). The actions of the regulator can be analogized to contracts and other bargains. More than for run-of-the-mill industries, the contractual understanding of regulation is fundamental to capital-intensive industries, such as electric power and

[1] Legal scholars are perhaps guilty of using the term "contract" in the regulatory context with less precision and caution than it deserves. The scholarly literature uses the notions of contract in regulation as a rough analogy to describe the nature of various relationships but not necessarily as a legal term of art. Like most legal scholars, I do not intend to imply that regulatory contracts necessarily entail legal duties, obligations, and remedies – an issue I return to in Chapter 5.

telecommunications.[2] For these infrastructure industries, capital investments comprise a large portion of the firm's costs. The firm is only able to pay for these investments over a sustained period of time, making contract a useful way of approaching the finance issue faced by firms and regulators (Gómez-Ibáñez, 2003). To the extent it encourages investment, commitment is fundamental to any account of economic regulation. Contract – a legal tool for establishing commitment – is thus an obvious mechanism for regulatory law to invoke in order to promote investment.

Although notions of the regulatory contract are not foreign to regulatory law, discussion of the regulatory contract is highly polarized. Only at the fringes of regulatory law do contractual and other bargaining concepts enter into serious discussion. This may be due to overreliance on courts as the final arbiter of contracts and a narrow understanding of the scope of contractual bargaining. A bargaining account of government relations can shed light on the history of regulation, as well as on its operation and any changes in regulatory approach. With deregulation and other legal transitions, contractual aspects of regulation have taken on renewed vigor. However, in the context of electric power and telecommunications deregulation, litigants and commentators have made a distinctively legalistic turn in discussion of the regulatory contract and its enforcement. Their approach to the regulatory contract is typically limited to discrete bargains between the firm and governmental bodies, ignoring the bargaining process and other transactional settings, such as bargaining between governing bodies. Many of the important public law questions in economic regulation that are implicated by contractual bargaining remain largely unexplored.

A good example of the polarized nature of the issue is "deregulatory takings" – a prominent theory first advanced a decade ago by scholars and utility advocates. Writing at the height of electric power and telecommunications deregulation in the 1990s, J. Gregory Sidak and Daniel F. Spulber invoked the regulatory contract (which they refer to interchangeably as both a "compact" and a "contract") as a foundational concept for their account of the state's obligations in introducing competition to industries such as telecommunications and electric power. According to them, the regulatory contract between the firm and the regulator is comprised of reciprocal burdens and benefits:

[2] A growing literature addresses whether other regulated activities can benefit from analogies to contract (Freeman, 2000). Although this book is focused on economic regulation, its lessons may also be of relevance to regulation as contract in other settings.

> The regulated utility submits to various regulatory restrictions including price regulations, quality-of-service requirements, and common carrier regulations. In return the regulated firm receives a protected franchise in its service territory, and its investors are allowed an opportunity to earn revenues subject to a rate-of-return constraint. Without the expectation of earning a competitive rate of return, investors would not be willing to commit funds for establishing and operating the utility.... Once the utility invests these funds, the long depreciation schedules typical in electricity and telecommunications regulation credibly commit the utility to performing its obligations under the regulatory contract by denying it the opportunity to recover its capital before the end of its useful life.[3]

This argument for deregulatory takings is a modern application of an implied regulatory contract in which the terms of the bargain are not necessarily express. Critics of this view, writing mostly from a legal perspective (Chen, 1999; Hovenkamp, 1999b; Rossi, 1998b), stake out an alternative view of the explicit regulatory contract that would allow regulators to change the terms and conditions of the regulatory contract with little or no attention to the costs this may impose on incumbent firms. In the 1990s, the debate represented by these two polar positions was among the most significant issues facing regulatory law.

Although this debate may have been the rage among regulatory lawyers during the 1990s, the issues faced today in industries such as electric power and telecommunications have little or nothing to do with deregulatory takings. As we near the end of more than a decade of legal transitions, dismantling old regulatory structures and replacing them with new ones, the short-lived theory of deregulatory takings might lead us to question whether the regulatory contract on which deregulatory takings is premised retains any relevance for these industries. That is, once old regulatory structures crumble, can the regulatory contract still be brought to bear on the conflicts infrastructure industries face, or is it a relic of an older economic and legal order with little modern application? In this book, I set out to advance government relations bargaining – a political process theory of the regulatory contract – as relevant to the deregulatory context and other legal transitions. Contract remains relevant, I argue, but bargaining accounts of regulation are challenged to tackle new issues in a changing regulatory environment. Bargaining accounts of government relations will bring important new insights to bear for public law in the context of economic regulation.

[3] Sidak & Spulber, 1997: 109.

I. DISTINGUISHING POLITICAL FAILURE FROM MARKET FAILURE

In the summer of 2003, a massive blackout left 50 million customers in much of the Northeast and portions of the Midwest without electric power. The blackout affected an area extending from New York, Massachusetts, and New Jersey west to Michigan, and from Ohio north to Toronto and Ottawa, Ontario, Canada. The economic costs it imposed are staggering.[4] Media accounts were quick to blame the blackout on deregulatory policies the electric power industry adopted throughout the 1980s and 1990s.[5] Although intuitively appealing, efforts to blame deregulation for the problem fail to explain the mechanism by which deregulation might have contributed to the problem. There is, for example, little reason to expect traditional rate regulation would have fared better in avoiding the 2003 blackout.[6]

How, if at all, has deregulation failed? Has deregulation made industries such as electric power better (cheaper, more reliable, etc.) or worse for consumers, investors, and firms, and what role, if any, has the law played in this? Notions of the regulatory bargain can shed light on the issues faced by deregulated industries, such as electric power, and by other industries in transition. The conventional account of deregulation's weakness suggests that enhanced competition between firms will sometimes – perhaps even frequently – lead to predatory market conduct that harms consumers (Kuttner, 1999). This account might be applied to critique electric power deregulation, perhaps as much as in any other sector of the economy affected by deregulation. In California's newly deregulated electric power market in the late 1990s, energy supply firms were able to manipulate supply and prices, seeking short-term gain at a cost to

[4] Refer to http://www.electricity.doe.gov/news/blackout.cfm?section=news&level2=blackout. Some estimated the costs of the 2003 blackout to be as high as $5 billion. Nancy Gibbs, *Lights Out*, TIME MAGAZINE, Aug. 5, 2003, at 30.

[5] On one account, "The current industry-centered deregulation of the national power grid has created market-driven chaos, with electric bills skyrocketing as high as 300 percent in California while power systems become less and less reliable – all at a time when the shrinking cost of renewable energy should be providing lower costs and a more reliable system." Michael I. Niman, *Why the Lights Went Out*, THE HUMANIST, Nov. 1, 2003, at 4.

[6] Indeed, for many Americans older than 45 years of age, the blackouts of 2003 were reminiscent of the blackouts of 1965, which left millions in eight Northeast states without power for almost 24 hours, or the blackout of 1977, which plunged New York City into darkness and brought about violence in several communities. For comparison between the 1965 blackout and the 2003 blackout, see Sillin (2003). The analogy between the blackout of 1977 and the blackout of 2003 is discussed in Goodman (2003).

consumers and others (Weaver, 2004). Similarly, in deregulated wholesale power markets (structured primarily by federal as opposed to state regulators), private greed certainly contributed in part to a serious shortage in generation supply and transmission capacity, exacerbating the blackouts that left New York City and much of the northeastern United States in the dark in the summer of 2003.[7] On this account of deregulation's weakness, private greed is the core cause of failures in the transition to competitive markets.

This account of deregulation's weakness is controversial. It may or may not have merit, but it is not the full story. Deregulated markets face another challenge that is underexplored in the popular and academic press. Most economists believe that properly designed markets can curtail the negative impacts of greed in the competitive process. Changes to regulatory structure are not only relevant insofar as they influence how private firms compete with each other in the unregulated sphere of the marketplace. Regulatory change also affects how firms interact with and influence governmental bodies in the formulation and implementation of regulatory law. Government relations bargaining in this context have serious consequences for the regulatory process and for public law.

For example, the failure of electric power deregulation in California was as much a consequence of ill-conceived government competition policies, frequently framed by public law doctrines, as it was a consequence of private greed in deregulated markets. Like most deregulated markets, California's plan to deregulate retail electric power did not dismantle government regulation. Instead, it emphasized new types of regulation, such as a state-supervised power pool that prohibited certain types of transactions and sanctioned others. Wholesale power supply markets, largely deregulated by the federal government in the 1990s, before California's retail market opened, are subject to market-based supply decisions by private firms and large price swings. California retail power suppliers, however, were subject to a price cap imposed by state lawmakers and were also prohibited from using long-term contracts to serve retail customers. Due to the state-imposed price cap, California utilities were precluded from passing on their costs to customers, forcing them to absorb monumental losses in highly volatile short-term supply markets when wholesale

[7] Matthew L. Wald, *A Question Still Unanswered: How Did the Blackout Happen?*, New York Times, May 10, 2004 (online edition) (quoting Robert Blohm, an electricity consultant who questions whether deregulation impaired reliability and caused the blackout to spread).

power prices skyrocketed. Several electric power utilities in the state – previously considered risk-free investments – went bankrupt. Undoubtedly, state policy decisions in California to cap retail prices and prohibit long-term contracts were influenced by strategic lobbying and other regulatory maneuvers on the part of private stakeholders in the California law-making process. Private manipulation of government regulation is as significant as, and may even eclipse, private abuse of competitive markets.[8] To the extent public law invites such manipulation, it shares responsibility for failed market policies.

Most accounts of California's failed deregulatory policies focus on private greed in the marketplace. In contrast, a government relations bargaining story of California's failed deregulation plan highlights weak links in the political processes leading to the formation and implementation of competitive retail power markets in the state. Firm–government interactions had significant influence on the path of California's competition policies as it implemented its deregulation plan. So did government–government interactions, as utilities in the state were brought to the brink of financial disaster while federal and state regulatory bodies faced off in inaction – each attempting to pass the blame to the other for the failures in California's deregulated markets, with neither one stepping up to the plate to address the serious regulatory problems that had been created. Public law doctrines, such as the filed rate doctrine (see Chapter 6) and federal preemption (see Chapter 8), were central to this crisis.

A government relations bargaining account can also be used to explore the issues of transmission reliability – perhaps the greatest problem competitive markets in electric power will face in the coming decade. A massive blackout in the summer of 2003 left large portions of the Northeast and Midwest without power due to a cascading failure of the interstate transmission grid. The 2003 blackout may have been triggered by individual negligence (and perhaps even greed, although that is doubtful), but private market behavior was certainly not the immediate reason the blackout spread from Ohio, where it is widely reported the initial event leading to the blackout occurred, to New York and other states. Consequences were made far worse for areas like New York City due to both public

[8] Accounts of California's failed deregulatory scheme focus on tensions and gaps between state and federal deregulatory policies (Joskow, 2001; Rossi, 2002). Other accounts emphasize California's failure to allow long-term contracts to serve the retail market (Borenstein, 2002). These accounts share a focus on California's failed government policies, not an inherent failure in power markets.

and private failures to expand transmission facilities over several decades. These failures were influenced by private conduct in a regulatory process – both preceding and following deregulation – as much as by deregulation itself. As one author observes, "[e]lectricity consumption increased by 35 percent in the 1990s alone (and is twice the level of the early 1970s), with transmission carrying capacity increasing by only 10 percent" (Sillin, 2003: 34).

Private utilities – owning both transmission, a natural monopoly network, and generation, which is competitive – frequently resist the expansion of transmission when it is not in the interest of their profits. Their influence is magnified, perhaps even masked, by environmental interest groups, who are allied with powerful incumbent firms in favoring state and local regulation of the industry. As James Madison predicted long ago in Federalist No. 10, if left to its own devices the state regulatory process is particularly vulnerable to the influence of powerful private interest groups. Where federal regulators also lack plenary authority to solve transmission problems, both federal and state regulators can readily fall into a cycle of evading difficult network congestion problems.

For example, the state of Connecticut has strongly opposed the Cross-Sound Cable, a 23-mile merchant transmission line that would allow Long Island Power Authority to import power from New Haven, Connecticut. Some Connecticut officials cite environmental concerns in support of their opposition to the project, such as impacts on shellfish beds and dredging operations in the New Haven Harbor; however, the project complies with all state siting and environmental statutes. The cable, already in place, was authorized to operate under a temporary emergency order issued by the Secretary of Energy following the August 2003 blackout, which was lifted in early 2004. There is reason to believe that the issue is within the jurisdiction of the Federal Energy Regulatory Commission (FERC), but the scope of federal authority over the matter is not clear because the FERC does not site transmission lines. Connecticut's Attorney General, backed by environmental interest groups and a major incumbent utility serving Connecticut customers (Northeast Utilities, which owns an older, parallel transmission line), threatened litigation if the Cross-Sound Cable was allowed to go live again.[9]

As electric power transmission illustrates, the behavior of private stakeholders is not only relevant in the market sphere, but also in the

[9] Bruce W. Radford, *Cross-Sound Cable Puts Feds on the Spot*, FORTNIGHTLY'S SPARK, June 2004, at 1.

regulatory process that implements the constitutive governance of deregulated markets and the public law doctrines that frame this process. Because states retain jurisdiction over the siting of power plants and transmission lines, public law defines the range of permissible regulatory responses in state politics and thus plays a central role in framing disputes over the location and expansion of transmission lines (see Chapter 7). As in the case of California's deregulation plan, prior to the 2003 blackout, interactions between governments were a major impediment to the expansion of transmission; long-standing jurisdictional conflicts and gaps under extant public law doctrines have left both state and federal regulators unable to take action to expand transmission (an issue addressed in Chapter 8).

Focus on private interactions with governmental bodies and interactions between governmental bodies – what I collectively refer to in this book as government relations bargaining – is not a new insight for regulatory lawyers and economists. A large literature explores private bargaining with the government. Since public choice theory came into its own in the 1960s, economists and political scientists have increasingly paid attention to how private firms interact with the government. Most applications, however, focus attention on a specific moment of change – for example, a regulator's decision to regulate or deregulate, the passage of a major piece of legislation, the repeal of previous regulatory approach. Public choice theory is downright cynical about the ability of regulation to enhance social welfare. Apart from condemning capture of the regulator, the literature rarely focuses attention on the continuing and recurring interactions between private firms and the government in a deregulatory environment. However, because deregulation seldom entails the complete dismantling of government – the general literature on regulation broadly defines deregulation as including restructuring initiatives that depend on government for some implementation and oversight (Borenstein & Bushnell, 2000; Cudahy, 2002a; Hirsh, 1999)[10] – such interactions regularly occur in the adoption and implementation of policies designed to enhance competition. A growing literature also explores interactions among governmental bodies, such as interactions between the

[10] Throughout, I follow this convention, using "deregulation" to refer to a variety of government competition policies regarding utility industries – for example, lifting restrictions on entry and exit, mandating open access to networks, and unbundling vertically integrated services – few of which require complete dismantling of regulation, although with deregulation prices are no longer determined under traditional cost-of-service standards and may be left entirely to the market.

federal government and states (see Chapter 3). Focusing on bargaining in the regulatory process shines light on a different kind of greed than popular critics of market transitions condemn. Rather than focus on private market greed, government relations bargaining focuses on private behavior and incentives in public ordering. Even in times of regulatory system stability, greed in politics may pose as a much of a challenge to market transactions as greed in private transactions. With deregulation and other legal transitions, however, focus on government relations bargaining brings to the fore important issues that other contractual accounts of regulation largely obfuscate.

II. LIMITS OF THE LEGALISTIC TURN FOR BARGAINING ACCOUNTS OF REGULATION

Predominant accounts of utility regulation focus on three interrelated projects. Traditional progressive accounts view regulation as ensuring private markets do not ignore the public interest (Mitnick, 1980; Posner, 1974). Neoclassical economic approaches view regulation primarily as correcting for market failure in the interest of promoting economic efficiency or enhancing social welfare (Posner, 1974). Public choice theory focuses on the incentives and consequences of regulation (Farber & Frickey, 1991; Mashaw, 1997; Quirk, 1981). The more cynical strand of public choice embraces a "capture" thesis that sees regulators as beholden to the powerful firms they are charged with regulating (Stigler, 1971). These approaches first emphasize the ends of regulation (intentional and otherwise), and then pay attention to process only insofar as it is useful to achieving these ends.

More than 10 years ago, George Priest argued that the project of two of the predominant accounts of the origins of regulation – "public interest" theory, which sees regulation as a solution to market failure, and "public choice" theory, a strand of which views agency regulators as operating under the dominant influence of (or "captured" by) the private firms subject to regulation – are misplaced. Rather than attempt to identify a singular theory of the origins of regulation or of exogenous substantive ends, Priest (1992) imagined a research agenda in which scholars make an effort "to understand the mechanics of a change in regulatory regime before deriving a theory of it" (323). Implicit to this project is the recognition that theories of regulation place inordinate attention on the substantive content of regulation. In contrast, a research agenda that focuses on mechanism of evolution and change in regulated industries poses a fundamentally different series of questions than conventional accounts.

An account of government relations bargaining places more emphasis on such questions than conventional accounts of economic regulation, such as public interest or public choice theories. Focus on government relations bargaining is not dismissive of ends – of course they are important – but recognizes that ends are not necessarily prior (or exogenous) to the theory of regulation. Process can matter as much as ends. Rather than begin with externally generated ends, analysis of economic regulation might take on different emphasis and realize fresh insights from paying attention to process first.

The goals of regulation are numerous; however, public interest, efficiency, and pluralist preference aggregation are most prominent. Public interest theories of regulation have intuitive appeal as a starting point for understanding the goals of regulation, although at best they are ambiguous. They focus almost exclusively on the substance of regulation rather than how it evolves and or promotes stable solutions to regulatory problems. As Bruce Mitnick's (1980) extensive study of regulation puts it, "there remains no accepted definition of the phrase ['public interest'], much less an accepted operational definition offering indicators that we may use to determine empirically whether something is in the public interest" (259). Approaching regulation as a bargain challenges us to focus not only on the substance of the public interest, but also on its evolution and, in particular, its ability to promote coordinated voluntary solutions to conflicts (its "equilibria" characteristics).

In addition, a government relations bargaining approach to regulation diverges from neoclassical economic theory in that it views natural monopoly regulation not merely as an efficiency-promoting solution to market failure, but also as a negotiated equilibrium that is the product of bargaining conditions and incentives. Such an approach also departs from many public choice accounts in that it does not embrace a strong capture thesis or condemn all rent seeking; instead, it acknowledges the reality of continuing interactions between firms and the government, and the incentives faced by private firms, as strategies used by stakeholders to sustain the commitments of the incomplete contracts surrounding the firm and its institutional arrangements in an industry.

It is certainly not a new insight for regulatory law to focus on bargaining. However, discussion of regulatory contracts generally assumes that the terms of the contract are complete, or downplays the incentive implications of incompleteness for the regulatory process. The contract and the regulatory ends it reflects are assumed to exist independent of the mechanisms of regulatory evolution and enforcement. For example, Sidak and Spulber take Priest's invitation seriously to observe that regulation might be analogized to a "contract," but they interpret bargains in a legalistic manner to rely on third-party enforcement (typically courts) to deter or compensate for renegotiation (Sidak & Spulber, 1997). This approach leads them to make numerous recommendations for regulatory law, most of which rely on judicial enforcement of a preexisting substantive bargain. Most prominently, Sidak and Spulber argue that courts have a primary role to play in enforcing regulatory commitments, under both contract law principles and the Takings Clause of the U.S. Constitution, a topic to which I return in Chapter 5.

Simple legal analogies between regulation and contractual obligations and enforcement might also lead to misleading explanatory and normative suggestions. For instance, as Daniel Cole (2003) observes, regardless of whether regulation can be described as anything approaching a legal contract, the practical obligations and remedies contract law affords do not give rise to meritorious claims for compensation for industry transitions, such as a decision to deregulate in most cases. Debates over judicial enforcement of regulatory contracts fail to confront that regulatory history is often partial or incomplete, presenting complex contract interpretation issues. As regulatory lawyers are well aware, contracts are frequently renegotiated in the regulatory process. A rich literature on incomplete contracts plays this out in commercial and corporate law settings, but incompleteness also has far-reaching implications for regulatory law (see Chapter 2). If the reality of incompleteness in the regulatory contract is acknowledged as a starting point, we might envision a very different role for courts and other government institutions than traditional accounts of regulation as contract suggest.

In the legal literature, it is commonly acknowledged that deregulation of industries such as telecommunications and electric power poses a fundamental challenge to theories of regulation and doctrines of regulatory law (Kearney & Merrill, 1998). Scholars of regulatory law have also failed to fully engage Priest's invitation in this context. We have yet to completely explore the implications of the regulatory contract for the regulatory process and for deregulated industries undergoing transitions. A regulatory law that draws from literature on government relations bargaining, relating this to incomplete contracts and institutional governance, would ask different questions and generate different conclusions for regulatory law than conventional analogies between regulation and judicially enforced, or legalistic, contracts.

The legalistic turn in discussions about enforcement of the regulatory contract, as embraced by modern commentators such as Sidak and Spulber, looks primarily to courts as the institutional enforcer of the regulatory contract. Although intuitively appealing – as we look to courts for answers to all kinds of social problems – such an approach also invites a type of judicial arrogance in completing the terms of the contract; judges, perhaps juries, become the final arbiters of history in filling in the contract's gaps. At most, though, the regulatory contract represents a long-term contract with poorly specified terms – what the legal literature has recognized as a "relational contract" (Macneil, 1978). However, if bargaining is the norm in regulatory contexts, public law may have very little role to play. Even where public law does play an important role, courts will not always serve as the primary enforcer of duties and obligations. In fact, to the extent the conception of the regulatory contract embraces certainty as one of its virtues, courts may not be the most likely institutions to provide it; indeterminate legal approaches to contract interpretation and remedies could work to undermine rather than enhance predictability (see Chapter 5). Perhaps courts have little to do with enforcing bargains in the context of economic regulation. The parties to any regulatory bargain – private firms and stakeholders, as well as governmental bodies such as agencies and legislatures – might play as much of a role in honoring contractual commitments as courts.

III. REGULATORY LAW AS AN INCOMPLETE BARGAIN

The legalistic turn in enforcement of regulatory contracts places enormous emphasis on the commitment represented by the regulatory contract, along with third-party enforcement of this commitment by courts.[11] This quest for substantive contractual completeness has an advantage – for example, it can reduce the costs of transacting in the political process – but it also obscures public law issues that frame the bargaining process.

[11] Third-party enforcement of the commitment by courts does not mean that every bargain, or even most bargains, will be litigated in court. As Chapter 2 suggests, with iterated bargains between a firm and regulator, firms may look to the regulator as much as courts for relief from undesirable terms – much as private firms in ongoing commercial relationships rely on self-enforcement mechanisms.

During the last 20 years, an alternative account of contractual bargaining – often referred to as "incomplete contracts" – has emerged in the law and economics literature. Instead of focusing on whether courts should limit their enforcement to express or implied contractual terms, incomplete contracts (discussed further in Chapter 2) provide fresh insights that can return bargaining to the core of debates about the role of public law in regulation and deregulation.[12]

A. Renegotiation, Institutions, and the Reasons for Incompleteness

Three main themes are of fundamental importance to any account of government relations bargaining that draws on incomplete contracts. First, and most obvious, an incomplete contracts perspective recognizes that parties to a contract cannot commit indefinitely not to renegotiate a contract into the future. In law and economics, the incomplete contracts approach has made important advances by addressing how renegotiation has implications for the firm. Applied to law making, the incomplete bargaining perspective does not seem to be controversial. No law, after all, can be said to be entirely complete because lawmakers will always fail to understand some future circumstances and conditions. Further, practical trade-offs in the political process may lead to ambiguities in any law-making bargain, sometimes leading agents to prefer incompleteness as a strategy that allows passing a law or regulation although it is imperfect. Even if it is not descriptively controversial, however, incompleteness has some important methodological and normative implications for regulatory law that this book explores.

The incomplete contracts literature has made two additional contributions that a government relations bargaining perspective can bring to bear for regulatory law. Central to this book, it allows an emphasis on comparative institutional questions; and, perhaps most significant for the regulatory law questions raised in this book, by focusing on reasons for incompleteness it pays attention to reciprocity and incentives in the contracting process.

To varying degrees, scholars using the incomplete contracts approach have emphasized the comparative institutional aspects of governance decisions. Oliver Williamson (1996a), for example, draws on incomplete contracts to address the "mechanisms of governance" – the private and

[12] For an application of this framework to regulated industries, see Gómez-Ibáñez, 2003.

public institutional order within which contracting occurs. Williamson warns against placing exaggerated emphasis on judicially enforced ordering. His effort dovetails with the contributions of legal theorists who eschew an approach to legal analysis that is focused on a single decision-making institution (Komesar, 2001). In addition to courts, other institutions, including legislatures, agencies, and state and local entities, may play an important role in the bargaining process.

The incomplete contracts approach is also mindful of incentives in the bargaining process – an insight that has important implications for regulatory law in a deregulatory era. As the law and economics of contracts has noted for more than a decade, the reasons for incompleteness in bargains matters. Attention to "default" rules in the contractual and corporate settings highlights the relevance of reciprocity and incentives to the incomplete contracts account of regulation.[13] Where the contracting parties are in a truly reciprocal relationship – each possessing equal access to information – the incomplete contracts literature says little about how to address the problem of incompleteness, if it is indeed a problem. In such contexts, the optimal default rule for courts may be no judicial role – deferring to idealized, Coasian-type bargaining between the private stakeholders and governmental bodies. Where these ideal bargaining conditions are prevalent, as they may well be among homogenous, repeat players in a negotiation, it might be predicted that regulatory law will be largely irrelevant.

In contrast, if idealized bargaining conditions do not exist, courts might have more to contribute to the bargaining process. One solution to regulatory incompleteness might be for regulators or courts to fill in the terms of the bargain with efficient or fair substantive default terms. Historically, courts have looked to fairness and efficiency in attempting to complete the express or implied regulatory bargain. Another approach is for courts to look to default rules that are designed with incentives in mind, such as clear statement rules designed to encourage more accountable decisions by one or both parties in the bargaining process, or penalty defaults, which penalize one or both parties with the idea of encouraging them to reveal information in the bargaining process (see Chapters 5 and 6).

Incentive-based default rules have much to contribute to discussions of judicial review in this context. A government relations bargaining

[13] "Default" rules – gap-filling measures that parties can contract around – are frequently contrasted with "mandatory" rules, which parties generally may not voluntarily waive within the legal system.

account of regulation – which, like incomplete contracts, takes a neutral position toward contracts renegotiation – reveals how deregulation creates new opportunities for opportunistic private behavior vis-à-vis the government in the deregulatory environment. In a nonreciprocal situation – where there is an asymmetry of information – incompleteness presents a more substantial problem for both contract law and the theory of the firm.[14] Incompleteness may exist for good reasons, but may also be the result of strategic behavior, such as one contracting party's nondisclosure or an effort to preserve discretion to act in that party's self-interest in the future. In their effort to devise optimal rules for information disclosure at the time of contracting, Ian Ayres and Robert Gertner (1992) illustrate the connection between information asymmetry and ex ante incentives. The legal literature focuses predominantly on "gap filling," but the incomplete contracts literature also advances other insights, such as emphasizing the effect of ex post incompleteness on ex ante incentives. As Eric Posner (2003) observes, the literature reveals a tension between efficient trade and efficient relationship-specific investments. In the parlance of regulatory law, there is sometimes a tension between efficient levels of participation in the regulatory process and efficient investment; if the law of economic regulation is designed to protect commitments at all costs, parties to a regulatory process may overinvest in expensive assets, leading to a potential reduction in social welfare. Reciprocity and incentives are key variables in any analysis of incompleteness in regulatory law. An account of regulation that is informed by incomplete contracts acknowledges how commitment relates to incentives for investment and influences ex ante behavior in the bargaining process.

Extension of the insights from incomplete contracts to regulation and the regulatory process provides several new research insights for regulatory law and has particularly important – but underexamined – implications for deregulated industries. A government relations bargaining approach recognizes that regulation itself is the beginning, not the end, of an inquiry into legal ordering. It also concedes that regulation is never exhaustive, nor should it be, because there is an optimal amount of specificity to rules and at some level precision comes at a serious cost to regulatory flexibility (Diver, 1983; Gómez-Ibáñez, 2003; Goodin, 1982). In contrast,

[14] The problems presented for corporate organization and contract law differ. In contrast to the Hart/Williamson approach to incompleteness, which emphasizes how incompleteness influences ex ante incentives to invest in firm-specific capital, Ayres and Gertner focus on how incompleteness influences ex ante incentives to reveal information in bargaining.

the traditional regulatory contract approach frowns on renegotiation and, by giving contract a legalistic status, invites a type of judicial arrogance. It empowers courts to revise history, filling in gaps with terms that may or may not reflect what was actually promised, often based on a narrow definition of efficiency.

Rather than look to courts as the primary arbiter and enforcer of substantive commitments, the incomplete contracts approach is agnostic toward contract negotiation. Such a renegotiation-neutral approach leads to a very different account of the goals of public law in the economic regulation context. Instead of protecting contracts – which even many legalistic contracts commentators acknowledge to be incomplete – regulatory law might broaden its agenda by paying attention to the behavioral incentives and welfare consequences of renegotiation, distinguishing between ex ante and ex post incentives and welfare states. Process is as just as important as substance in an incomplete contracts analysis of regulation. By focusing on bargaining incentives, such an analysis could introduce an insurance perspective to the study of regulation. Much as the insurance perspective reveals problems for the torts system, such as moral hazard, ex post compensation or liability for regulatory change – advocated by those who embrace legalistic contracts – influences regulated firms' ex ante interactions in the regulatory process and has consequences for ex post welfare (Posner & Rosenfield, 1977). Courts will have an important role to play for regulated industries but merely protecting regulatory commitments is not their primary task, to the extent it is relevant to the judicial enterprise.

B. Some Basic Analytical Observations

Before moving on to subsequent chapters, some analytical observations about the approach of this book are in order.

First, throughout this book, I present government relations bargaining as an approach to regulation invoking a comparative institutional analysis of the governance of deregulated markets to draw out the insights of incomplete bargains for regulatory law. A government relations bargaining approach envisions regulation not just as a "tool" responding to a context-specific problem (Breyer, 1982) but as an institutional alternative to market-based ordering. Within the market, such ordering can be external, in the form of interfirm contracts, or internal, in the form of intrafirm transactions. José Gómez-Ibáñez (2003) makes a substantial advance in the application of incomplete contracts to regulated industries by focusing on the conditions under which private contracting will fail and emphasizing the relationship between monopoly regulation and procurement contracting. As his comparative case study of incomplete contracts in a variety of regulatory contexts suggests, where private contracting fails, a need for discretionary government regulation, often by an administrative agency, will be necessary. Even if discretionary governmental regulation is chosen as a regulatory mechanism, however, bargaining questions continue to arise. Contractual bargaining is relevant to public governance issues, as well as to private governance within the market. In the public governance sphere, rather than look to judicially enforced contracts as the default mechanism for governance, courts should compare the effectiveness of contract with other institutions, such as federal or state courts, federal or state agencies, the legislature, and the firm itself.

Although the comparative institutional approach is not a necessary feature of incomplete contracts analysis of regulation, by combining the two analytical approaches, government relations bargaining brings to light many possibilities for analysis of public law questions that other approaches obfuscate. The literatures on incomplete contracts – primarily in economics – and on institutions – primarily in political science – are largely distinct, but there is an important conceptual convergence between the two projects. Transaction costs is one of the primary reasons for contractual incompleteness. Similarly, institutional theorists focus on how transaction costs affect the efficiency of alternative institutional arrangements (Eggertsson, 1996). Although the institutional literature is less formal in approach to modeling than much of the literature on incomplete contracts, incompleteness may be understood within the institutionalist framework, perhaps most prominently identified with the work of Douglass North (1996). Although much of the institutionalist literature treats contracts as a "theoretical fiction" (Eggertsson, 1996: 9, at n. 3), the bargaining framework can provide a lens for analysis that is complementary to an institutional approach to the same problems.

Second, and related, this book takes a broad approach to the definition of regulatory law. The scope of regulatory law includes not only substantive regulation itself, but also the structural decision rules and networks – the political process, including constitutions – that generate regulation and changes to it. Regulatory law defined broadly includes what agencies and legislatures do, as well as the constitutional order that defines the mechanisms for public governments, both state and federal, and the antitrust laws that, when properly enforced, frame the private ordering of the marketplace. This definitional approach to regulatory law, much like the comparative institutionalist literature, distinguishes between "institutions" (defined broadly as "formal and informal rules that constrain individual behavior") and "institutional environment" (subject to longer-term modification) (Eggertsson, 1996: 7). Some political scientists have referred to this as the distinction between "ordinary" and "constitutive" decisions (Laswell, 1971: 77), a dichotomy that perhaps maps more directly onto a legal ordering.

Such a broad approach to regulatory law presents a formidable challenge. The government bargaining account cannot ignore the implications of renegotiation for regulation. If regulation is subject to constant renegotiation, a bargaining account of regulation may fail to provide any stable solutions to regulatory problems. With constant renegotiation of every commitment, any decision by regulators and firms is only tentative, at best, or always shifting, at worst. To the extent this is the case, regulatory decisions may have little coercive, precedential, or expressive value for a legal system or for private actors (e.g., firms) or for a legal system. At the extreme, renegotiation could undermine incentives for private firms to invest in critical infrastructure, leading to a loss of investor confidence in major industries such as electric power and telecommunications. As a glance at the history of natural monopoly regulation would suggest, though, not all rules are always up for grabs.[15] Within a regulatory system, some equilibria between regulators and firms, or between governmental bodies, can be understood as having source in implicit, self-enforcing agreements. Even where bargaining does not generate a simple Nash equilibrium due to the repeat player effects, it may be characterized as "subgame perfect" due to the existence of credible third-party threats.[16] For instance, a regulator and a firm bargaining against the backdrop of future judicial review (with similar or different expectations about the applicable rule a court might apply) may reach a very different bargain than parties bargaining without any expectation of judicial redress. The identification of such equilibria can be helpful in evaluating the rules and

[15] Just as the famous astronomer presented with the claim that the earth rests on the back of a great turtle, we must address whether "it's turtles all the way down." The story is commonly attributed to William James (Cramton, 1986).

[16] Subgame perfection "implies that all threats are credible because it is in the player's best interest to carry them out, even if doing so is costly in the short run" (Mahoney & Sanchirico, 2003: 1284). As Mahoney and Sanchirico observe, the N-player repeated prisoner's dilemma has many subgame perfect equilibria that rely on third-party enforcement to induce cooperative play. These equilibria may only reveal themselves after several iterations of a game but illustrate the importance of law as a mechanism for third-party enforcement.

implications of the given regulatory system. Institutional insights might suggest that some features of a regulatory system are more likely to change than others – for example, constitutions are more difficult to modify than legislation – and this can be a relevant factor in assessing the practical path for bringing about desirable bargaining.

Third, although this book sets out to imagine an agenda for regulatory law that draws on bargaining, this book does not attempt an independent, systematic defense of the formal incomplete contracts model of economic behavior. To be sure, economists do not agree that incompleteness will necessarily plague contractual relations. As Eric Posner astutely observes,

> Why would rational parties choose noncontingent contracts when more sophisticated contracts would enable parties to obtain better results? And if parties did choose more sophisticated contracts, why would courts need to do anything other than enforce the terms of these contracts? If courts only enforced the terms of contracts, much of contract doctrine, and much of the law-and-economics literature, would be irrelevant.[17]

Indeed, as the distinguished economists Eric Maskin and Jean Tirole (1999) argue, under certain assumptions transaction costs do not necessarily prevent the formation of complete contracts. The argument in this book does not depend on a formal articulation of the incomplete contracts model but instead is exploratory of the implications if and where we might expect incompleteness in regulation and regulatory law. In this vein, the book attempts to generate questions and hypotheses, rather than provide formal answers regarding the implications of an incomplete contracts model for government relations bargaining.

Finally, this project has both explanatory and normative dimensions. At the explanatory level, the book explores the promise of research ideas from incomplete contracts and institutional analysis that fit extant legal doctrine concerning regulation in ways that equal, if not exceed, their conceptual competitors. Recognizing that the key questions are fundamentally empirical ones, the book uses a case study approach. In theory, economics or political science might suggest a certain approach to understanding regulation, but how does this play out in practice? Throughout the book, the electric power industry is used as a primary example for illustrating the interplay of economics, politics, and law in contractual bargaining. On occasion, telecommunications is also addressed. It is hoped that the case study approach will provide a focused opportunity for

[17] Posner, 2003: 85.

examinanation of the implications of specific legal doctrines on certain types of firm and institutional structures. Of course, the risk of any case study approach is that the generalization that can be developed from it will be misleading due to unrepresentative selection. Although large data sets across industries would be ideal for drawing such generalizations, such data are not readily available. Until it is, a case study examination of similarly structured industries – such as electric power and telecommunications – is well suited to generate tentative hypotheses for further empirical study, if not to call into question conventional attitudes and beliefs about regulatory law.

There is also a normative dimension to the project that becomes clear in later chapters. This book is not concerned so much with the substance of regulation in any given context as it is with the process that produces the bargaining conditions for regulation. Although the focus is not on answering every normative question posed by regulation, the approach has a fundamentally different normative focus, and thus leads to different questions and recommendations than competing accounts of regulation as contract. For example, the approach is much more aligned with – and may reflect a normative preference for – government experimentalism and flexibility (Dorf & Sabel, 1998) than previous accounts of regulation as contract that risk ossification of regulatory policies. Further, although applying the contractual account to public governance issues is predicated on a basic pluralist vision of politics as incorporating the vector of competing interest groups (i.e., it does not always condemn rent seeking), I also do not always see the protection of industry rents as a legitimate end for regulation. To that extent, my normative analysis rejects thin pluralism as a solution to bargaining problems for every public law issue. A challenge for public law is to recognize when social welfare might require overriding thin pluralism. In some instances, such as in evaluating regulatory tariffs, I argue that informational asymmetries in bargaining make a compelling case for rejecting thin pluralism in favor of a more robust substantive account of regulatory law, such as a thick (public interest-oriented) pluralism.

C. Unmasking the Core of Regulatory Law

Government relations bargaining sheds light on several different dimensions of regulation and regulatory law. Economists routinely look to incomplete contracts to analyze the structure of the firm and markets. In political science, game theorists and rational choice modelers have made efforts to understand law making as an activity that occurs in bilateral and multilateral bargaining spaces. Sociologists focus on the network interactions of groups, which political scientists also increasingly address in their efforts to understand and model interest group behavior and influence. The law-making sphere readily lends itself to bargaining analysis. Regulations and laws can be analogized to contracts between firms in an industry and different governing bodies, as can interactions between governmental bodies, such as interactions between federal and state governments or interactions between states.

Government relations bargaining provides an umbrella framework for applying the insights of these various disciplines to various public law doctrines and processes in economic regulation. The fundamental project of regulatory law is organized around interactions between private firms, interactions between firms and the government, and interactions between different government entities. Each interaction gives rises to a type of behavior – contracting between private firms, private firm or interest group participation in the political and regulatory process, or interjurisdictional gaps and conflicts – with which regulatory law is concerned during the formation of regulation, its application and operation, and transition periods, such as in the context of deregulation. Each type of behavior may yield benefits for social welfare, but also may reduce overall social welfare. A primary point of regulatory law is to minimize the types of interactions that lead to overall reductions in social welfare, such as inefficient private contracting, interest group capture or manipulation of the regulatory process, or inefficient regulation or ossification in the interjurisdictional context. The subject matter of this book thus differs from many other accounts of regulatory law, which focus almost exclusively on firm–government interactions, going beyond the history of regulation or its substance. Instead, the approach of this book is much more process oriented – focusing on the institutional implications of regulatory doctrine – and defines the core of regulatory law more broadly than traditional accounts of regulation. Although some have defined regulatory law broadly to include law, policy, and politics (Tomain & Shapiro, 1997), regulatory law traditionally focuses on regulation and the intersections of the overlapping spheres of antitrust and federalism with regulation. This book urges a more extended framework for regulatory law, particularly as industries are deregulated. What goes on in the realms of antitrust law and federalism, even outside the realm of conventional regulation, is of fundamental importance in deregulated industries. In addition, the framework of this book raises important issues for industries in regulatory transition, where institutional instability and conflict replace traditional norm of coordination.

Traditionally, applications of incomplete contracts to regulation focus on the type of incompleteness that is internal to a firm. As Part I of his book argues, insights about the role (and relevance) of regulatory law can be gained by extending incompleteness beyond just the firm to encompass public governance issues, including general issues of public order and the role of law in markets. Three main bargaining eras are relevant to the analysis. First, before economic regulation of an industry arises, firms bargain primarily with state, local, and federal legislatures. Second, once economic regulation is in place for an industry, firms bargain primarily with regulatory bodies – that is, state and federal agencies. Third, during a period of regulatory transition in which the scope and purpose of regulation changes or regulation is dismantled, firms again look to legislatures for relief.

Much analysis of regulation focuses on one of these bargaining eras but does not make connections across them. Most regulatory law assumes the second type of bargaining, thus paying little or no attention to the first and third eras of regulatory bargains. As we embark on a new era of competitive markets in electric power and telecommunications, most regulatory relations take place in the first and third bargaining eras. In a traditional environment governing regulated industries, the boundaries between antitrust law, economic regulation, and federalism were largely stable. To a degree, this is a function of clear legal rules, but it is also owing to the voluntarily coordinated behavior of private stakeholders within the industry and governmental bodies. The era of natural monopoly regulation presented nearly ideal bargaining conditions – a relatively small number of homogenous private stakeholders, along with government actors, working out cooperative, stable solutions to regulatory boundary problems in repeated (and largely predictable) negotiations. In the era of natural monopoly regulation, the combination of legal rules, implicit contracts, and cooperative solutions provided a relatively stable framework for regulatory law. However, as traditional regulation is dismantled or modified, the old order faces new challenges. As firms (some established, others emerging) begin to compete in restructured industries, regulatory boundaries are increasingly uncertain. In the parlance of contracts, they are increasingly subject to renegotiation, but the possibility of shifting boundaries is not something regulatory law has focused much attention on.

Chapter 2 sets the stage for later discussion by applying government relations bargaining to the natural monopoly structure of the electric power industry and the rise and operation of its regulation during the twentieth century. Discussion focuses on vertical integration of the industry, the evolution of regulation, and the concomitant stability of rate regulation. Cost-of-service regulation is firm specific. In fact, for more than 50 years, it worked as a forum for negotiating any tension between public and private interests; individual firms were deterred from conduct that undermined the regulator because this could have negative implications for their approved rates. During the era of natural monopoly regulation, which focused its attention on the outputs of the firm (in the form of service prices and quality), regulatory law formulated doctrines to constrain private actors, such as service obligations, as well as doctrines to constrain public actors, such as the takings clause (constraining federal and state regulators), the filed tariff doctrine (constraining courts), and the dormant commerce clause and antitrust immunities (constraining state regulators). Given the idealized bargaining conditions of the rate regulation process, however, these structural constraints were largely hidden and explicitly invoked only rarely.

Chapter 3 argues that a government relations bargaining approach can also shed light on the movement toward deregulation in electric power. By creating strong ex ante incentives for investment, the natural monopoly model encouraged overinvestment in certain sectors of the industry. Moreover, the rate-making and regulatory process – which historically focused on regulating the firm-specific outputs of the firm – worked to foreclose competition and new innovation by existing and potential competitors. In contrast to the traditional regulatory approach, the movement toward deregulation places its focus on the regulation of inputs (e.g., network access) for certain sectors of the industry and increased reliance on competition for other sectors, rather than on regulation of outputs (e.g., service prices, quality). It also changes the number and diversity of private actors interacting in markets and with the state. These firm–government interactions are more frequent and less visible, and thus less likely to lead to a convergence of private and public interests. The realm of regulatory law thus may be expected to be invoked more frequently in a deregulatory environment.

The remaining chapters use concrete vignettes from economic regulation to illustrate how government relations bargaining challenges us to revisit many doctrines of public law in the deregulatory era. If improperly applied, extant legal doctrines – many of which were hidden from the regulatory order for much of the twentieth century – can have adverse consequences for social welfare in deregulated markets or other markets in transition. Should the doctrines of regulatory law be embraced, reformed, or abandoned, given deregulation's more salient tension between private and public interests? By taking a neutral stance toward regulatory renegotiation, an account of regulation informed by incomplete contracts provides some insight into these questions. Given the increased scope and intensity of private behavior in the deregulatory environment, reform or clarification of these legal doctrines will be necessary for deregulation to fulfill its promise. At a minimum, regulatory law must more carefully approach ex ante behavior by private firms. However, government relations bargaining might also provide a way of setting out basic default rules to guide courts in reviewing regulatory disputes.

In Chapter 4, it is argued that universal service obligations – a classic "public good" – must be approached by lawmakers with greater caution in a deregulatory environment than under natural monopoly regulation. Universal service goals can be implemented in a deregulatory environment, notwithstanding the elevation of private interests over public welfare in the everyday working of deregulated markets. Chapter 4 suggests not only a national tax on power distribution to pay for universal service in a deregulated power market, but also argues that universal service would be best approached through a voucher system for low-income customers rather than an ex ante service mandate imposed by regulators or courts at the state level.

The chapters in Part II of this book directly explore the role of public law doctrines in deregulated markets. Shifts in boundaries have important implications for courts and their approach to judicial review. The government relations bargaining approach envisions a more modest approach for courts in a deregulatory era than many conventional contractual accounts of regulation, such as the legalistic contract approach. The role of courts is not to interpret and enforce preexisting regulatory bargains, as advocates of deregulatory takings suggest, nor is the judicial role limited to enforcing bargains only where there are explicit clear statements on the part of a governmental body, as some might suggest. On the government relations bargaining approach, the role of courts is also aimed at providing bargaining conditions that are likely to assist the political process in developing stable regulatory commitments in competitive markets. Default rules for courts reviewing the regulatory decisions are a way of facilitating legitimate political solutions to regulatory commitment problems. In addition, regulatory law is mindful of how institutional enforcement choices affect regulatory law. Traditionally, these enforcement choices were determined by fairly clear legal rules, given the structure of price jurisdiction and transparency in jurisdictional territory among regulatory bodies. With deregulation, ambiguity abounds and enforcement choices are increasingly influenced by private stakeholders, raising serious problems for regulatory law. Courts must referee such choices in the regulatory process in order to safeguard the public interest.

In contrast to those who conceptualize regulation as a "regulatory contract," particularly Sidak and Spulber, Chapter 5 cautions against strong majoritarian default rules – especially rules rooted in constitutional law, such as the constitutional takings or breach of contract constraints some would impose on governmental bodies in the deregulatory environment. Regulatory contract advocates envision the government paying damages for regulatory and deregulatory transitions; in contrast, an insurance perspective illustrates how the ex ante incentives created by such compensation can be harmful. Chapter 5 argues that recovery for a utility's stranded costs, whether based on constitutional or policy arguments, creates perverse ex ante incentives by encouraging overinvestment in infrastructure, and might also discourage competition and innovation. This chapter also favors a process-based majoritarian default rule of judicial deference in such contexts, coupled with a clear statement rule as a way for courts to evaluate breach of contract claims against the government.

Chapter 6 takes on a steadfast doctrine of regulatory law – the filed tariff doctrine. This doctrine is frequently invoked by federal courts as a basis for refusing jurisdiction over cases involving utility conduct. Thus, it has a particularly important role to play as legal conflicts arise in deregulated markets. The filed rate doctrine is not a single rule but is a legal amalgam of several independent objectives, including protecting against price discrimination, federal preemption-related concerns, and nonjusticiability concerns. An incomplete contracts analysis exposes a serious problem with the filed rate doctrine. Because tariffs are rarely complete, courts must fill in the gap regarding their enforcement mechanism. As a default rule, the filed tariff doctrine designates the regulatory agency, not the courts, as the enforcement institution for tariffs. This might be what a majority of bargaining entities, particularly regulated firms and government agencies, prefer; however, such a default rule leaves the ex ante choice of institutional forum for governance of the industry largely to private firms. The conventional account views the filed tariff doctrine as an impediment to deregulation. In contrast, Chapter 6 argues that the default rule of the filed tariff doctrine encourages firms to engage in strategic behavior in tariffing, leaving courts powerless and even resulting in more radical deregulation than either Congress or agencies would prefer.

If the filed tariff shield is relaxed where there a one-sided opportunity for a firm to forum shop in tariffing with little or no third-party monitoring of enforcement, federal courts could serve the public interest by playing an important enforcement role in deregulatory markets. In such contexts, a inventive-based default rule – allowing courts to consider antitrust and other legal claims against the backdrop of tariffs even when both the regulator and firm might prefer otherwise – would encourage better disclosure and monitoring in the tariff context.

Chapter 7 examines the dormant commerce clause, which constrains state regulators from adopting protectionist policies that impede interstate commerce. It relates this doctrine to an independent rule: state action immunity from antitrust enforcement, which precludes antitrust challenges to private conduct that is consistent with certain state regulatory schemes. The dormant commerce clause will play an important role in the deregulated environment to the extent that it limits the ability of state and local regulators to impede competition, especially from out-of-state suppliers. I focus on the similarities between this goal and antitrust immunity for state regulation. Specifically, courts must more carefully evaluate state action immunity in order to guard against private actors' ex ante use of state regulation to shield their conduct from antitrust law, limiting the gains to social welfare from competition.

Many of the problems that plague electric power deregulation arise due to jurisdictional gaps and overlaps in enforcement that can be traced to the dual-jurisdictional approach to the regulation of electric power in the United States. For example, where states such as California have deregulated retail power markets, the behavior of firms in wholesale power markets, deregulated by federal authorities, may allow for manipulation of downstream prices and supply in ways that escape the scrutiny of both state and federal regulators. Even where states have not deregulated electric power at the retail level, strategic use of deregulated wholesale markets may harm consumers and escape the scrutiny of regulators. Recalcitrant state legislatures, which frequently adhere steadfastly to outdated regulatory statutes that limit the ability of state and local agencies to even consider the needs of deregulated interstate power markets, present one of the greatest challenges for wholesale competition in electric power. In the Telecommunications Act of 1996, Congress endorsed cooperative federalism, an alternative regulatory regime designed to both encourage experimentation and to clarify jurisdictional authority by encouraging great coordination between federal and state and local regulators. However, in other contexts with widespread jurisdictional confusion, such as electric power, Congress has failed to pass legislation clarifying jurisdictional ambiguities, enhancing even further the power of a state legislature to defect from competitive power markets. In Chapter 8, it is argued that a judicially imposed set of default rules could help to improve the regulatory solutions for network industries such as electric power. This chapter recommends a presumption against preemption of state regulation, while endorsing a presumption in favor of state or local agencies acting on behalf of federal goals as a way of closing jurisdictional gaps, enhancing incentives for jurisdictional coordination, and overcoming recalcitrant state legislatures in the regulation of infrastructure.

Chapter 9 concludes by reflecting on the promise of a government relations bargaining framework for understanding regulatory law vis-à-vis competing predominant accounts of regulation: public choice theory, public interest theory, and collaborative governance. Regulatory incompleteness is a reality of complex industries. The economic literature on the economics of the firm has produced multiple insights for the substance of regulation itself. However, by highlighting how bargaining is fundamental to many problems of public governance, extension of some of these insights to government relations bargaining can help to inform the doctrines of public law in the context of economic regulation, thus helping to improve the functioning of markets – especially deregulated markets and other markets in transition.

PART I

EXTENDING INCOMPLETE BARGAINS FROM THE ECONOMICS OF THE FIRM TO PUBLIC GOVERNANCE

2

Regulatory Bargaining and the Stability of Natural Monopoly Regulation

During most of the twentieth century, utility firms in industries such as electric power and telecommunications were characterized by two primary features: vertical integration of the industry and regulation of rates based on cost of service. Cost-of-service regulation of telecommunications and energy utilities was firm specific. It occurred primarily in individual state and local jurisdictions as opposed to at the national level and, due to the structure of the industry, applied in governing jurisdictions where a single utility possessed substantial market power. For more than 50 years, traditional natural monopoly regulation worked as a particularized forum for negotiating any tension between public and private interests; individual firms were deterred from engaging in conduct that undermined the regulator because this could have negative implications for their approved rates. Richard Hirsh, a historian of the electric power industry, describes this as "a consensus between utilities and reformers concerning the nature of the American electric utility system" (Hirsh, 1999: 11). The same sort of consensus appears to have also existed in telecommunications (Noam, 1997).

To the extent that the bargain between the firm and government was stable, it is not clear what role public law played for economic regulation during the twentieth century. During the era of natural monopoly regulation, regulators focused their primary attention on governing outputs of the firm (in the form of mandated service prices and quality). These agency decisions were subject to judicial review, but courts largely deferred to agency regulators. On rare occasion, regulatory law also looked to constitutional and structural doctrines as default rules to frame bargaining for private actors – such as service obligations for firms – and governmental bodies – such as the U.S. Constitution's Takings Clause (constraining federal and state regulators), the filed tariff doctrine (primarily constraining courts), the dormant commerce clause and various immunities from antitrust regulation (limiting both state and federal regulators), and jurisdictional limits on regulatory authority (constraining both federal and state regulators, depending on their legal source).

Regulatory law had a distinct form, but the stable consensus behind the rate regulation process and its ability to promote cooperative solutions to most regulatory conflicts left many of its structural constraints hidden. As Robert Ellickson's (1994) classic study of disputes in rural Shasta County, California, puts it, "members of tight social groups will informally encourage each other to engage in cooperative behavior" (167). The farmers and cattlemen in close-knit Shasta County had little role for judicial intervention in resolving their disputes over animal trespass and "lawful fences" (Ellickson, 1994). Similarly, Professor Lisa Bernstein (1992, 2001) found that merchants in the cotton and diamond trades, with well-developed background norms, largely opt out of the formal legal system. Like merchants contracting against the backdrop of well-developed norms, similarly situated utility firms contracting with regulators may not have a need for judicial enforcement of the bargain.

During the natural monopoly era of price regulation, courts were rarely asked to invoke the formal doctrines of regulatory law to resolve disputes; even when they were called on, courts largely avoided intervening in disputes that would resolve themselves on their own within the public and private institutional environment. Legal doctrines may have been important in framing basic bargaining conditions for firms and governmental bodies in the realm of economic regulation, but the role of regulatory law was only significant where transaction costs were so high that bargaining could not solve conflicts on its own within the institutional framework of the regulatory agency. Under natural monopoly regulation, bargaining rarely failed to solve conflicts on its own.

I. THE REGULATORY CONTRACT, THE LAW AND ECONOMICS OF VERTICAL INTEGRATION, AND RATE REGULATION

Among regulatory lawyers, natural monopoly regulation is often understood by reference to a "regulatory compact," a fictional contract between the utility and the state (Sidak & Spulber, 1997). Under this compact, the utility consents to certain obligations, such as the duty to serve, in return for its geographic franchise and expected recovery of its costs of service through regulated rates (Hirsh, 1999). In the parlance of economists, the relationship between a utility and government can be understood within a long-term contract framework, given the large amounts of capital required for network infrastructure and the complexity of the underlying environment, leading to poor specification of contractual terms (Goldberg, 1976; Williamson, 1979). Some modern commentators argue that this contract, although tacit if not metaphorical, must be honored by the state as any other legal contract (Sidak & Spulber, 1997; Spulber & Yoo, 2003). As George Priest (1992) suggests, however, the regulatory compact rationale is perhaps best understood not only as a legal obligation (if it is that at all – see Chapter 5), but also as an account of the evolution of utility regulation. Priest's evolutionary approach to regulatory bargains finds support in the incomplete contracts account of bargaining.

A. Incomplete Contracts, Bargaining Renegotiation, and Regulatory Flexibility

Early law and economics scholars, such as Ronald Coase, recognized the importance of transactions costs in framing discussion of organizational form (Coase, 1937) and legal rules (Coase, 1960). Few debates in law and economics stray far from issues raised in Ronald Coase's two seminal works, "The Problem of Social Costs" (Coase, 1960) and "The Nature of the Firm" (Coase, 1937). Although "The Problem of Social Costs" dominates many modern discussions of legal rules, the impact of Coase's earlier work, "The Nature of the Firm," is equally important. Coase set out to explain why the private firm emerges in a market economy. According to Coase, the main reason the firm emerges is that there is a cost to external exchange using the price mechanism of the market. Taking inspiration from Coase, law and economics scholars have systematically favored discussions of private law – corporations, torts, contracts – over larger-scale legal issues, such as the nature and scope of public law and the processes that lead to its enactment. Within the context of these discussions, the incomplete contracts framework – viewing legal rules as a response to incompleteness in contractual bargaining – is an undeniably important theoretical development in the law and economics of corporations and contracts.

A second important set of framework tools for evaluating incompleteness in contracting comes from decision theory. Herbert Simon, an early decision theorist, tempered traditional assumptions of self-interest with the notion of bounded rationality: that actors are "*intendedly* rational, but only *limitedly* so" (Simon, 1961: xxiv, emphasis in original). If human rationality is bounded, it is impossible to know every possible state of affairs at the time of contracting. Under circumstances where there are substantial transaction costs or where rationality is bounded, comprehensive bargaining – in design of the firm's organization and in its private and public governance – is not feasible.

Transaction costs and bounded rationality are two reasons that transactional bargains are incomplete. Within the economics literature, the incomplete contracts framework has been most rigorously, if not exhaustively, applied to the economics of the firm. Drawing on this insight, in the 1970s, Oliver Williamson sketched a transactional framework for a new approach to industrial organization. Williamson's transactional cost framework acknowledges the relational nature of the enterprise of contracting, while also recognizing the comparative institutional task of assessing transaction costs in the contracting process. For Williamson (1975), markets – an endless cycle of private transactions – and hierarchies are the two main institutional options for facilitating the integrity of a transaction. Williamson (1979) recognizes that transaction-specific governance rules would be likely to be more developed in contexts in which transactions are recurrent, entail idiosyncratic investment, and are executed under greater uncertainty.

In similar vein, Oliver Hart (1988, 1995) looked to incomplete contracts – that there are transaction costs to writing contracts – to explain how residual rights of control over the corporation are related to its ownership. Hart's approach emphasizes how renegotiation is almost endemic to most intrafirm transactions, as well as interfirm and firm–government transactions. In other words, the incomplete contracts model is based on the assumption that, due to limited knowledge about future states of affairs, the parties to the contract cannot commit not to renegotiate the contract in the future (Hart & Moore, 1999).

The formal incomplete contracts model, commonly attributed in economics to Eric Maskin and Jean Tirole (1999), has limits. Where the state and private parties both have access to information and have mobility to exit relationships, completeness could evolve in regulatory relationships. Where parties do not have the mobility to exit relationships, however, as may be the case in the context of the process of contracting for government regulation, even incomplete contracts critics such as Maskin and Tirole concede that contracts may be incomplete.[1] The iterated nature of regulation against the backdrop of judicial review – firms contracting with

[1] For the more general argument that the Maskin and Tirole critique does not undermine the transaction costs literature, see Hart and Moore (1999).

the state know that they will have future opportunities to influence the regulator or courts, and the regulator knows that it may need to preserve discretion to change course in the future – also make incompleteness a likely, if not necessary, result in the context of regulation.

Indeed, in the context of regulation, incompleteness is not only conceptually possible. It may be desirable as well. As any legislator, regulator, or judge knows, it is not feasible to write a law with such detail that it can encompass and take care of most, let alone every, issue in its express terms. In fact, in the context of public law, excessively detailed specifications in law can be costly if they are under- or overinclusive. One cost of overinclusive retails in law is complexity (Ruhl & Salzman, 2003). Detailed specifications may also cost at the cost of experimentation and flexibility in regulatory policy (Dorf & Sabel, 1998). Thus, any system of public law will settle on an optimal degree of precision (Diver, 1983; Gómez-Ibáñez, 2003; Goodin, 1982). At some point, the costs of precision in the bargaining process will exceed their benefits. A system that anticipates renegotiation may be more efficient and hence desirable – as long as litigation costs do not become exorbitant.

B. An Incomplete Contracts Account of Vertical Intergration in the Utility Industry

The incomplete contracts framework is a helpful way of understanding the rise of vertical integration in utility industries. In the preregulation era, firms negotiated primarily with state and local legislative bodies, and eventually with legislators at the national level. For example, the modern, investor-owned electric utility was conceived in late nineteenth-century Chicago by Samuel Insull, an associate of Thomas Edison (Platt, 1991). Insull is much maligned in history for his financing tactics in consolidating ownership of the electric power industry. However, like many other monopolists, his innovative ways of approaching the business side of electric power were novel and his influence lasted long beyond the collapse of his holding company empire. By 1890, economists such as Richard T. Ely and Henry Carter Adams had written that monopolies result from economies of scale achieved by technological innovation (Adams, 1887; Ely, 1887; Hovenkamp, 1991). Indeed, the historian Harold Platt (1991) observes that Insull's approach "represented a practical application of a novel economic and constitutional theory of 'natural' monopoly" (74). Initially, large Chicago electricity users, such as apartment buildings, hotels, fancy shops, and department stores, generated power locally

(Platt, 1991). Eventually, Chicago Edison (Commonwealth Edison's predecessor), competing for increased service territory, realized that ownership of multiple generators within the same horizontal firm structure allowed significant coordination economies (Platt, 1991). Hence, Insull was able to horizontally consolidate a geographic service territory for a single utility, Chicago Edison; the utility was required to provide service, and in return the utility was given an exclusive franchise, precluding others from providing service within its franchise area.

In addition, integration of generation, transmission, and distribution functions within the same vertical firm allowed significant operational economies. In addressing the economic arguments for vertical integration, it is useful to consider electricity's technical characteristics. First, electricity transmission follows physical, not economic, relationships. Because electrons travel in the path of least resistance, the physical transmission of electricity defies a predefined contract path linking particular buyers and sellers to physically identifiable products. Thus, analogies to highways, railroads, or pipelines can be misleading. Second, electricity cannot be feasibly stored. Although high-voltage cells are physically capable of storing large capacities of electricity, their cost is prohibitively high. It is also not feasible to simply let electricity travel through the grid until it finds a user because kilowatts are quickly lost with every mile of transmission and the risk of overload (and accompanying blackout) is great. It is far more efficient to use electricity as it is produced, requiring tight coordination between power supply and demand. Third, the transmission of electricity is sensitive to the generation input acting upon the grid. For these reasons, electricity must be moved on a closely coordinated, integrated transmission system that displays large economies of scale.[2]

Under these technological conditions, widely accepted throughout the twentieth century, vertical integration of generation, transmission, and distribution functions within the same firm was almost universally believed to create significant operational economies within the industry. The vertical integration of generation and transmission is the market's recognition of two technical phenomena that make separation of these functions potentially costly: (1) "Electrical equilibrium," the transmission

[2] Although important, the economic relevance of these technical characteristics should not be exaggerated. The differences between electricity and other commodities are only differences in degree. For instance, other industries face physical constraints on transportation (e.g., railroads), and other commodities are difficult and costly to store (e.g., natural gas). Firms in the electricity industry, like firms in other industries, have found ways to economize on the costly technical characteristics of electricity.

stasis necessary to avoid blackout, requires that the sum of power demanded must equal the sum of power supplied at generation buses minus the amount of power lost in transmission; and (2) individual generators cannot physically direct their output to any particular customer or demand point. A vertically integrated generation and transmission utility is able to economize on these technical complexities by engaging in "economic dispatch" (using the least expensive generator to meet its customer demands), monitoring generation to maintain internal electrical equilibrium, and diversifying its contracts to allow an operationally flexible combination of generation capacity to meet its customer load. Of course, vertical integration was not without costs. For instance, under this scenario, a utility could make a decision to build generation facilities near its customers as a substitute for expanding the capacity of power transmission lines, possibly resulting in transmission bottlenecks in transmission-constrained areas. Nevertheless, the reasons for vertical integration were believed to demand the natural monopoly system, which by the middle of the twentieth century was virtually universal in the industry (Grossman, 2003).[3]

Beginning with Insull's efforts at integration to grow business, utility firms rapidly began to realize economies through the vertical integration of generation and transmission and the horizontal integration of multiple electric power generators. In his famous article "The Nature of the Firm," Ronald Coase (1937) observed that all transactions in an economy are not necessarily most efficiently realized through explicit exchange in the market.[4] Oliver Williamson generalized Coase's observation to present a framework for analyzing the costs of market contracting and the optimal degree of vertical and horizontal integration, or internal contracting. Williamson observed that the costs of market contracting vary with uncertainty, the frequency of transactions, asset specificity (the extent to which durable assets are tailored to specific transactions), and problems caused by private opportunism. Transactions exhibiting a higher concentration of these characteristics require complex contracts and tend

[3] As of the 1980s, it was common acknowledged that "[v]ertical integration between generation and transmission is virtually universal" (Joskow & Schmalensee, 1983: 113).

[4] There is, in principle, no need for the market to organize around firms. Instead, market actors could organize through arms-length transactions with the guidance of price mechanisms. A firm simply bypasses (or internalizes) the system of market prices and coordinates production without the use of explicit prices. Essentially, Coase was taking exception to the then-dominant understanding that the "natural" evolution of the firm was defined by technology and its costs, and could be taken as given.

to favor integration within organizations. As the need for contractual complexity rises, so does the cost of bilateral contracting, making internal control more attractive (Williamson, 1996a). The Coase/Williamson framework provides one explanation for the high degree of vertical integration in the twentieth-century electric utility industry, central to the traditional framework of natural monopoly regulation. This high degree of vertical integration in the industry minimized the costs of contracting by internalizing costs, many of which are informational (Casson, 1997), within a single firm.

Samuel Insull also recognized that significant economies could be realized from the horizontal integration of electrical generation, distribution, and transmission. Much of this, too, is internal to the firm. Originally, it was difficult to achieve high degrees of horizontal integration because power systems could not be coordinated. However, with technological innovations the central station became a feasible technology for integrating adjacent electricity transmission systems (Platt, 1991). Ownership of multiple generators within the same horizontally integrated firm structure results in greater efficiency if there are significant coordination economies. In the early years of the electric power industry, technological innovations permitted the integration of large central power stations and adjacent electric generators into a single horizontally integrated transmission system.[5] The technology that allowed such a high level of horizontal integration appeared to offer some scale economies. However, the attraction of vertical and horizontal integration also had its limits. Typically, a given local or state jurisdiction could only sustain between one and three investor-owned utilities, so the limited jurisdictional reach of governmental regulation served as a natural limit on the firm's desire to merge. So did "power pooling" – voluntary external contracting with adjacent utilities that worked to diversify power supply options while also preserving some flexibility for firms.[6]

[5] As Platt (1991) suggests, such horizontal integration was dependent on the development of AC current, allowing the extension of electricity transmission beyond a mile and a half, and the technology of central station coordination. In addition, a large degree of horizontal integration has been externally established through informal coordination and contractual pooling (Platt, 1991). For example, it is commonplace for vertically integrated utilities to functionally and operationally integrate with other separately owned utilities through long-term cooperative activities and long-term contractual arrangements governing transmission (Joskow & Schmalensee, 1983).

[6] In addition, a large degree of horizontal integration has been externally established through informal coordination and contractual pooling. "Power pools" – formal and informal agreements among independent utilities to coordinate their investment and operating

Although economic rationales favored high degrees of vertical and horizontal integration in the electricity industry, an integrated firm structure also presents potential problems. The integration of constituent services and a geographic franchise under the rubric of a single firm called for some degree of franchise and price regulation to control market power and welfare-reducing monopolistic behavior and to provide stability for the firm (and its investors) over time. Under the traditional approach, regulators define a franchise service area for a public utility, guaranteeing it access to customers within this area (Phillips, 1993). Once a franchise is defined, the traditional approach to regulating the electric utility was to regulate rates in a manner designed to approximate the results of a competitive market. In a competitive market, price equals long-run marginal economic cost, including a normal rate of return on capital. In contrast, though, a monopolist can increase its profits by charging prices that exceed marginal cost. Because marginal cost is difficult to measure directly, regulators approximate marginal cost by computing the utility's invested capital ("rate base"), determining an allowable rate of return on that invested capital and setting rates designed to produce the prescribed rate of return on capital.

As historians such as Richard Hirsh (1999) describe it, utility managers in the electric power industry sought the proliferation of the natural monopoly price regulation model in individual states. Insull headed a

activities – also provide certain economies for the industry. "Electrical equilibrium" between adjacent systems can only be achieved through the operational coordination pooling provides. Moreover, the efficient operation of power generation requires adjacent systems to engage in "economy interchanges," the alteration of generation levels to equate line loss adjusted marginal cost (operationally known as "system lambda"). The pooling of separately owned vertically integrated generation and transmission resources facilitates such economy interchange. Thus, it is commonplace for vertically integrated utilities to functionally and operationally integrate with other separately owned utilities through long-term cooperative activities and long-term contractual arrangements governing transmission (Joskow & Schmalensee, 1983). Paul Joskow and Richard Schmalensee, perhaps the leading U.S. commentators on the economic structure of the electric utility industry, have observed that as of 1979 formal power pools, governed by interutility contracts, accounted for nearly 60 percent of U.S. generating capacity. Informal cooperative pools between utilities also exist in certain geographic areas (Joskow & Schmalensee, 1983). As Joskow and Schmalensee note, power pooling is a substitute for vertical integration. In addition to power pools, federal regulators have established nine regional reliability councils that facilitate information exchange within their interconnected member systems and establish reliability criteria for system interconnections and power supply. Together, these nine regional groups form the North American Electricity Reliability Council (NERC), whose members include utilities, public authorities, and representatives of the federal government. NERC continues to play a major role in deregulated power markets.

trade association called the National Electric Light Association (NELA), which played a key role in proposing and lobbying for state regulation of electric utilities throughout the United States. The NELA viewed municipal ownership of utilities as the main alternative to price regulation but opposed public ownership. A compromise position, forged by the University of Wisconsin economist John Commons, who worked together with Insull, supported state price regulation of privately owned utilities in states such as Wisconsin and New York (Bradley, 2003). Eventually, regulation shifted from legislative bodies to expert regulatory agencies, which adjudicated entry into the industry and the appropriateness of rates charged by existing firms.

This regulatory approach had – and although no longer the ideal, continues to have – a major impact not only on the public utility firm (Chen, 2004) and the substance and stability of regulation (Hirsh, 1999), but also on the structure of the electric power industry. The vertically integrated utility provides generation, distribution, and transmission to its customers. Transmission is the long-distance network that allows access to power supply in the form of generation. For a vertically integrated utility, local or regionally sited power plants can serve as a substitute for expanding transmission networks to allow access to other power supply options. Over much of the twentieth century, investment decisions by the vertically integrated utility were made with this crucial economic trade-off in mind. As a result, transmission "bottlenecks" arose in many areas of the United States. With the vertically integrated firm as the norm, these deficiencies were largely hidden, if they were problems at all, but it is fair to say that because of this history in the industry the modern national transmission grid is not designed with sufficient network capacity to make power supply options substitutable in every area of the country. This has important implications for any transition to competition in the industry because competitive markets in the electric power industry look to the transmission network as the transportation infrastructure for market-provided power supply. To the extent the industry today has inherited a network that was designed with the trade-offs of the vertically integrated firm in mind, market access will be limited until transmission capacity is reallocated.

II. BARGAINING IN THE SHADOW OF REGULATORY LAW

It is conventional wisdom that the incomplete contracts approach to regulation provides a powerful explanation of the natural monopoly structure of twentieth-century regulated industries and their regulation. How an incomplete contracts account of natural monopoly regulation might explain the stability of regulatory law for much of the last century is much less acknowledged and much less explored. Law and regulation do not exist in isolation of the political process that develops and sustains them. During the twentieth century, natural monopoly regulation provided a relatively stable type of government intervention for price-regulated utilities. The stability of this regulatory order relegated many of the doctrines of regulatory law to a dormant status. Indeed, history suggests that many of these doctrines were of questionable value, given the largely self-correcting regulatory system of rate setting.

Against the backdrop of the vertically integrated firm with service obligations, three features of the regulatory contract influenced the course of twentieth-century regulatory law: jurisdiction-matched market monopoly (along with barriers to entry), output regulation of the firm, and iterated negotiations between the firm and the regulator. Together, these features worked to relegate many of the nonspecialized doctrines of regulatory law – administrative law, constitutional law, antitrust, and federalism – to the shadows of the regulatory process during the era of rate regulation.

First, market monopoly for utility industries was the norm, both as a matter of fact and law. In most jurisdictions, a single firm exercised market power with respect to telecommunications or electric service. Further, within local jurisdictions regulators identified a single firm (sometimes two or three, depending on jurisdictional size) as a de jure monopolist operating free of interfirm competition as the provider of service for all customers. A single firm in most jurisdictions allowed for lower cost of bargaining with the local regulator than would have been the case in more complex markets or if regulation were national in nature. For example, in many states one or two vertically integrated electric utilities served the entire market, allowing firms to procure state or local regulation at a lower cost than federal regulation, while also making the regulator's task at the state level far less expensive and simpler than national regulation. The bargaining procurement account of state regulation can explain both the supply and the demand for state (and local) public utility commission regulation of firms – as opposed to more extensive national regulation – early in the twentieth century. Because state or local regulation was the norm, the electric utility industry grew up with a tight degree of coordination between the regulatory jurisdiction (typically statewide) and the conduct regulated (typically a handful of firms with monopoly power operating only in an individual state or locality). Eventually, national regulators were extended some jurisdiction over specific transactions – primarily to close regulatory gaps that existed given the state-based ratemaking process – but for much of the twentieth century the regulatory process remained based at the state or local level, where most regulatory barriers were implemented and retail prices for utility services were determined.

Second, the nature of regulation was focused almost exclusively on the control of the firm's outputs (Spulber & Yoo, 2003). Specifically, rate regulation, or regulation of the firm's prices, was the primary forum for regulatory decisions, including decisions about the firm's expansion. Such regulation emphasized prices and their relationship to the firm's costs, but rarely did regulators focus on alternative regulatory strategies, such as input regulation, regulation of market structure, and disclosure. Output regulation influenced the kind of information and mechanisms that regulators used (Pechman, 1993). Because outputs were firm specific, negotiations between the agency regulator and individual firms – not industrywide regulation – were the norm. Regulators focused primarily on the regulation of entry and price, but during the era of natural monopoly regulation input decisions by the firm were largely left to private decisions in the marketplace.

Third, regulatory decisions were iterated negotiations between a single firm, a small number of stakeholder groups with largely homogenous interests, and the agency regulator. In contrast to noneconomic regulation, this presented a relatively stable equilibrium for two reasons. To begin, the iterated structure of rate regulation created expectations of stability for the firm and helped to reduce the asymmetry of information between the firm and the regulator. If in one period the firm was undercompensated for its activities, the regulator could make up the difference in the next period. Likewise, if the firm incurred windfalls, regulators might recoup some of these in a future period. In this sense, repeated iterations made the rate-making process self-correcting from the perspective of the firm and its costs. This might explain part of the traditional preference of regulatory agencies for case-by-case regulation of the firm over industrywide rulemaking (Quirk, 1981).

The iterated negotiation of rate making was also stable due to the historical structure of industry and interest group stakeholders. Although traditional rate regulation had significant costs (some of which are discussed in Chapter 3), price regulation of natural monopolies concentrated the benefits and dispersed the costs of regulation. As Martha Derthick and Paul Quirk (1985) observed about regulated industries generally, "[t]he predominant view of both economists and political scientists was that regulation presented a case in which the benefits of government policy were concentrated in a few well-organized interests – the firms and unions that were protected from competition – whereas the costs were widely dispersed among consumers whose incentives to organize to protect their interests were insufficient to induce political action" (9–10). Price regulation presents problems such as errors in assumptions in the rate-making process, regulatory lag, and overinvestment (discussed in Chapter 3), but to the extent these problems are correctable or dispersed, price regulation can also provide an equilibrium state of affairs for firms in the industry.

It also provided a stable equilibrium for the primary nonfirm stakeholders, such as consumer and environmental interest groups. Rate making provided rate stability for customers, but as is discussed here it also subsidized access to service for low-income and rural customers. For environmental interest groups as well, the rate making process produced great opportunities. With only a few large firms providing service in any given state jurisdiction, the politics of environmental regulation at the state and national levels could portray large monopolies as the primary targets for pollution control and other environmental mandates. Although utilities were not always complacent with pollution controls – especially those imposed on existing plants with little or no guarantee of cost recovery – firms were also not unaware of the low stakes most locally sanctioned, forward-looking environmental controls presented to them. Through the rate-making process, the cost of complying with these mandates could be spread among all customers, rather than concentrated on the firm or its shareholders. Thus, nonfirm stakeholders had a role to play in the iterated bargaining process; however, these interest groups often stood to benefit substantially by using the rate-making process to subsidize the things they valued most.

Combined, these three features had important implications for the shape of twentieth-century regulatory law. Because the homogenous, vertically integrated utility could negotiate for regulation at relatively low costs, coordinated solutions to most conflicts were worked out before regulatory commissions, not courts.[7] Public utility law – in the contexts of telecommunications, electric, and natural gas services – became a highly

[7] Other factors may also have contributed to the stability of rate regulation. Even if we do not accept the strong version of the capture thesis, the relationship was, as public choice theory reminds us, quite cozy. Further, as discussed in Chapter 3, rate regulation was relatively quiet until the late 1960s because the economy was expanding and strong growth in demand was predictable.

specialized area of legal practice, in which lawyers in Washington, DC, and state capitals focused their attention and skills on practice before a singe jurisdictional agency. Lawyers often specialized even further within a specific industry. For instance, energy lawyers and telecommunications lawyers were rarely one in the same; each developed their own specialized bar groups, practice areas within larger firms, and boutique law firms in Washington, DC, and larger state capitals. The specialized nature of legal practice worked well under the traditional natural monopoly model because the lawyer's main contribution was to ensure stability of the regulatory bargain within an industry.

Although the features of the regulatory bargain may have allowed specialization to proliferate, they also relegated much public law to near invisibility in the regulatory process. Because traditional public utility law was a highly specialized area, other legal doctrines played only a peripheral role in its development and implementation. The doctrines of regulatory law blended in close harmony with the regulatory contract and were invoked rarely to override or change the regulatory process; private parties to the negotiation – monopoly firms – had little reason to explicitly invoke litigious doctrines when a negotiated or cooperative solution could yield equal, if not better, results for them. Stronger yet, public law doctrines may have been mere background rules, framing the negotiation but providing little direct benefit themselves. Whatever account of these doctrines is correct, if public law is understood as a set of default rules invoked where bargaining fails to produce a coordinated solution, its doctrines were largely relegated a secondary role to the negotiated process of regulation for much of the twentieth century.

For example, for all the rhetoric in American law about "universal service" and the "duty to serve," during the era of rate regulation consumer service obligations were frequently undertaken voluntarily by utilities – not adopted because they were required by regulatory law. Companies (beginning with Samuel Insull's Chicago Edison) relied on the scale economies claim to support their monopolies but, in return for an exclusive franchise (precluding others from providing service within a defined geographic area) and rate regulation (guaranteeing recovery of capital costs), these firms understood that they were agreeing to an important condition: the extension and continued provision of service to all customers. Universal service was considered a key part of the natural monopoly franchise bargain (Platt, 1991) – a default rule frequently imposed by regulators and courts – even where it was not an express term of the bargain. Prohibitions on direct competition increased system stability and reliability, minimizing some of the costs of vertical coordination, and decreased horizontal coordination costs by ensuring only a few adjacent utilities are parties to any power pool. Prohibitions on competition also hid any costs associated with using generation as a substitute for transmission expansion. In return, though, customers must be guaranteed access to power supply and distribution services if requested because these services are bundled together and provided by a single firm.

Twentieth-century U.S. regulators built on an ancient common law duty that applied to public utilities such as ferries, flour mills, and railroads, imposing on electric utilities a "duty to serve" – an obligation to provide extraordinary levels of service to customers, especially small residential customers. As applied by courts and regulators in most states, the public utility duty to serve entailed several obligations, among them duties to interconnect and extend service if requested, to provide continuing reliable service, to provide advanced notice of service disconnection, and to continue service even though a customer could not make full payment. Unlike other obligations that applied to private firms, including those such as inns and restaurants representing or holding themselves out as serving the public,[8] in the public utility context the duty to serve required service where it was not ordinarily considered profitable.

The link between the public utility concept and the duty to serve survived many different regulatory eras and institutional arrangements, garnering a variety of intellectual explanations (Arteburn, 1927; Burdick, 1911; Robinson, 1928; Wyman, 1903). There are strong fairness or distributional arguments supporting a duty to serve. Many of these overlap with the goals of the civil rights movement, without which many customers would not have had equal access to quality utility service. However, in the classic era of public utility regulation (beginning with the Gilded Age and lasting through the 1990s), the economics of the

[8] Of course, civil rights laws may preclude service exclusion for some groups of individuals (Singer, 1996), but their scope is limited. Also, to the extent a public utility is a state actor (e.g., a municipal utility), the Due Process and Equal Protection Clauses of the U.S. Constitution may impose some limitation on service exclusion. Apart from these exceptions, under antitrust laws ordinary private businesses may unilaterally refuse to deal with particular customers and set the terms and conditions under which they contract. See *United States v. Colgate & Co.*, 250 U.S. 300, 307 (1919). The duty to serve, however, imposes significantly more rigorous dealing and service terms and conditions on utilities than other private actors.

regulatory contract, on which natural monopoly regulation is based, provided the predominant intellectual framework supporting extraordinary obligations for providers of utility services.

Under the natural monopoly regulatory framework, the duty to extend service, even where it is not immediately profitable, can be economically efficient. As Richard Epstein (1997a) suggested, "the obligation of universal service to all comers is the obvious and effective way to overcome the holdout advantage that common carriers would otherwise possess against their customers" (2118). Law and economics scholars distinguish between property rules, which include a right to exclude others from use, and liability rules, which include no right of exclusion but a right to compensation for use (Calabresi & Melamed, 1972). Utilities subject to a duty to extend service are not given an ordinary property right to exclude. Instead, the utility is protected by a liability rule, which allows customers to take service on demand in return for compensation, as determined through an elaborate rate-making system. Effectively, service extension obligations are imposed on the utility, rather than assumed by the consumer, because the utility is better positioned to spread the costs of extension among multiple customers thus minimizing the wealth impact on poorer customers.

Cost spreading is a primary rationale behind the extension obligation applicable to utilities, but "service continuation" obligations are understood by analogizing to long-term bilateral contracts between a supplier and a buyer and the identification of the superior risk bearer (Williamson, 1976). In industries with large upfront capital investments, long-term contracts are necessary to entice suppliers to make investments. Without long-term contracts guaranteeing a reliable pool of buyers of a good, many suppliers would not make the necessary capital investments to produce or distribute the good. For example, in the natural gas industry, long-term contracts between pipelines and local distributions companies were essential to financing the national pipeline infrastructure (Pierce, 1988).

As is ordinary in practice, long-term contracts in private industries are often negotiated to allow flexibility in either price or quantity. The extended durations of such contracts pose problems for planning risk management, and "gaps" in such contracts will always exist. For sales of goods, once service under such a contract commences, a supplier has an obligation to continue to meet reasonable demands for services and not renege on this obligation if a more profitable alternative comes along (U.C.C. § 2–306). For example, assume a seller has agreed to supply a buyer's coal requirements for a 20-year period. The parties base their price-per-ton figure on a Department of Labor price index. However, over time incidents such as oil embargoes and inflation cause the supplier's production costs to exceed the agreed index, so if the seller continues to perform it will suffer substantial losses. Nevertheless, the approach of some courts in reviewing such contracts has been to hold the seller completely responsible and to grant specific performance.[9] Thus, in the long-term contract context, some courts have in effect enforced a service continuation obligation, even in the face of substantial economic losses to the seller (Joskow, 1977).[10]

This approach to enforcing contracts has some efficiency basis in the long-term contract context where the seller is the superior risk bearer (Posner & Rosenfield, 1977; Speidel, 1981). In the electric utility context, the long-term agreement was endorsed by an understanding between a utility and its customers, which regulatory lawyers refer to as the regulatory compact. One of the parties to this hypothetical agreement, the utility, is a rate-regulated monopolist. Vis-à-vis the end use customer, the utility is the superior risk bearer with respect to changes in the supply of electricity and the technological aspects of transmission and distribution. The customer, though, may be the better risk bearer with respect to its unforeseeable uses of the utility's service. At the same time, as between the utility and customers, the utility is in a better position to spread any losses associated with service cut-off among multiple customers, especially where those losses might have an impact on low-income rate payers or small businesses. A general utility obligation to continue service and to pay for foreseeable damages places the risk of shut-off on the superior risk bearer and cost spreader.[11] The utility, then, can attempt to seek compensation for these risks and costs through regulated rates, while also providing customers adequate opportunities to contest service curtailment or to seek an alternative supplier.[12]

[9] *Missouri Pub. Serv. Co. v. Peabody Coal Co.*, 583 S.W.2d 721 (Mo. Ct. App. 1979); *Iowa Electric Light & Power Co. v. Atlas Corp.*, 467 F. Supp. 139 (N.D. Iowa 1978).

[10] Accord U.C.C. § 2–306, comment 2. This comment notes that requirements to "curtail losses" may constitute breach.

[11] With respect to service continuation, the utility is not only the superior risk bearer, but also the superior cost spreader. In most cases it will be desirable to impose continuation obligations on the utility, except when the customer is, on average, the superior risk bearer and the gains from requiring customers to bear the risks of shut-off exceed any loss spreading gains from imposing the obligation on the utility.

[12] Although under traditional franchise and price regulation a general duty to serve has some economic efficiency grounds, one of the economic problems created by a service extension and continuation obligation is cross-subsidization. Customers who may not

The service continuation obligation facilitated intraclass cross-subsidization by building into all customers' rates the costs of customers who cannot afford to pay the full costs of their bills. Although this likely led to mismatches between any one customer's costs and rates, it allowed utilities to spread these risks among all customers. When a utility removed a customer who could not afford full payment from its system by disconnecting service, two things occurred: First, the utility avoided the variable costs of producing energy, typically the price of the fuel required to deliver the units of energy to the customer; and second, because service continuation gave the utility leverage in collection, the utility forewent any revenue that it might have been able to collect from the household if service were continued. So, assuming excess capacity, there may have been a general economic advantage to all rate payers in keeping as many customers as possible on the system. Service continuation obligations allowed the utility to spread fixed costs (for existing capacity) over a larger number of customers and to reduce the portion of each customer's bill allocated to fixed costs (Colton, 1991). Thus, even in the event of underpayment, it may have been cost effective for a utility with excess capacity to continue service to a customer and to accommodate the customer who could not afford service at cost by working out a partial payment plan, as long as it was reasonably expected that the customer could pay at least the variable cost of service.

Cross-subsidization was a necessary result of the duty to serve, but the impact of cross-subsidization was minimized by contribution requirements, the rate-making process, and cost-effectiveness considerations. Although cross-subsidization costs associated with the duty to serve were inevitable, regulators had to strike a balance to ensure the benefits of universal access to utility service offset these costs. The duty to serve (discussed further in Chapter 4) thus had a relatively continuous and stable coexistence with franchise and price regulation under natural monopoly regulation. As consumer service obligations illustrate, the general approach of the traditional rate regulation model aligned many consumer interests and the interests of the regulated firm. For similar reasons, the

benefit from service extension may be allocated a portion of the fixed costs of extension, which are built into the fixed-cost component of their rates. However, contribution requirements, imposed by many regulators, limited the degree to which utilities can subsidize service extension by increasing rates for all customers. The traditional rate-making process, in which the impact and cost effectiveness of intra- and interclass cross-subsidization are litigated, also minimized the degree of cross-subsidization resulting from the service extension obligation.

rate regulation process lived in harmony with many environmental interest groups because it was generally expected that the costs of environmental controls would be approved by state regulators in the rate-making process.

Under the natural monopoly rate regulation process, many other doctrines of regulatory law lived in harmony with the regulatory contract. Later chapters discuss these doctrines in further detail, but a brief description of their convergence with the bargain struck during the rate regulation era suffices to make the point. Constitutional takings and breach of contract claims against the government for undercompensation of the firm in rate cases (discussed in Chapter 5) were largely redundant, given the self-correcting nature of the rate-making process. Because the firm operated as a monopolist for a service territory in which the regulator was also visible, the regulator had a strong incentive to maintain the firm's financial viability. Rather than sue for takings – a utility claim the Supreme Court has failed to award a single victory since the New Deal – firms could (and routinely did) use the rate-making process to seek compensation for their losses due to the regulator's actions.

Other doctrines of regulatory law led a similarly peaceful coexistence with the regulatory contract during the era of rate regulation. The filed rate doctrine – which gave regulators exclusive jurisdiction over tariff matters – worked to benefit both regulators, by keeping courts off their turf, and the firms subject to the regulatory process, by insulating them from consumer claims (discussed in Chapter 6). Because interfirm competition was rarely the norm during the era of rate regulation, the antitrust laws rarely applied, thus relegating state action immunity (discussed in Chapter 7) a secondary role in regulated industries. Without a norm of interstate competition, the dormant commerce clause (also discussed in Chapter 7) played a minor role in regulated industries. Federalism disputes (discussed in Chapter 8) arose from time to time, but they were easily resolved by giving regulators exclusive jurisdiction over matters involving certain territories or types of service.

Through the rate-making process, the utility consensus or regulatory contract was well suited to promote voluntary cooperative solutions between firms, between firms and government, and between jurisdictional authorities. Other interest groups, primarily consumer and environmental concerns, were able to address their concerns adequately in the rate regulation process and litigious relationships were the exception, not the rule. Certainly litigation under the doctrines of regulatory law was not extinct, but stakeholders rarely resorted to litigation outside the regulatory process by which rates were set. Stakeholders demanded regulatory law solutions only when the regulatory bargaining process failed to produce a stable equilibrium on its own. In this sense, utility rate making was a type of bargain against the shadow of regulatory law (Ellickson, 1994), but public law cast a relatively faint shadow over regulated industries. For most firms operating under natural monopoly regulation, regulatory law was largely epiphenomenal to the regulatory process that sustained the equilibrium of the regulatory contract. Public law entered into the picture only when transaction costs were so high that bargaining could not solve conflicts on its own. This was rare under natural monopoly regulation, given a locally managed regulatory system in which state agencies dealt with only a handful of homogenous firms on an iterated basis.

By the late twentieth century, the law of economic regulation was little more than a description of the rate-making process, sprinkled with a few broad administrative law principles to manage a highly specialized agency regulatory process. Much of the regulatory law scholarship produced during the past few decades is sophisticated – some of it very technical – but its primary focus is on the welfare or fairness implications of different pricing and cost rules applied by regulators. Even in more recent decades, there is little or no discussion of the larger role public law might play in ordering the industry or regulatory process, particularly given changes in the stability of the regulatory system.

3

The Incompleteness of Regulatory Law

Moving Beyond the "Small World" of Natural Monopoly Regulation

In addition to explaining the traditional utility firm's vertically integrated organization and the stability of legal order in the natural monopoly regime, a government relations bargaining perspective provides important insights for the process of enactment and reform of regulatory law. Specifically, a bargaining approach provides a fruitful way of understanding many of the interactions between firms and governmental bodies, as well as among governmental bodies, in the political and legal process. It also presents a fresh way of understanding the demand for public law against the backdrop of deregulation and other legal transitions.

The bargaining approach to public governance issues is hardly novel and is certainly not foreign to law, economics, or political science. Gómez-Ibáñez (2003) advances the application of incomplete contracts to regulated industries by focusing on the conditions under which private contracting will fail and emphasizing the relationship between monopoly regulation and procurement contracting. His analysis, attentive to the general public/private institutional question, suggests that there will be a need for discretionary government regulation, often by an administrative agency, where private contracting fails. Even where an institutional approach of discretionary governmental regulation is chosen, however, bargaining retains relevance as a conceptual tool in understanding the regulatory process and its relationship to legal doctrine.

The relevance of contractual bargaining for the regulatory process has been explored by economists and political scientists, and increasingly by legal scholars. Economists have addressed the implications of incompleteness for the public procurement process, where private enterprises directly contract with the state (Laffont & Tirole, 1990, 1993). Legal scholars and political scientists have extended the incomplete contracts idea to the public law-making context more generally, analogizing statutes and regulations to "contracts" or "bargains," which presumably are incomplete given vagueness in regulatory language [Epstein, 1995 (bargaining in regulatory licensing and permitting); Farber, 1991 (legislative deals); McNollgast, 1992 (legislative bargains); Baron & Ferejohn, 1989 (majoritarian legislative bargains); Easterbrook, 1988 (statute as contract); for criticism, see Movsesian, 1998]. Economists have looked to incomplete contracts models to address incentive issues surrounding the passage of statutes and adoption of regulations (Laffont & Tirole, 1993; Martimort, De Donder, & de Villemeur, 2003).

Although these analyses come from a variety of disciplines – law, economics, and political science – they rarely speak to each. The various discourses all accept the premise that incompleteness is not limited to private transactions or the economics of the firm. Jonathan Macey aptly sketches their common ground:

> Where interest groups compete in a political marketplace, legislative institutions behave like firms whose output is law. As such the theory of the firm, rather than the theory of market exchange, guides the public choice analysis of institutions such as Congress. Like all firms, Congress organizes its internal affairs to minimize the costs of ensuring contractual performance.[1]

Macey (1986) recognizes that the bargaining analysis is not limited to Congress, but also includes regulatory agencies. Nor is the range of analysis limited to transactions between private stakeholders and a regulatory agency. A bargaining context can also provide a useful lens for addressing transactions between governmental bodies and across jurisdictions. For example, economists have analyzed political constitutions as incomplete contracts that coordinate conflicts between public bodies through legal rules such as separation of powers doctrine (Persson, Roland, & Tabellini, 1997). A few legal scholars extend the incomplete contracts account to argue that important insights for the law-making process can be gained by acknowledging that all law is inherently incomplete (Baker & Krawiec, 2004; Sunstein, 1995; for criticism, see Wright, 1996). Discourses from law, economics, and political science increasingly share the common ground of viewing political transactions as bargains when examining public ordering issues such as interactions between private firms and governments, as well as interactions between public regulatory bodies.

Particularly with deregulation of network industries, such as telecommunications and electric power, an account of regulation that

[1] Macey, 1998: 177.

acknowledges incompleteness in bargaining brings to bear important insights about public governance in competitive industries. To begin, the interest group story surrounding the movement toward deregulation remains puzzling. What interest group story could possibly explain why policy makers would favor deregulation if the benefits of regulation are narrowly focused on a few interest groups and its costs are diffuse among many less powerful interests, creating a powerful equilibrium in favor of the regulatory status quo? A regulatory relations bargaining approach provides a way of reframing debate about the movement toward deregulation in industries such as telecommunications and electric power. Its insights focus on two primary phenomena relevant to industry governance in a deregulatory era: incentives and bargaining conditions.[2]

To the extent that regulation is the product of bargaining, it is helpful to distinguish between ex ante incentives and ex post states of affairs. Ex ante, the natural monopoly model (and rate regulation in particular) created strong incentives for investment in capital facilities, and may even have encouraged overinvestment in certain sectors of regulated industries or in technologies facing obsolescence. Moreover, the rate-making and regulatory process – which historically focused on regulating the firm-specific outputs of the public utility – worked to foreclose competition and new innovation by existing and potential competitors. The neoclassical economics and the cynical public choice accounts of regulation both suggest that the failures of natural monopoly regulation are somehow inherent to regulation itself. A government relations bargaining approach recasts the issue not as an inherent flaw with regulation, but as a failure of the conventional approach to regulation to balance ex ante incentives and ex post welfare concerns in the rate regulation process, particularly given changes in technological and economic conditions.

The bargaining conditions surrounding regulation and its enactment in a deregulatory world also bolster the relevance of such an approach. In contrast to the traditional regulatory approach, the movement toward

2 In applying incomplete contracts to public law actors, complex issues arise. Public bodies, such as a legislature or an agency, have a more complex set of motivations for their behavior than do private actors, such as the shareholder and the firm. The principal agent aspects of a decision by a public actor, such as an administrative agency, are complicated, involving not only the agency and its employees, but also the executive branch, the legislator, and the electorate. Public actors may change frequently, as is the case with state legislators facing term limits, thus undermining the commitment of any public contracting decision. These problems with behavior and commitment are not intractable but must be kept in mind when exploring a regulatory relations bargaining account of public governance.

deregulation places its focus on the regulation of inputs (e.g., network access) for certain sectors of the industry and increased reliance on competition for other sectors, rather than on regulation of outputs (e.g., service prices and quality). Given this regulatory goal, state and local agency regulation lacks the comparative advantage it might have had when the focus was output regulation. As new firms arise to challenge incumbent monopolists, the new regulatory dynamic changes the number and diversity of private actors interacting in markets and with governmental bodies. Firms and regulators will find agency adjudication a less effective mechanism for implementing their bargaining objectives. Instead, agency regulation and other legislative mechanisms – including mechanisms outside the agency decision-making process – will increasingly be used. Thus, with deregulation, firm–government interactions are more frequent, less consistent, and (in all likelihood) less visible.[3] These interactions may also present a greater risk of potential divergence between private and public interests in the formulation of regulation. They also pose a greater potential for conflict – between firms and government or between regulatory bodies and jurisdictions – that will not be as likely as the old agency-based adjudication regime to allow for coordinated voluntary solutions to conflicts. A bargaining approach to regulation thus predicts that traditional aspects of regulatory law, rarely invoked during a period of natural monopoly regulation, will be invoked more frequently in a deregulatory environment and may be in need of reassessment.

I. EX ANTE INCENTIVES, OVERINVESTMENT, AND INDUSTRY RESTRUCTURING

Traditional accounts of regulation from economics and political science have a problem explaining the rise of deregulation in industries such as electric power. Take the neoclassical economics account that regulation is

[3] In other words, increases in the frequency of interactions between government and a more heterogeneous range of interest groups will introduce new inefficiencies to public decision making. The frequency and increased heterogeneity of interactions may complicate the formulation of regulatory law, but there are also important benefits to deregulation. The regulatory process will no longer be dominated by a handful of powerful firms, making capture of the regulatory process less likely. This micropolitical benefit to deregulation, oft-touted by public choice theorists, is not irrelevant, but much of the empirical literature suggests that the capture thesis is not validated by empirical evidence (Quirk, 1981). Because deregulation will not entail complete dismantling of government and will depend on regulatory process for its implementation, any micropolitical benefit to deregulation must be weighed against the micropolitical costs.

designed to correct for market failures. If deregulation is due to a failure with regulation to achieve this goal, regulatory theory is challenged to explain more than 50 years of natural monopoly regulation as a failure in economics and its assumptions, or as policy makers' mistaken understandings of economic principles. The public choice interest group of account of regulation also faces a challenge in explaining any move toward deregulatory policies. Because the benefits of regulation are concentrated on just a few interest groups – primarily firms and unions – and the costs of regulation are dispersed among multiple groups, regulation seems to present an equilibrium point for policy makers and interest groups. One of the major challenges for political scientists is to explain how, despite this equilibrium, deregulation – initially opposed by large firms in many industries, including airline, trucking, and telecommunications – happens in industries such as electric power (Derthick & Quirk, 1985).

Indeed, the predominant public choice account of deregulation echoes public choice's dismal general story of regulation's general promise, as has been observed by others (Mashaw, 1997). At its best, on this cynical account regulation is fundamentally ineffective, although many in the public choice school also see regulation as an abysmal failure in which regulators begin to mimic the preferences of the private firms they regulate (Mitnick, 1980). Electric power regulation is no stranger to this thesis. One of the earliest empirical studies in the public choice literature, by George Stigler and Claire Friedland, focused on the electric power industry. They evaluated the establishment of state utility commissions and found no significant variation in any measure associated with regulation (including prices and revenues) across states, with or without commissions, or across periods, before or after the initiation of commission regulation (Stigler & Friedland, 1962). Stigler and Friedland's findings raise a serious question about regulation's purpose. If regulation does not lower rates or revenues, then what purpose does it serve? Public choice scholarship eventually answered this question by embracing a cynical attitude toward regulation. In advocating government auctioning of monopoly franchises, Harold Demsetz (1968) argued that "the rivalry of the open marketplace disciplines more effectively than do the regulatory processes of the commission" (65). Later, George Stigler (1971) took Demsetz's cynicism a step further, arguing that regulation can be understood as a commodity and is prone to capture by powerful interest groups.

Although data on the history of the electric power industry is not entirely inconsistent with the capture story, at best, empirical support for regulatory agency capture is mild. For instance, economists have noted that traditional price regulation may create incentive for an industry to adopt a higher than optimal capital-to-labor ratio in the industry. This phenomenon, known among economists as the Averch-Johnson effect (Averch & Johnson, 1962), has some empirical support.[4] Its magnitude, however, is widely debated among economists.[5] Regardless of whether the Averch-Johnson effect is empirically widespread, it is commonly recognized that many firms in the electric power industry overinvested in certain types of capital, such as power generation. In the 1960s and 1970s, utilities made many investments (often with the blessing of regulators) that, in hindsight, did not seem prudent. For instance, in the late 1960s and early 1970s, power plants in excess of 1,100 megawatts were designed and installed using extrapolation by growth methods (Hirsh, 1999). The new machines were not as efficient as previously installed plants; however, once decisions were made to site and build these plants, customers were forced to pay for the older, less efficient plants. Regulators approved many of these decisions to build mammoth power plants. In many circumstances, regulators used extrapolation by growth to predict continuing growth in electricity sales and even encouraged them, although sales growth figures declined drastically post-1960. For instance, the 5-year moving average of sales declined from around 7 percent in 1960 to 2 percent in 1996 (Hirsh, 1999), so if regulators used these data they would greatly overestimate growth rates in certain generation markets. The result of the regulators' decisions was a higher than optimal capital-to-labor ratio in the industry. However, this result seems driven primarily by informational failure and other biases on the part of regulators, such as historical data and technology biases, rather than capture by regulated industry.

Regardless of what motivated overinvestment in capital, the investment decisions of firms under the old regulatory order continue to have an enormous practical impact on the structure of the electric power industry. To the extent that regulators approved a vertically integrated utility's investments, this benefited firms and their shareholders by guaranteeing them a return on investment while limiting access to any market in power supply by both consumers and other firms. Equally important – and more relevant to the industry's problems as it is deregulated – decisions

[4] Economists have found some empirical support for the Averch-Johnson effect (Courville, 1974; Peterson, 1975; Spann, 1974).

[5] If the expected rate of return used by regulators is less than the cost of capital, the empirical results seem mixed at best (Boyes, 1976; Dechert, 1984). For a review of the evidence, see Joskow and Noll (1981).

to approve utility-operated power plants for local customers served as a substitute for investing capital to expand transmission facilities to wheel power from more remote sources have a continuing effect on the structure of the industry today. For most of the twentieth century, the vertically integrated utility treated on-system generation as a substitute for the expansion of transmission, leading to serious underinvestment in transmission infrastructure in key regions of the United States. Limited transmission capacity – a constraint shaped by the old regulatory order – today remains the most significant obstacle to effective competitive markets in electric power. Private incentives for expanding transmission, which remains a natural monopoly, are widely seen by industry experts as somewhere between nonexistent and inadequate. Clearly, the old regulatory order and its public choice incentives contributed to this failed modern incentive structure.

However, although elegant and not without its attraction, the cynical capture public choice story is not the only account of regulation that can explain the investment decisions of utility firms under rate regulation. Indeed, outside electric power regulation, careful empirical efforts to operationalize interest group influence on regulation do not support the thesis that regulatory agencies are captured, or even that they have a consistent tendency to favor regulated industry interests over other concerns (Quirk, 1981). If rate regulation is understood as a bargain between the firm, the regulator, and other stakeholders – a bargain with many incomplete terms – the investment decisions of firms can be isolated as responses to incentives created by the regulatory environment. Perhaps rate regulation provided nearly complete terms, in which both the firm and the regulator knew exactly who bore the risk of any given investment decision (a possibility explored in Chapter 5). At the same time, regulation and the assumptions and information on which it is based was also incomplete in many respects. Similar to private parties bargaining in the sphere of the marketplace, regulators [many of whom were state-level political appointees with little expertise (Gormley, 1983)] could not anticipate every future condition and state of affairs. For instance, they could not perfectly foresee the limits on technological efficiencies from increased plant size. Nor could they anticipate the decline in the growth rate of electricity sales that would ensue in the late twentieth century.

Under natural monopoly price regulation, the approval of a utility's rate by regulators typically did not include any express promises beyond a license to charge and recover costs subject to the regulators continued approval. The "terms" of the contract, to the extent they were mutually understood, were largely derived from the repeat relationship of rate regulation, in which a specific firm, other stakeholders, and the regulator worked out a mutually understood balance between profit and the public interest. The firm was constrained by the prospect of the regulator reneging on previous rate commitment that might later be deemed overreaching. The regulator was constrained by the prospect of a utility devoting lobbying resources to limiting the discretion of regulatory agencies, by looking to either federal or state legislatures, or devoting resources to appellate litigation as a way of delaying regulatory action.[6]

In the end, the political story behind the movement to deregulation is not one of simple economic enlightment of the regulator. Nor is it a simple story of economic capture. As even one of the strongest early proponents of the capture thesis suggests, the story is fundamentally one about coalition politics (Peltzman, 1989), which lends itself to a bargaining analysis. For most of the twentieth century, electric power was regulated by state commissions, who were dominated by political appointees without expertise. Growth and demand were relative predictable, and consumers were relatively happy because rates declined (Gormley, 1983). Eventually, though, exogenous changes in economic conditions and technology led to price differentials in various states, leading to shifts in the political coalitions that previously sustained natural monopoly price regulation.[7] As one economist, Matthew White (1996), puts it in his careful empirical study of state deregulation of electricity, "to observe deregulation, the magnitude of the price gap must be sufficiently large that the pressure to bring existing prices into line with the market equilibrium cannot be accommodated within the institutional regulatory process" (231). Price gaps and cost differentials changed the incentives for interest groups – consumers and new entrants, such as independent power producers – to look for relief beyond the framework of price regulation by state and local utility commissions. For regulated firms themselves, changes in economic conditions contributed to an erosion of the utility consensus; from the 1940s through the 1960s, electric power prices declined in both real and absolute terms, but beginning in the 1970s fuel costs began to rise

[6] Given widespread comity by courts for the expertise of regulators, as well as deference to political and policy decisions, appellate litigation was a delaying tactic at best, but one that kept pressure on regulators and undeniably influenced their decisions.

[7] Ideology played an undeniably important role in these shifting coalitions. Mavericks, such as Robert Crandall in the airline industry, captured the imagination of reform-minded politicians, as well as new incumbents; however, deregulation was not merely an issue for one side of the political spectrum.

substantially and, when firms sought major rate increases, regulators faced increasing political pressure from consumer and environmental groups to rewrite the utility consensus, leading to an increasingly adversarial relationship between utilities and rate regulators, particularly in states (Sillin, 2003).

Although state commission approval of a rate based on cost of service cannot possibly encompass all future state of affairs, this does not mean that it necessarily failed to adequately promote efficiency or protect the public interest within its bargaining framework. Over time, a private firm contracting with a regulator in the rate-setting process may face strong ex ante incentives to exaggerate its capital expenditures, seeking license to build these costs in its rates. Such rate increases, if approved, would provide the firm a substantial cushion for sustaining its profits against unanticipated economic conditions in the future. Further, when technology changes, allowing more efficient plants to complete with previously approved and more expensive facilities, a new state of affairs – an exogenous condition unanticipated by the contracting parties – would require the contracting parties to reassess the terms of the bargain. The incomplete contracts model emphasizes the en ante incentives one or both parties may have in the bargaining process, but also recognizes how the contract's completeness or incompleteness will influence these incentives.

The incentives facing a firm may constitute endogenous bargaining conditions to the extent that they were understood to be within a transactional framework between the contracting parties. Consistent with public choice theory, rate regulation may have encouraged a certain amount of "strategic incompleteness" (Bernheim & Whinston, 1998) – for example, when there was uncertainty about future conditions, a firm may have encouraged the regulator to be incomplete in its decisions, thus maximizing the firm's flexibility and ability to influence the regulator in future decisions concerning rates. Incompleteness could arguably provide even greater opportunities for the firm to maximize its profits, but if the firm possesses better information than the regulator regarding the risks of technological and future market conditions it could better hedge its bets against the future by retaining a certain degree of incompleteness in the end result of the regulatory process. In such circumstances, verification costs for the regulator are relatively high. Changes to bargaining conditions – for example, forcing the firm to reveal to the regulator information about changing technology or market conditions – may improve the ability of cost-of-service rate regulation to protect the public interest.

However, not all conditions surrounding bargaining are endogenous. Parties cannot, for instance, bargain over the rate of inflation; as a result, they frequently may leave terms open because they are simply outside the realm of the negotiation over rates. At the time of contracting, although there is always a possibility of change, neither the regulator nor the firm may have sufficient information to evaluate the risks of a change in technology or economic conditions. These conditions may be uncertainties that are exogenous to the transaction. If a firm or the regulator has no experience on which it can build assessments of future risk, exogenous factors will be more likely to prevail as bargaining conditions, increasing overall uncertainty on both sides of the bargaining space. However, even where conditions are exogenous, it still may be relevant to evaluate how the existence of a condition – such as technological, economic, or political change – will impact current and future incentives on the part of contracting parties.

As both endogenous and exogenous changes necessitate, the rate regulation process creates some need for ex post evaluation of an incomplete bargain. Not all incompleteness is strategic – indeed, due to uncertain future conditions and transaction costs, a lot of incompleteness can be understood as necessary, if even efficient. The government relations bargaining account focuses on how we structure legal institutions to maximize welfare against the backdrop of such incompleteness, not how legal institutions are inherently unlikely to maximize welfare. Over time, policy makers have given serious consideration to proposals designed to give regulators the same quality information as firms, to adjust rates more regularly to changing conditions, and to minimize or reduce the profit incentives that may be motivating firms in the rate regulation process; in most jurisdictions, such reforms have been implemented. Despite this, the acceptable administrative costs and costs of error in the rate regulation process simply did not keep pace with rapidly changing technological and economic conditions. In addition, the rate regulation process does not directly address the economic structure of the firm and how previously tacit contracts associated with vertical integration may, under different technological and economic conditions, be more efficiently provided through the marketplace and other institutional arrangements.

So understood, a government relations bargaining account recasts how we account for the move from rate regulation to deregulation. Although some public choice accounts see rate regulation as inherently flawed, to the extent it licenses overinvestment by self-interested firms who have largely captured the agenda of regulators, an incomplete contracts approach puts its emphasis on a different problem. If there is a fault, the problem with rate regulation is not government regulation itself. Instead, the instability of rate regulation can be traced to the necessity of incompleteness in rate regulation and, more specifically, how this incompleteness relates to current technology, changes in an industry, and future incentives for the firm and the regulator; specifically, as incentives for private participants in the regulatory process change, some of the tacit coalitions that may have supported a specific institutional arrangement will also change. The bargaining conditions and incentives that may support an institutional arrangement are not fixed, or inherently flawed, but may be modified to enhance ex post social welfare; however, the successful recasting of bargaining conditions depends on the contracting parties having access to information that can overcome regulatory inertia, a task that regulatory law has historically ignored, but one that it may be well equipped to pursue in the era of institutional instability that deregulation has brought about.

II. SKETCHING THE DEREGULATORY LANDSCAPE

In the electric power industry – as in telecommunications and many other industries – one response to sustained failures with the rate regulation process has been to deregulate, or restructure, the industry in the direction of a more competitive environment. Deregulation does not imply the dismantling of regulation but does necessitate some fundamental change in its focus. Although some attention of reformers has been directed at state and local rate regulation, many (if not most) deregulatory reforms are directed at using regulation to change the structure of the firm itself and the industry overall, often at the national level. Due to improvements in technology and information access, many of the economies associated with power generation that were previously provided through vertical integration can increasingly be provided through private decisions in the marketplace. Beyond power generation, however, regulation remains highly relevant to the operation of power transmission and distribution. Thus, since the late 1970s, the electric power industry (in the United States and elsewhere) has undergone a substantial facelift from the vertically integrated utility that dominated throughout the twentieth century.

The government relations bargaining approach provides a plausible explanation of how interest groups came to support deregulation in industries such as electric power. The original consensus in the industry relies heavily on state regulation, which is firm specific. As a matter of interest group politics, the consensus – or regulatory contract – behind natural monopoly regulation began to unravel (Hirsh, 1999). With the unraveling of this largely state-based bargain, stakeholders increasingly looked to the U.S. Congress and federal regulators for solutions. Against the backdrop of high fuel prices in the 1970s, Congress passed the Public Utility Regulatory Policies Act of 1978 (PURPA), a part of President Carter's energy plan, which fueled the growth of new entrants in power generation, known as cogeneration facilities.[8] PURPA fueled the growth of a significant independent power producer sector, which challenged incumbent utility market power in electric power generation. Congress again expanded efforts to develop power markets when it passed the Energy Policy Act of 1992, expanding the FERC's authority to mandate transmission access.[9] The FERC began to explore mechanisms for introducing competition to wholesale generation markets, culminating in the adoption of Order No. 888 in the mid-1990s, which mandated access to transmission for wholesale power supply markets.[10] The Energy Policy Act of 1992 and Order No. 888 further encouraged the growth of independent power producers and have also led to the proposal of merchant power plants and transmission lines across the nation.

Meanwhile, throughout the 1990s, many states also began to experiment with retail deregulation. Due to the incentives created by PURPA and technological innovations, independent power producers began to proliferate in the industry in the 1980s. As new entrants entered the industry, the limits of state-maintained price regulation became more obvious. Cost-of-service regulation may have worked well to align consumer interests when prices were decreasing; however, when costs began to increase, costumers were no longer a single homogenous interest group but began to fragment into different interest groups reflecting their usage patterns and substitute elasticities, primarily industrial, commercial, and residential consumers. In some states that deregulated, such as California, large industrial customers lobbied heavily for low-cost power, demanding reforms to the traditional state approach to regulating electricity prices, while residential consumers generally opposed deregulation.

[8] Public Law No. 95-617, 92 Stat. 3117 (1978) (codified as amended at 16 U.S.C. §§ 824 a-1 to a-3, 824 i-k).

[9] Public Law No. 102-486 (amending sections 211 and 212 of the Federal Power Act, 16 U.S.C. § 824 j-k).

[10] 61 *Federal Register* 21, 540 (1996) [codified at 18 C.F.R. parts 35 and 385 (1997)].

The practical economic consequence of the state side of deregulation was exacerbated by the price differentials that emerged across states by the mid-1990s. Fuel costs began to rise drastically in the 1970s. Over time, states adopted different mixes of power generation (ranging from hydro to natural gas, coal, and expensive nuclear plants), and made a range of commitments to approve the building of plants using different size and technological assumptions. By the early 1990s, the costs of power generation differed drastically from state to state, varying from around $.02 per kilowatt hour to over $.08 per kilowatt hour. As one economist describes it:

> Changes in the economics of power generation have undercut the cost structure of incumbents to the point where the costs of small-scale entry into the power generation business are well below the average costs of many incumbent utilities. The result is a substantial increase in the opportunity cost of statutory entry barriers and political pressure on regulators to close the price gap. In high-cost states the magnitude of the price gap suggests fairly strong incentives for consumers to press for regulatory changes, and regulatory reforms are the natural result.[11]

The price gap was not only a differential between new supply entrants and incumbents. Incumbents often had some ability to purchase power on the wholesale market at a fraction of the cost of generating their own on-system power, but the incumbent was frequently locked into long-term contracts or, even if it was not, faced little incentive to procure power at a more competitive cost because it owned its own generation facilities and stood to benefit by expanding its own generation rather than opening transmission to new entrants. Price gaps and cost differentials also worked to change the incentives for stakeholders in the existing natural monopoly scheme of price regulation.

New entrants certainly had an impact on the unraveling of the utility consensus, but their power in the reform process was bolstered by the decline of the homogenous public utility firm, which typically operated in a single state jurisdiction. By 1990, even the incumbent utility firms in the industry were no longer homogenous. Due to mergers in the industry, many utilities operated in multiple states. Although some operated their own systems to allow generation to act as a substitute for transmission, others possessed excess transmission capacity and relied on off-system generation procured through wholesale market transactions. The former generally opposed competitive reforms, whereas the later embraced them.

[11] White, 1996: 230.

Utilities increasingly merged to bolster their efficiency and market position, including their control over transmission. The historical approach of a firm limiting its operations to a single state regulator's jurisdiction was no longer the norm. State-led deregulation was not a unified movement across the United States. States experiencing excessive price and cost gaps (along with a large industrial and commercial rate base) deregulated quickly, but other states adhered to the old framework of price regulation. Against this backdrop, wholesale markets (regulated at the federal level) were increasingly deregulated at the federal level due to similar cost differential pressures bolstered by the political lobby of recently deregulated states. By the late 1990s, a complex range of regulatory solutions across states created much uncertainty regarding the ultimate regulatory approach. However, one thing was certain: State and local governments retained jurisdiction over the siting of both power plants and transmission lines, but apart from this the glue that created stability in the industry for much of the twentieth century no longer held.

Together, new entrants without service obligations (e.g., independent power plants, merchant facilities), large industrial customers demanding lower-cost power, and utilities possessing excess transmission capacity forged an informal alliance favoring reforms to the industry. A large focus of this effort involved looking to federal regulators for a consistent national policy that would overcome the equilibrium of the state-centered natural monopoly model and stabilize the disequilibrium of heterogeneous regulatory approaches between states. Apart from isolated incumbent utilities, only residential consumers and environmental interest groups, both of whom benefited from the taxation allowed by the old locally run system, continued to prefer the traditional approach.[12] This newly aligned set of interests led to demand for many new regulatory approaches, including the possibility of a new system of federal regulation. At the same time, firms that had begun to rely on state-by-state negotiated contracts would not support federal price regulation; in some regions, new interest group alliances – including utilities, industrial customers, and new entrants – were forged to favor restructuring. In other areas, isolated utilities that owned transmission facilities steadfastly resisted change. "Deregulation" was co-opted by the reform coalition as a

[12] Even then, the local-based approach was seen as having limited utility, mostly as a tool for financing other regulatory requirements or for forming local-based grass roots consumer or environmental coalitions. Environmental groups, for instance, were among the first to recognize that national mandates were necessary to overcome state and local barriers to environmental regulation.

nonthreatening way to package these restructuring efforts, many of which (contrary to the decentralized ideals of deregulation) involved increased federal authority over the industry. Yet, at best, the reform coalition favoring deregulation of electric power was a loose one. It has had modest success in influencing the FERC (which had signed on to most of its agenda by the mid-1990s), but has failed to garner sufficient support for clear congressional action on important deregulation issues, such as whether the FERC has the authority to mandate expansion of power transmission networks. Thus, imperfect as localism may be, state and local regulation remain an essential component of the process in which competitive markets are being implemented in the United States (see Chapters 7 and 8).

Deregulation also led to substantial changes in the firm and industry-wide structure of the electric power industry. The traditional utility was a vertically integrated natural monopoly, typically legally sanctioned to operate as a monopolist within a geographically defined service territory. Beginning with technological innovation in the 1980s and continuing through the 1990s, however, generation sector of the electric power industry increasingly came to be recognized as structurally competitive (Joskow & Schmalensee, 1983). Today, it is no longer considered economically efficient for a single firm to provide power generation, but most markets can efficiently sustain two or more firms generating electric power. In more recent years, the generation sector of the industry has grown remarkably and is currently seen as competitive in nature. New firms, such as independent power producers and merchant plants compete aggressively with incumbent utilities in many markets. Rate regulation of generation has largely been abandoned in wholesale power markets (regulated at the national level), and many states have also begun to deregulate the prices of retail generation. Although prices have largely been deregulated in the United States, many states continue to actively regulate the environmental aspects of locating, or siting, power generation, and emissions remain heavily regulated at the federal and state levels. In larger power markets in the United States, there may be dozens of options for purchasing electric power. Small consumers may not have these options, to the extent a state has not deregulated its retail markets, but utilities have them and they are increasingly available to large industrial customers as well.

In contrast – and presenting a particular challenge for regulatory law – the transmission and distribution sectors of the industry continue to be seen as natural monopolies. Previously, transmission and distribution were often (but not always) provided by the same, vertically integrated firm, but today they are more frequently disentangled. A local distribution utility often provides the service to the end use retail customer, whereas transmission is frequently provided by a larger, multistate utility. Both transmission and distribution continue to be heavily regulated. Although there is some jurisdictional overlap, transmission prices are most extensively regulated by the federal government, through the FERC, whereas distribution prices are regulated most extensively by the states. Transmission and distribution remain to be considered classic network infrastructure networks, physical access to which will be essential for competition to thrive. The FERC may regulate many transmission access and pricing issues, but much of transmission (including whether to build and where to locate it) – and nearly all issues regarding power distribution – remain entirely within the jurisdictional realm of state and local regulators.

Given this multijurisdictional landscape, in assessing the bargaining conditions for public governance issues, it is important to make explicit the horizontal and vertical axes along which regulators operate. The horizontal axis of regulation describes regulation by the same jurisdictional level of government, such as state regulators. An incomplete bargaining situation may exist at the horizontal level to the extent that states fail, implicitly or explicitly, to adopt a coordinated norm to overcome jurisdictional conflicts. Along the vertical axis of regulation, incompleteness may also exist. For example, incompleteness may exist to the extent that there are gaps between federal and state regulators. Further, jurisdictional overlaps between federal and state regulators may create bargaining problems, where each jurisdiction may attempt to exercise its regulatory authority, thus leading to a conflict in which regulation imposes spillover costs on another regulator. Jurisdictional overlaps may also create a potential free-rider problem: If each regulator expects the other to take the initiative in addressing difficult and complex regulatory problems, an equilibrium in which neither regulator chooses to act may ensue.

In the United States, jurisdictional tensions between federal and state regulation have been brought to the fore by deregulation of industries such as electric power and telecommunications. In the context of electric power, federal regulators have unabashedly embraced a deregulatory policy – even with respect to power transmission, despite its network characteristics. States such as California have sometimes embraced deregulatory policies, but today the approach of states (which have substantial jurisdiction over retail transactions) is probably best described as a patchwork of different solutions. Some states have deregulated electricity, allowing every customer a choice of provider; some states have partially deregulated, allowing some customers choices; and other states have ardently opposed deregulation. Previously, this tension between federal and state regulation (and between individual states) was largely hidden because firms frequently operated within the jurisdiction of a given state, and state and federal regulatory policies were consistent.

This partially "deregulated" structure has invited the need for new market participants to play a role in coordinating the balance between supply and demand. In addition to the enormous across-the-board growth in the power generation sector, at the wholesale level, where markets are most pervasive, brokers and marketers have played an active role for some time. In the states, brokers and marketers may also play an important role, depending on the degree of retail deregulation. The jurisdictional difficulties surrounding deregulation have also given rise to many interstate associations – some commercial, such as multistate transmission utilities, whereas others are more public in nature, such as regional transmission organizations that coordinate interstate transmission service between firms.

III. CASTING A NEW SHADOW FOR REGULATORY LAW

With the institutional instability produced by deregulation, regulatory law confronts many new challenges. Although the old regulatory order of natural monopoly regulation allowed coordinated, voluntary solutions to latent conflicts between firms and governmental bodies, largely in the context of adjudication, deregulation ironically presents a new demand for public law solutions to some conflicts. Most of these public law solutions will not involve agency adjudication. With deregulation and other legal transitions, coordination norms between individual firms and the regulator do not already exist, so the transaction costs of coordinated solutions to conflict will be higher. Given higher transaction costs, deregulation increases the likelihood of regulatory incompleteness. Demand for public law to mediate between stakeholders and governmental bodies is greater. The shadow of public law, once faint, now looms more significantly over government relations bargaining.

Cost-of-service regulation provided a certain amount of stability for the relatively monolithic utility. Its rate-making process facilitated a higher degree of convergence between the preferences of the regulated firm and the regulator than will exist in the formulation of regulatory solutions in deregulated markets. To the extent that preferences failed to converge in the setting of a firm's rates, the firm could hold out for the promise of favorable regulatory treatment in a later rate proceeding. If, with the passage of time, a firm was substantially undercompensated for its expenses, the rate-making process provided opportunities for adjustments in the form of retroactive rate increases or rebates.

As competition policies have evolved since the late 1970s, regulators have increasingly focused their attention on network access issues – a range of issues that can only be resolved at the national level. Physical networks, such as electric power transmission and distribution, serve as a downstream market "bottleneck" for competitive electric power supply. Physical and economic access to such bottlenecks are necessary for suppliers to reach their customers and for competition in upstream markets to thrive. Thus, with deregulation, regulators have increasingly focused their attention on the rules for network access, on regulating access to an input, rather than on regulating prices or an output (Spulber & Yoo, 2003). Antitrust law principles, such as the essential facilities doctrine, can play an important role in regulating input access. Because industries such as electric power and telecommunications have not abdicated ex ante regulatory enforcement by agencies, the balance between judicially enforced antitrust doctrine and regulatory standards enforced by agencies remains a topic of much contention, but one that a government relations bargaining perspective can help to clarify (see Chapter 6 and Chapter 7).

As these shifts in the substantive approach to regulation have occured, deregulation has also brought about substantial change in the micropolitics of the regulatory process. One major development is the loss of the self-correcting regulatory apparatus of rate making. To the extent the rate-making process corrected for regulatory mistakes, hence allowing for the convergence of preferences over time, the shift to regulating network access does not provide the same opportunities for correction in the future. Increasingly, regulators set general terms for network access through generally applicable rules, not in iterated individualized cases. Thus, the firm has much more at stake in the establishment of standards by rule than it did in the setting of rates in individualized cases. Under such circumstances, it is more likely that firms will approach the regulatory process with strongly held preferences that diverge from those of the regulator. At best, the repeat player effect is substantially weakened. Thus, the incompleteness of regulation in a deregulatory era may be more likely to produce ex post mistakes than it did in a regulatory environment.

Another development that increases the complexity of the regulatory process is the proliferation in the number and diversity of new entrants in competitive markets. Under rate regulation, for instance, state regulators considered the cost of service for a handful of investor-owned utilities operating within their jurisdiction. Each utility was relatively similar in its structure – vertically integrated – and faced similar operational and economic issues. Competition will lead to decreases in market power, but also has implications for power in the regulatory process. With the introduction of competition, the concentration of political power among the traditional suppliers has become diffuse. The monolithic investor-owned utility is no longer the prototypical stakeholder bargaining with the regulator. Instead, regulators face a larger number of stakeholders – dozens rather than a handful – with greater diversity. In the electric power context, for example, firms including generation suppliers, transmission utilities, local distribution companies, merchant plant companies, and marketers and brokers have actively participated in the regulatory process in states such as California. Nor are consumer groups a single homogenous interest group because residential and industrial consumers no longer always see eye-to-eye on utility pricing.

The implication of this is to greatly enhance the complexity of conditions surrounding the regulatory bargaining process. With the proliferation of new entrants, it is more difficult for an agency regulator to predict the repeat players in the regulatory process. A more diverse pool of private stakeholders will frequently (but certainly not always) provide a check on extreme preferences because participants in the regulatory process criticize or refute positions taken by others. Arguably, technical expertise on the part of the regulator will be less valuable because regulators will increasingly be called on to broker political compromises; certainly, it will be more complex for the regulator to possess expertise encompassing the entire range of issues stakeholders will raise. Hence, legislative bargains will be preferred over adjudicative ones, but the legislative bargaining process is a less orderly, often less visible, and less predictable process than many firms in regulated industries have come to expect.

To borrow a term from the sociology of networks (Watts, 2003), from the perspective of both the private and public governance sides of the bargain, the "small world assumption" is less likely to hold in a deregulatory world. Under what network sociologists refer to as the small world assumption, actors are able to understand the consequences of their actions and to assign probabilities to each state of nature (Savage, 1972; Watts, 2003). Much of this literature emphasizes the communication network between agents (and there is no necessary affinity between a small number of bargaining agents and the number of communication nodes), but there is also some similarity to small world conditions and the idealized bargaining conditions of low transaction costs and perfect information. When bargaining occurs in complex situations with multiple parties whose rationality is bounded, the small world assumption is more questionable. As W. Bentley Macleod has argued, in situations in which the small world assumption does not hold, complete contracts may be even more difficult, if they are not altogether impossible (Macleod, 1996).

Although the historical role of regulators can be understood through a bargaining lens, in a deregulatory environment, transaction costs or bounded rationality are even more likely to make bargains – in both private and public governance spheres – incomplete due to high transaction costs. In newly constituted sectors of formerly regulated industries, political power may be less concentrated and monolithic, but powerful interest groups may still have an influence on the process leading to deregulation and its implementation, leading to problems that will increasingly demand the attention of lawyers and courts. A government relations bargaining account thus presents a new and exciting challenge for public law in a deregulatory era. It is not a challenge that legal scholars or courts have fully confronted.

4

Refin(anc)ing Retail Service Obligations for the Competitive Environment

The traditional natural monopoly paradigm may have viewed electricity itself as a public good. In a competitive market, however, certain public goods previously associated with electric power will not necessarily be provided on their own. A challenge for deregulated markets is to evaluate how these public goods will continue to be offered within a competitive market. This chapter uses a bargaining perspective to address the provision of an important public good – universal access to retail power – in deregulated electric power markets.[1]

Universal service obligations can be implemented in a deregulatory environment, notwithstanding the elevation of private interests over public welfare in the everyday working of deregulated markets. Along these lines, a government relations bargaining framework raises two new concerns for provision of this public good. First, it advises against the imposition of across-the-board ex ante service obligations, favoring instead cautiously adopted and narrowly tailored service mandates for deregulated markets. Second, to the extent that service obligations are not efficiency promoting, the government relations bargaining approach makes trade-offs between efficiency and other goals more explicit in the political process. In this sense, a government relations bargaining approach is more attentive to political accountability than previous accounts of public good provision in the industry.

During the twentieth century, the privately owned electric utility was allowed to operate as a monopolist, but it also had certain responsibilities:

[1] Later chapters return to the more difficult issue of reliability in wholesale power supply markets. This issue is far more complex than retail service obligations to the extent it depends on transmission capacity issues that require solutions to other regulatory problems, such as jurisdiction of national and local regulators.

It submitted to price regulation and assumed obligations to extend service to all customers within its geographic service territory and to continue providing service, once service had commenced (Haar & Fessler, 1986). With the advent of deregulation, it is assumed that markets will largely displace price regulation, but little discussion focuses on the implications of deregulation for utility service obligations in the electricity industry. Today, electric utilities' extraordinary service obligations – often collectively referred to as the "duty to serve" – face their largest challenge ever.

The potential conflict between universal service and retail competition in electricity bears analogy to a tension in other industries, such as natural gas and telecommunications. In the natural gas industry, deregulated by the FERC in 1992,[2] local gas distribution companies have begun to offer many customers retail choice in many states (Costello & Lemon, 1996; Hall & Pierce, 1997). In New York, the natural gas industry's more recent introduction of retail competition is alleged to adversely affect the quality of gas service essential to many New Yorkers for heating, leading to a legal challenge against the state by consumer advocates (Norlander, 1998).[3] Although competitive reforms to the electric power industry lag behind the natural gas and telecommunication industries, as electricity is deregulated, particularly at the retail level, similar problems can be expected to arise. Many reformers look askance at the duty to serve in competitive retail utility service markets (Bouknight & Raskin, 1987; Norton & Spivak, 1985; Pace, 1987), often pointing to conflict between retail competition in electricity and the duty to serve.[4]

[2] See Pipeline Service Obligations and Revisions to Regulations Governing Self-Implementing Transportation and Regulation of Natural Gas Pipelines After Partial Well-head Decontrol, 57 *Federal Register* 13,267 (1992), order on reh'g, 57 *Federal Register* 36,128 (1992), order on reh'g, 57 *Federal Register* 57,911 (1992), reversed and remanded, *United Distribution Companies v. FERC*, 88 F.3d 1105 (D.C. Cir. 1996), order on remand, 78 F.E.R.C. (CCH) ¶ 61, 186 (1997). Order No. 636 is codified at 18 C.F.R. Part 284 (1997).

[3] The case, brought by consumer taxpayers and a consumer advocate nonprofit group alleging illegal expenditure of public funds under the state finance law, was dismissed for lack of standing. *See Public Utility Law Project of New York, Inc. v. New York State Public Service Commission*, 681 N.Y.S.2d 396 (App. Div. 3d Dep. 1998).

[4] There is little, if any, disagreement that retail wheeling is incompatible with an obligation to serve. A utility cannot be obligated to meet the energy needs of potential customers within its service territory without some guarantee of recovering the costs associated with that obligation. To do otherwise would clearly result in economic inefficiencies. It would also lead to further inequities because the costs and risks of meeting a standing obligation would be borne either by the utility's remaining customers or its stockholders (Lesser & Ainspan, 1994).

Can vigorous retail competition of the type public utility deregulation envisions coexist with extraordinary obligations to serve customers in industries such as electric power? If so, at what costs? Who will bear these costs? These questions are central to the law and economics of networks, of paramount importance as regulators and courts implement competition in traditional public utility industries, including electricity, where the natural monopoly model is being abandoned or reformed. Application of extraordinary service obligations to electric distribution companies in a competitive retail framework can coexist with improved efficiency in retail power markets. At the same time, the abandonment of the natural monopoly framework challenges regulators to narrowly tailor service obligations, to articulate new rationales for service obligations, and to devise new ways of paying for them. A tax on power distribution is probably the most efficient way to pay for universal service in a deregulated power market, but universal service could be approached through a voucher system for low-income customers rather than an across-the-board ex ante service mandate for firms in deregulated industries.

I. RETAIL WHEELING AND UNIVERSAL SERVICE IN ELECTRICITY

The dawn of competition in electricity raises a tension for the common law duty to serve, historically protected by natural monopoly regulation (see Chapter 2). Traditional economic efficiency arguments in favor of imposing extraordinary service obligations must be reassessed in light of structural modifications to the industry. As regulators move away from the natural monopoly paradigm (see Chapter 3), the retail duty to serve faces a threat that was largely foreign to its twentieth-century existence.

It is tempting for regulators addressing the obligations of firms in electric power markets to look to other markets in which they have experience. In telecommunications, for instance, universal service is widely accepted as consistent with retail competition. However, one of the primary network efficiency rationales for universal service in telecommunications is inapplicable to physical energy network markets, such as electricity and natural gas. To the extent extraordinary service obligations continue for electricity and natural gas in the same manner they have been since the early 1900s, regulators need to articulate alternative economic efficiency justifications. Alternatively, they will need to explicitly embrace goals outside economic efficiency, such as fairness, in support of maintaining this public good in a competitive environment.

A. The Tension Presented by Retail Markets

Wholesale transmission access and competition among wholesale suppliers has not posed any immediate threat to the public utility retail duty to serve,[5] but the introduction of retail competition requires some reassessment of the intellectual foundations for, and practical application of, traditional retail service obligations. The California Public Utility Commission's first order leading to the adoption of retail choice legislation acknowledged the need for consideration of this issue as customers begin to shop for power:

> To allow eligible customers to choose without restriction between the regulated price for a bundled utility service and the price offered by the generation services market may severely reduce the utility's ability to plan for, and reliably serve, its remaining customers. Absent modifications to the compact's traditional duty to service, consumers may make choices about electric services which they find economically attractive, but which are undesirable with respect to the broader goal of allocating society's resources efficiently.[6]

The possibility of such uneconomic bypass – bypass that might work to lower costs for a single shopping customer, while raising average costs for other customers[7] – necessitates consideration of the costs of the traditional duty to serve. Moreover, a system that allows power suppliers and customers to choose to deal with each other, especially if left unregulated, may allow suppliers or distributors to elect never to serve certain classes of customers, such as low-income residents, or to cease service however they want, consistent with retail power sales agreements.

Of course, perceived conflicts between vigorous retail competition and the public good of customer access can be avoided to the extent

[5] Since the FERC's Order No. 888, wholesale access and supply competition occur under the FERC's open access policies, which require a transmission utility to offer transmission service to customers and suppliers at terms and conditions comparable to the service it offers its own power supply. See Promoting Wholesale Competition Through Open Access Non-Discriminatory Transmission Services by Public Utilities and Transmitting Utilities, 61 *Federal Register* 21,539 (May 10, 1996) [codified at 18 C.F.R. Parts 35 & 385 (1997)]. In the past, competition at the wholesale level may have had potentially adverse impacts on service obligations. Bouknight and Raskin (1987) note "to the extent that existing obligations are inconsistent with a system of free and fair competition the Congress and the FERC must address the issue" (239).

[6] Re Proposed Policies Governing Restructuring of California's Electric Services Industry and Reforming Regulation, 151 P.U.R.4th 73, 92 (Cal. Pub. Util. Comm'n 1994).

[7] Uneconomic bypass has been defined as bypass that reduces costs to one customer but increases overall average network costs, thus creating costs for other customers (MacAvoy, Spulber, & Stangle, 1989).

that one of these seemingly incompatible goals is simply abandoned. Unless the movement toward retail competition in traditional public utility industries ceases, one option in the face of the tension between retail competition and common law service obligations is to abandon the duty to serve for competitive markets, treating traditional utility services as any other service in a competitive market. After all, as retail markets open up, it will be increasingly possible for suppliers and distributors to provide a variety of service qualities to end users. Without a duty to serve, utility markets might operate much like other deregulated markets, such as oil, trucking, and banking, which rely on contractual obligations and general consumer protection laws to ensure service delivery. For example, if an electricity supplier refuses service to a customer the customer must find alternative suppliers, and competition in power generation will likely provide customers a range of power supply qualities.[8] If a power distributor (known as a "DisCo") refuses to extend or discontinue service to a customer because it is not profitable, the customer may also attempt to find alternatives. For example, large, heavy load customers of electricity may find alternatives, such as self-generation or wheeling around the DisCo, to be cost feasible. Markets flourish with bilateral relationships, while the duty to serve imposes a unilateral obligation on the incumbent utility. Customers already have a variety of safeguards, including credit financing and consumer protection statutes, such as the Uniform Commercial Code.[9]

[8] Some suggest that traditional rate regulation has had an adverse effect on the average quality of service. Carron and MacAvoy (1981) chronicle a decline in service quality throughout the 1970s. Notably, in England, which deregulated its electricity industry through privatization in 1991, service disconnections fell by 95 percent over the first few years of deregulation (Costello & Graniere, 1997). Any decline in service quality associated with rate regulation is closely related to the Averch-Johnson effect, as well as the tradeoffs between expanding transmission and expanding generation made by the traditional vertically integrated firm (see Chapter 3).

[9] For example, express and implied warranty protections appear in both state and federal law. See U.C.C. § 2–313 (express warranty); § 2–314 (implied warranty of merchantability); § 2–315 (implied warranty of fitness for particular purpose); § 2–318 (extension of warranties to third-party beneficiaries expected to use goods); see also 15 U.S.C. §§ 2301–2312 (Magnuson-Moss Warranty Act, regulating explicit and implied warranties). In addition, federal law prohibits "unfair methods of competition and unfair or deceptive acts or practices in or affecting commerce" [15 U.S.C. § 45(a)]. All states have similar statutes protecting against unfair trade acts. The federal Equal Credit Opportunity Act, 15 U.S.C. § 1691–1691e, and the Fair Credit Reporting Act, 15 U.S.C. § 1681, establish minimum standards that prevent discrimination in the granting of credit and consumer safeguards. See also 15 U.S.C. ch. 41 (Consumer Credit Protection Act); 15 U.S.C. §§ 1692–1692o (Fair Credit Debt Collection Act); 15 U.S.C. § 1637 (Fair Credit Billing Act). State regulation

However, although it is a challenge, it is not an impossible task for regulators to establish public goods such as extraordinary service obligations for competitive retail industries. Many sectors of the financial, insurance, and health industries have experience with implementing universal service pursuant to national policy through various sorts of assigned risk pools. For example, the Community Reinvestment Act of 1977 mandates that banks are required to serve the "convenience and needs" of their local communities for deposit and credit services.[10] The property insurance industry has developed Fair Access to Insurance Requirements (FAIR) plans.[11] In the health care industry, the obligation of hospitals to serve the indigent is explicitly made a condition in the awarding of federal construction grants.[12] Nonprofit health care providers take on an obligation to provide indigent health care, in part as a condition to the grant of certain governmental benefits, such as federal, state, or local tax benefits (Simpson & Strum, 1991). It is questionable how successful these approaches to promoting universal service have been, but their existence suggests that the duty to serve can coexist with retail competition if we are willing to bear the costs. Notably, in each of these cases, service obligations are typically imposed pursuant to national, as opposed to state, legislation.

B. The Limits of the Telecommunications Analogy

The public good of extraordinary service obligations has found an efficiency explanation that may be compatible with competitive markets

of finance charges, credit terms, and the federal Truth in Lending Act (TILA), 15 U.S.C. § 1602(f), have historically not applied to public utilities because these laws contain a stricter definition of credit designed to capture transactions in which both parties intend that payment will be delayed and finance charges imposed as a part of a lengthened payment schedule. In competitive markets, though, retail electricity suppliers and distributors may devise payment plans that resemble credit sale transactions or sponsor open-ended credit plans for the sale of electricity, which could trigger TILA disclosure and disputed bill procedures.

[10] Public Law No. 95-128, 91 Stat. 1147 (codified as amended at 12 U.S.C. §§ 2901–2906).

[11] The FAIR plan was created under the Urban Property Protection and Reinsurance Act of 1968, Public Law No. 90-448, 82 Stat. 555 (codified as amended in scattered sections of 5, 12, 15, & 42 U.S.C.). For discussion, see generally, Austin (1983).

[12] The Hill-Burton Act conditioned the funding of hospital construction on the provision of uncompensated care to indigent citizens. See 42 U.S.C. § 291. In addition, a federal law called the Emergency Medical Treatment and Active Labor Act, adopted in 1986, required Medicare-participating hospitals to examine and treat all emergency room patients and women in labor. See 42 U.S.C. § 1395dd.

in the telecommunications context. Extraordinary obligations applicable to service providers in telecommunications have come to be known as "universal service," endorsed by the U.S. Congress in the Telecom Act of 1996.[13] The rationale for universal service in telecommunications is independent of the natural monopoly rate regulation structure, used to rationalize service obligations for electric power (see Chapter 2).

In the telecommunications infrastructure context, the predominant economic rationale for a universal service obligation is that pervasive access increases network system benefits for all customers (Lemley & McGowan, 1998). Basically, the idea is that a service obligation on providers of telecommunications service enhances the value of network service for all customers to such a degree that customers are willing to pay a premium to subsidize universal access. The Federal Communications Commission (FCC), in its 1997 universal service order, recognized this economic rationale:

> Universal service support mechanisms that are designed to increase subscribership by keeping rates affordable will benefit everyone in the country, including those who can afford basic service. At the simplest level, increasing the number of people connected to the telecommunications network makes the network more valuable to all its users by increasing its usefulness to them. Increasing subscribership also benefits society in ways unrelated to the value of the network per se. For example, all of us benefit from the widespread availability of basic public safety services, such as 911.[14]

Because the value of telecommunications service increases to customers with greater degrees of system interconnectivity, universal service is regarded as economically valuable by telecommunications firms and customers, even those who can afford market-priced services. Put another way, universal service creates a positive externality, which inures to the benefit of all customers through pervasive interconnectivity. For example,

[13] Telecommunications Act of 1996, § 254, Public Law No. 104-104, 110 Stat. 56 (Feb. 8, 1986) directed the FCC to define "universal service," consistent with principles in statute. This provision was the subject of deliberations of a joint federal/state board and FCC rules issued in 1997. See In re Federal-State Joint Board on Universal Service, FCC Docket No. 96-45 (May 7, 1997). These rules have been clarified in several orders on reconsideration. See, e.g., In re Federal-State Joint Board on Universal Service, FCC Docket No. 96-45 (Dec. 31, 1997). For criticism of this new statutory provision, see Mueller(1997). Additional papers and comments regarding universal service are available through the Benton Foundation website at http://www.benton.org/publibrary/policy/uniserv/home.html.

[14] In re Federal-State Joint Bd. on Universal Serv., FCC Docket No. 96-45, slip op. at p. 8, ¶ 8 (May 7, 1997).

the more pervasive access to the Internet, the more valuable the Internet is as a communications tool, everything else being equal.[15]

Although intuitively attractive, this rationale is not without its problems. First, clearly there is some limit on the amount the average consumer is willing to pay to subsidize universal service. At some point, the marginal benefits of enhanced access will not justify the additional cost. For example, expansion of a network initially financed by middle-class customers to include the poor, particular those with whom middle-class customers rarely interact, will likely provide few benefits of the sort the average middle-class customer will be willing to pay. The average middle-class customer who can afford to pay for his or her own access will likely not be willing to pay a significant premium to enhance access for others unless there is some cognizable benefit to the network system or to the value of service. Empirically, it is unclear how much the average consumer is willing to pay to subsidize universal service. Clearly there are some limitations on the willingness of consumers to pay for system benefits but, without empirical study, this theory fails to provide a clear criterion for limiting its extension. For example, taken to its extreme it could require not only subsidization of the network, but also a redistributive tax to pay to provide computers or other electronic devices to customers who cannot afford to pay for these. Although such a tax may seem desirable as a matter of fairness or distributive justice, it is hardly required by economic efficiency.

A second limitation with this rationale for universal service in the telecommunications context is that it does not factor in network congestion costs and network degradation. If the infrastructure is already in place to accommodate additional customers at a low incremental cost, the positive externality rationale provides a powerful rationale for enhancing access. However, with limited infrastructure, additional participants may actually cause the value of service for incumbent customers to decline if congestion ensues or if the quality of service is otherwise adversely affected. As Amitai Aviram (2003) suggests, networks present a unique kind of opportunism in their potential for degradation. In the Internet context, for example, the congestion bottlenecks resulting from mass access to system networks are obvious.

Although the argument has its limits, the positive externality rationale for universal service might explain why some consumers, in an

[15] So, too, with the fax machine, an appliance that only became valuable once it was distributed among multiple persons connected by a network (Kelly, 1997).

unregulated market, may be willing to pay for cross-subsidization of universal service in telecommunications. However, it is a tenuous argument, at best, for supporting a duty to serve in the natural gas and electricity industries. Under traditional public utility regulation, the consumption of gas and electricity commodities, unlike communications services, do not depend on interconnectivity for their value. Additional customers might make certain secondary markets possible – Circuit City would not exist if customers did not have circuits[16] – and this may stimulate demand for electricity or natural gas. Moreover, as discussed in Chapter 2, increasing the number of customers on a network decreases the fixed costs associated with providing electric or natural gas service, reducing the price each customer pays in a rate-regulated environment. However, any individual customer can obtain great value from using electrical or natural gas appliances in complete isolation. An electrical generator, for example, can easily power a home or office, as long as adequate fuel is available. Thus, although some economic benefits to pervasive access can be identified for these industries, they relate primarily to the costs and supply of network service, not to its demand value or the amount customers are willing to pay for universal service. To this extent, the positive externality argument for universal service is weak when applied to commodities, such as electricity and natural gas, outside the natural monopoly framework – or, at least in this context, universal service demands some alternative economic explanation.

II. THE EFFICIENCY OF A DUTY TO SERVE IN DEREGULATED ELECTRIC POWER MARKETS

With deregulation of retail electric power markets, reformers are reluctant to abandon public goods that have historically been provided under natural monopoly regulation. For example, most states that have attempted to implement retail competition in power markets acknowledge the potential tension between the common law duty to serve and competitive retail markets without abandoning either goal. California stated in the preamble to its 1996 retail wheeling legislation, "[i]t is the further intent of the Legislature to continue to fund low-income ratepayer assistance programs, . . . in an unbundled manner . . . " and maintained 1996-level low

16 Thanks to Larry Garvin for putting it to me this way.

income and universal service expenditures.[17] New Hampshire, which considered similar legislation, was more explicit:

> A restructured electric utility industry should provide adequate safeguards to assure universal service. Minimum residential service safeguards and protections should be maintained. Programs and mechanisms that enable residential customers with low incomes to manage and afford essential electricity requirements should be included as part of industry restructuring.[18]

The task of formulating extraordinary service obligations in an era of retail competition is challenging. It should not, however, preclude consideration of retail competition by states, nor should it necessarily lead to the abandonment of public goods such as extraordinary service obligations. As Chapter 2 suggests, under cost-of-service regulation, many of these obligations were voluntarily assumed by utility firms, even without explicit regulatory mandates. The introduction of retail competition in some states may help to mobilize support for the legal enhancement of consumer protection obligations, perhaps from fear of the abuses markets may yield, and to make such protections more explicit in state law.[19]

Although the rationales applicable to the telecommunications industry are inapposite in competitive electricity markets, there are some plausible economic efficiency rationales supporting continuation of the duty to service in competitive retail power markets. Some understanding of a competitive electric power market's operational framework is a necessary predicate to understanding how extraordinary service obligations might apply in this context. The local distribution utility (or "DisCo") is often believed to remain a natural monopolist. In contrast, activities such as generation, power supply, marketing, and brokering are now regarded as competitive industries (Fox-Penner, 1997).

Because deregulation of the electricity industry acknowledges different market characteristics for these various firms, the traditional approach to implementing service obligations requires some reassessment. Equal

[17] Cal. A.B. No. 1890 (signed Sept. 23, 1996), at § 1(d).

[18] N.H. State Code § 374-F:3 VI.

[19] In Ohio, for example, the consideration of retail competition has mobilized consumer protection interests, leading to the proposal of minimum electricity service standards for the first time in the state's history. *Ohio Regs Set Service Standards*, ELECTRICITY DAILY, Feb. 9, 1998; Alan Johnson, *State Board Sets Service Standards for Ohio's Electric Companies*, COLUMBUS DISPATCH, Feb. 6, 1998, at 4E. Illinois' restructuring legislation also contains new low-income customer assistance charges. Cam Simpson, *Thousands Without Heat in Area*, CHICAGO SUN-TIMES, Dec. 9, 1997, at 1.

application of an ex ante service obligation to every institutional actor providing electric utility services in competitive retail markets can pose significant economic costs and may thwart the development of retail power markets. In particular, from an efficiency perspective, proposals endorsed by many consumer advocates that suppliers or marketers assume extraordinary service obligations (Alexander, 1996; Colton, 1997) are specious because this aspect of the industry no longer exhibits natural monopoly characteristics. However, this does not mean that service obligations are without any economic efficiency basis or that they cannot survive in deregulated markets. At a minimum, current state retail wheeling plans require that the power distribution sector of the industry assume some extraordinary service obligation. There is little agreement among the states about whether the various market institutions interacting with the DisCo in retail markets should also bear extraordinary service obligations. Extraordinary service obligations *can* facilitate access to power supply without undermining efficiency gains, but regulators need to carefully assess the limits of service obligations in competitive markets.

For small load customers such as residential customers, small business and single location offices, power distribution remains a monopoly service under most state restructuring plans. Put another way, a single utility (the DisCo) continues to provide distribution to power supply for the large bulk of power customers. For most smaller customers who do not have access to capital financing markets or own rights of way to build distribution lines, it is cost prohibitive to duplicate distribution lines as long as the incumbent DisCo itself owns the facilities.[20] Thus, even in competitive retail markets, DisCos initially remain monopolies for small residential and commercial customers, at least with respect to the horizontal distribution market.[21] Following California's approach, until now, every state retail wheeling plan has treated power distribution in this manner by defining a *de jure* monopoly for distribution, subject to fairly traditional regulation, effectively defining a new regulatory compact for power distribution.

Further, to date, every state that has seriously considered moving to retail competition in the sale of electricity has determined that a "basic

[20] As Vernon Smith (1993) argued, however, joint ventures may work to solve this problem.

[21] Fox-Penner (1997) cites recent reports by the FERC and the U.S. Office of Technology Assessment, as well as the conclusions of Joskow and Schmalensee (1983). However, not everyone agrees (Smith, 1993).

service" option must be provided by the DisCo to those who do not choose an alternative supplier for electricity, are refused service by a retail supplier, or have been disconnected.[22] The DisCo is effectively the supplier of last resort.[23] In some states, basic service will be regulated at a rate established to be less than the rates immediately prior to competition, thus minimizing the impact of stranded costs on small residential customers.[24]

For example, according to Vermont's retail competition restructuring order, "exclusive franchises for distribution" remain necessary. The DisCo "will retain its obligation to plan, build, and operate its local distribution system in a manner that ensures safe and reliable service to customers."[25] Vermont defines the basic service offer as "[s]ervice offered to customers by the distribution company but provided by a retail service provider through contract." This service "may be priced either to float with the spot market or fixed on a longer term basis."[26] After the transition to retail competition, this offer, which is limited to franchised customers of DisCos, "will be made available over a contracted period" and "through a retail service provider."[27]

Because retail competition envisions the fragmentation of utility service into different markets, from generation to transmission to distribution, the implications of continuing the duty to serve will need to be assessed in the context of each market. Given power distribution's *de jure* monopoly status under state retail wheeling plans, with little or no analysis most state regulators look initially to the DisCo as the primary bearer of the traditional duty to serve. However, given the inapplicability of the traditional rate regulation framework for understanding service obligations in the competitive market structure, coupled with the mobilization of interests likely to support imposition of new service obligations, the

[22] Basic service or the standard offer is independent of a "safety net" provided in many states for low-income customers. Unlike the safety net, basic service or the standard offer is designed to provide stable electricity service without major price fluctuations, while providing sufficient education about the available options and benefits of retail competition in electricity to stimulate consumer choice and interest. This approach to ensuring service access is similar to the minimum standard of coverage recommended in health care reform (Rockefeller, 1991).

[23] A similar model is emerging in the natural gas industry (Merrill, 1999).

[24] See, e.g., R.I. Gen Laws ch. 316, § 39-1-27.2(d) & (f); Re Electric Utility Industry Restructuring, Maine Pub. Util. Comm'n, Docket No. 95–462, July 19, 1996.

[25] Re Restructuring of the Electric Utility Industry in Vermont, 174 P.U.R.4th 409, 434 (Vt. Pub. Serv. Bd. 1996).

[26] Id. at 488.

[27] Id. at 427.

efficiency rationales for continuing to impose an extraordinary service obligation on the incumbent utility require reassessment. To the extent regulators can articulate only tentative justifications for service obligations within the contractual framework, explicit taxes coupled with vouchers for low-income service may be the best route to proceed with updating the duty to serve for a post natural monopoly era.

Consider, first, the economic rationales for imposing service extension obligations. Because the DisCo maintains a horizontal monopoly with respect to rights of way and essential network facilities, most customers will continue to have a need for access to distribution from it. At the same time, the DisCo will be in a better position than suppliers or others to spread the costs of service extension, minimizing the economic impact of the distribution network on customers, particularly the poor. Society's utility in the aggregate will be higher if resources are expended toward universal service than in maximizing the revenues of the DisCo; conceptually, this poses an aggregation problem that would be difficult to measure, but the disutility of service discontinuation to at least some consumers will exceed the total utility of a lower DisCo rate for all customers. So even in a competitive retail market, although it is probably impossible to quantify empirically, it seems that economic efficiency rationales for requiring the DisCo to extend its distribution network to at least some customers will continue in some circumstances. It should be noted, though, that in a deregulated environment where power supply is competitive the access and cost-spreading rationales for the extension obligation apply to distribution service only, not to competitively provided power supply. Put another way, despite an economic rationale for requiring the DisCo to assume some distribution service extension obligation, economic analysis does not require the DisCo to also provide power supply. Thus, without further exploration of the structure of retail power markets, there does not appear to be a strong economic rationale for requiring the DisCo to build generation facilities or procure power supply to serve customers. Nevertheless, to the extent regulators decide to impose basic service obligations on some institutional actor in competitive power markets, for at least some customers the DisCo may also be in the best position to spread the costs associated with basic service.

With respect to service continuation, the second obligation of the traditional duty to serve, the economic efficiency rationales behind the obligation also require some reassessment. One of the primary economic efficiency rationales for imposing extraordinary service continuation obligations relates to the utility's status as the superior risk bearer vis-à-vis the customer (discussed in Chapter 2).[28] In deregulated power markets, however, the long-term contract analogy that undergirds application of superior risk bearer analysis to the regulatory compact loses much of its relevance because customers themselves may select power suppliers on a month-to-month basis.

Further, in a competitive retail market, the same rationales cannot justify imposition of an obligation on a private firm to provide full service at a price below total costs, as often applied under rate regulation. There may be some continuing advantage to avoiding power shut off to the extent that a customer is able to pay the variable portion of the costs associated with the supply and distribution of power, as routinely occurred with rate regulation (see Chapter 2). This cost-sharing advantage, however, is significantly reduced in a competitive market where power suppliers face alternative customers for their capacity; it may apply to distribution service, which retains natural monopoly characteristics; however, absent excess capacity committed to DisCo customers, this rationale for a service obligation would not apply to competitive power supply.

Despite these structural and regulatory differences between a competitive market and the traditional regulated industry, efficiency arguments might support imposition of *some* service continuation obligation on the DisCo or other suppliers in a competitive environment. With respect to service discontinuation, the physics of power flow may require the DisCo to bear some responsibility, especially if its grid has not been modernized. Once power is supplied to a distribution grid without computerized customer metering, the DisCo is automatically the supplier of last resort to the retail customer; the customer will continue to receive power until it is physically disconnected by the DisCo. So in certain areas, technology may necessitate some DisCo service continuation obligation in order to ensure system stability.

Yet another rationale for imposition of a service continuation obligation is that retail power markets may yield poor information for market actors, precluding consumers or others from enjoying the full benefits of deregulated markets. Assuming customers have good information about power supply options and the terms of power supply sales contracts, vis-à-vis the DisCo, the customer will be the superior bearer of the risks of service shut-off. The customer can purchase supply plans that provide for early warning or, if necessary, insurance to cover the risks of property or

[28] Of course, to the extent that utility risk bearing is desirable, a cost-spreading rationale also applies.

other damage due to a loss of power. Many customers, though, may not have adequate information about power supply markets to react to the risks of shut-off, particularly where shut-off is due to technological failure or emergencies. In addition, in competitive power markets, consumers are unlikely immediately to possess the knowledge or experience to react to this information when some reaction, such as the purchasing of power insurance or backup supply options, is in order. Poor information or consumer discounting of risks may require the DisCo or a supplier to assume some service continuation obligation, even in a competitive power supply market. This is especially true as these markets initially evolve and as regulators embark on the task of educating consumers.

Further, given that a welfare system already exists in our market economy, the imposition of service continuation obligations in a competitive power supply market might work to mitigate the incentives the welfare system produces for taking excessive credit risks. As competitive power markets evolve, consumers are likely to be offered credit financing plans for electricity akin to many of the financing plans available for other purchases, such as purchase of an automobile. Offerers of such sales are likely to provide creative financing options, often offering consumers who are poor credit risks high-cost financing plans. To the extent such risks are repeatedly presented to low-income consumers in a competitive power supply market, they will also increase the incidence of payment default, especially because utilities will not face the same incentives as under rate regulation to continue service with acceptance of partial payment. As customers increasingly default and lose the basic necessities of life, such as electricity service, over time this could both increase the cost of the welfare system and undermine its poverty reduction goal (Posner, 1995). In this manner, imposition of a service continuation obligation, even in a competitive market, might be seen as a way of reducing the costs of other public welfare programs.

Thus, although some serious reassessment is necessary, economic efficiency arguments for continuing with public goods such as extraordinary service obligations in competitive markets are not completely irrelevant. To the extent economic arguments exist, though, they are no longer based in vertical integration and rate regulation; as with retail competition, the market facilitates many of the transactions that the traditional public utility previously coordinated within a single, vertically integrated firm. Instead, in a deregulated environment the rationales for service obligations relate primarily to horizontal integration and the quality of information consumers can be expected to possess.

Beyond these efficiency rationales for universal service in competitive electric power markets, most of which focus on the structural nature of efficient power markets, it must be acknowledged that, with deregulation, regulators will bear a heavier monitoring cost in implementing universal service goals for electricity. In contrast to the traditional regulatory structure, where a single natural monopoly firm provided service to all customers within its service territory, multiple firms will now provide a variety of services to these customers. In addition to the DisCo, generating companies, power supply companies, and energy service companies, as well as brokers and marketers, will enter power markets. Any obligation imposed on entities beyond the DisCo will entail significant monitoring costs for regulators.

To the extent regulators continue to adhere to the constituent obligations of the common law duty, they will also likely be challenged to articulate nonefficiency justifications in the political sphere, such as fairness, to support service obligations in a competitive retail environment. In this sense, retail competition is likely to force more explicit policy discussion of the costs and benefits of extraordinary service obligations than occurred under the traditional regulatory compact. For example, in Ohio the discussion of consumer service protections has become explicit with the dawn of competition, whereas previously consumer protections were often built into utility tariffs on a voluntary basis.[29]

Some consumer advocates have proposed that states extend service obligations to suppliers, marketers, and brokers, and that DisCos be required to procure basic service power for consumers through mandated bidding criteria or an allocation plan that accurately reflects market power. Although there are legitimate concerns that, in the provision of basic service, the DisCo may tend to favor any generation resources it owns over competitively supplied generation, from an efficiency perspective there is no sound basis for extending utility service obligations beyond the DisCo to power suppliers, marketers, and brokers.

Few states have been willing to require complete vertical disintegration; however, even absent complete vertical disintegration, unbundling of DisCo power sales and procurement can be achieved financially through requiring DisCos with generation to bid into a power exchange and to meet all basic power needs with power exchange purchases. A power exchange, such as that which existed in California's

[29] Alan Johnson, *State Board Sets Service Standards for Ohio's Electric Companies*, Columbus Dispatch, Feb. 6, 1998, at 4E.

deregulation scheme, prices based entirely on the spot market of supply and demand for power. If a DisCo is mandated to bid its power into the exchange before selling basic service to customers, customers purchasing basic service would realize more of the benefits of competition than they would under competitive bidding, because mandatory bidding into a power exchange facilitates decoupling of DisCo basic service power purchases from power sales. Under such an approach, the DisCo has an adequate incentive to purchase from the exchange the lowest-cost power or it will risk losing basic service customers to alternative suppliers if those customers opt to participate in the direct retail purchase market. With such institutional reforms, imposition of a duty to serve on DisCos, to be financed through a system benefits charge, can work simultaneously to facilitate the development of robust power supply markets and pass the new efficiencies of these markets on to consumers without sacrificing access goals. Now a notorious example of deregulation policies run amok, California was not an ideal laboratory for this model, because the state's restructuring plan precluded any markets from developing around long-term contracts and burdened the DisCo with a retail price cap (Rossi, 2002). Even absent these failures in California's deregulatory experiment, however, its approach to imposing service obligations on the DisCo was not a perfect solution. Regulators still must address the issue of how basic service power supply is procured by the DisCo. Without careful attention to market incentives, a DisCo may, as the utility did for much of the twentieth century, continue to see universal service as a way of insulating itself from power supply competition.

States might also consider innovating beyond the approach in California's power exchange, which relies on heavily regulated trading protocols to address the anticompetitive problems with service obligations, by establishing explicit taxes to support a service voucher program for qualifying customers. A tax, similar to a systems benefits charge, can be imposed on the DisCo. Rather than directly requiring the DisCo to provide default service, a state could make electric power vouchers available to low-income customers and others who qualify for universal service based on transparent criteria. Vouchers would allow customers to purchase power supply when needed, but prices would be determined based on the market. Under this approach, it is no longer necessary to impose a service obligation on the DisCo because revenues from vouchers will allow prices signals to work as incentives for service provision. Suppliers could continue to compete for universal service voucher customers – without a state imposing the service obligation on any single market actor, creating a risk for anticompetitive conduct, or attempting to procure power supply for universal service purposes (risking distortion of power supply markets).

To the extent a duty to serve continues to apply to the industry, on whatever rationales, competitively priced retail power markets will work to minimize many of the price distortions of cross-subsidization historically associated with extraordinary service obligations. Under the natural monopoly framework, utility service obligations were paid for through cross-subsidies, but rate regulation helped to minimize the market distortions of this practice. Utilities generally were not opposed to assuming service obligations, especially where they worked to enlarge the customer base, as long as they could recover the costs of these obligations from some customers. With retail competition and a movement to market-based pricing, cross-subsidization will continue to exist, but power supply markets will require DisCos to minimize the impact of subsidies on customers or risk losing customers, especially larger ones, to bypass or other suppliers wheeling on the DisCo system.[30]

Cross-subsidies are not without controversy, but the fiction of the regulatory compact coupled with the economics of natural monopoly price regulation have masked the redistributive nature of extraordinary utility service obligations for the past 100 or so years. Under this regulatory framework, public and private interests converged in maintenance of the duty to serve (see Chapter 2).

Following World War II, public choice theory began to question the orthodox understanding of government regulation generally and utility regulation in particular, providing the intellectual tools for smashing the regulatory compact in a variety of different industries (Farber & Frickey, 1991; Mashaw, 1997). One of the predominant accounts of the growth of utility regulation is regulatory capture – that utilities and other interests, such as consumer groups, secure protection of their interests through the political process by capturing regulation (Becker, 1983; Peltzman, 1976; Stigler, 1971). For example, as Eli Noam (1997) has suggested, in the telecommunications context there is a public choice explanation for the existence of a redistributive universal service obligation in the Telecom

[30] Most DisCos are not willing to accept the service obligations absent some compensation guarantee. "The most dangerous position for the disco would be as the backstop provider to customers not effectively served by the market. This scenario is almost assured if the disco does not convince those in power to remove the obligation to serve" (Pleatt, 1998: 44, 48).

Act of 1996. Although the capture thesis may overstate what actually has occurred (Quirk, 1981) – particularly because regulators could incur benefits outside industry from the provision of public goods – consumers and utilities may well have formed a loose coalition to secure legislative endorsement of the universal service requirement; this inures to the benefit of the average consumer, who now has more pervasive access through interconnectivity; it also benefits utilities because regulators allow recovery of universal service costs by guaranteeing minimum service access charges or rates. If this explanation is applicable to national legislation regulating telecommunications, it would seem even more plausible in the regulation of electricity and natural gas commodities that have developed service obligations primarily at the state level and likely more responsive than the U.S. Congress to the preferences, desires, and needs of state consumers and industries. Modern endorsement of the duty to serve in statutes and regulations in the electricity and natural gas contexts may have resulted not from some public-spirited regulatory compact, but from utilities, consumers, and their representatives forming a loose coalition to secure a regulatory benefit from the political process.

As this chapter suggests, once the regulatory compact has been reassessed to take into account emerging markets economic efficiency rationales for universal service in competitive retail telecommunications, electric power and natural gas markets remain plausible. Retail competition in most public utility industries, such as telecommunications, natural gas, and electricity, is here to stay. Thus, the laws and regulatory concepts we have invoked to regulate public utilities since the Gilded Age are also being transformed. Public goods that were previously bundled into the natural monopoly firm's services, as was the extraordinary service obligation imposed on utilities, need to be addressed independently. It will become important that, in addressing the financing of extraordinary service obligations, regulators avoid building into competitive retail markets structural mechanisms that harm consumers. As I suggest, in initial restructuring of regulated utility markets, to the extent regulators or courts extend the duty to serve beyond incumbent distributors, to suppliers and marketers, new inefficiencies may result. Imposition of narrowly tailored basic service obligation on the DisCo, to be fulfilled through voluntary procurement of power supply and financed through an system benefits charge or voucher, minimizes the inefficiency of imposing a service obligation in a competitive market.

Despite efforts to maintain the *de jure* monopoly status of power distribution, though, in the long run competition may prove inevitable for even this segment of the electricity industry. Increasingly, the availability of distributed generation threatens the need for power distribution because adequate substitutes may be available to customers who can afford generation. Due to the growth of distributed generation, the power generation industry may be set for a future similar to the current mainframe computer industry, which has been seriously threatened by the desktop personal computer industry.[31] Some even suggest that power distribution will ultimately become a competitive or contestable industry.[32] To the extent these developments occur, the ability of a single DisCo to recover the costs of its extraordinary service obligations through a system benefits charge for a geographic area will be weakened significantly.

In the end, as in other contexts – including banking, insurance, and health services, as well as telecommunications – a national service mandate will likely be the most efficient solution. In competitive power distribution markets, a national sales tax on power distribution or supply, coupled with federal voucher and service extension grant programs to guarantee minimum service quality would more efficiently provide service than locally financed universal service in competitive markets (Rossi, 1998a). However, as long as retail service in electric power remains within the jurisdiction of state regulators, carefully structured state and local finance mechanisms will be necessary.

Federal regulation of electric power extends to only wholesale transactions, so customer service obligations will likely remain a matter of state law for the foreseeable future. Enhanced retail competition in historically regulated markets will not mean the end of traditional doctrines of public utility law, such as the duty to serve. Yet regulators must be bold and creative in approaching the content and financing of extraordinary service obligations for new actors in these markets, with a keen eye toward minimizing the structural inefficiencies they pose. Careful study and

[31] Matthew Coralan and Raymond J. Keating, *Microturbines: The Engine of Deregulation,* Investor's Business Daily, Dec. 15, 1997, at A40; Laurence Zuckerman, *Tiny Turbine: The Next Generator?; Company Hopes Its Small Unit Will Dominate Power Market,* New York Times, Dec. 2, 1997, at D1.

[32] More than 30 years ago, Harold Demsetz (1968: 55, 59) observed that the history of utilities has been characterized by competition for service areas. Of course, the availability of distributed generation may make power distribution competitive in the sense that for some customers switching to self-generation may make distribution unnecessary, so distribution markets will begin to compete with the availability of affordable self-generation, as they already do for some large industrial customers. In addition, some economists suggest that power distribution networks can operate in a competitive manner if property rights are defined to facilitate the development of joint ventures (Smith, 1993).

appreciation of the distinct economic and institutional structures of various utility service markets will be necessary to provide sound guidance as regulators apply the duty to serve to competitive retail industries. At each step of this analysis, regulators must not only ask whether there are efficiencies to be gained. Clearly there are, but the challenge regulators will face is devising ways of passing these new efficiencies on to the average consumer. To the extent that the economic rationales for the duty to serve are lacking in the deregulatory era, increased political transparency for what are predominantly social welfare programs will be necessary. An explicit voucher program for low-income consumers, financed through a state tax on the DisCo, holds greater promise for enhancing efficiency and the accountability of regulatory policy than imposing ex ante obligations on market actors through regulation.

PART II

INCOMPLETE REGULATORY BARGAINS, INSTITUTIONS, AND THE ROLE OF JUDICIAL REVIEW IN DEREGULATED INDUSTRIES

5

Deregulatory Takings and Regulatory Bargaining

Regulatory law practitioners and scholars focus much of their attention on legal transitions. Since the mid-1980s, the prospect of governmental liability for private harms imposed by regulatory change has attracted the attention of leading scholars in a variety of contexts, including changes to corporate securities and tax laws (Ahdieh, 2004; Fisch, 1997; Kaplow, 1986; Symposium, 2003; Van Alstine, 2002). For more than a decade, transition issues have dominated discussions of the legal implications of deregulation for industries such as electric power and telecommunications.

In the context of economic regulation, it is now conventional to frame the transition issue as a "deregulatory taking" – a novel term used to describe potential legal claims against the government requiring financial liability for deregulatory policies that upset the settled expectations of private firms. In the leading treatise on the topic, *Deregulatory Takings and the Regulatory Contract*, J. Gregory Sidak and Daniel F. Spulber (1997) (who seem to have coined the term "deregulatory takings") make an explicit link between deregulatory takings and the regulatory contract to argue in favor of governmental compensation for regulatory change in the electric power and telecommunications contexts. If positioned within an incomplete contracts framework, deregulatory takings presents an occasion to evaluate the appropriate default rule for courts to apply in filling in gaps in the regulatory bargain as they consider the harms imposed by regulatory transitions. Understanding regulation as a bargain, however, does not commit or limit courts to the role of discovering and enforcing implicit contracts.

I. MAJORITARIAN VERSUS INCENTIVE-BASED DEFAULT RULES FOR INCOMPLETE BARGAINS

It is commonplace to frame discussion of the legal implications of regulatory transitions in terms of the regulatory contract. Writing at the height of telecommunications and electric power deregulation in the 1990s, Sidak and Spulber explicitly invoked the regulatory contract as a foundational concept for their innovative account of deregulatory takings in the telecommunications and electric power contexts. According to them, the regulatory contract between the firm and the regulator is comprised of reciprocal burdens and benefits:

> The regulated utility submits to various regulatory restrictions including price regulations, quality-of-service requirements, and common carrier regulations. In return the regulated firm receives a protected franchise in its service territory, and its investors are allowed an opportunity to earn revenues subject to a rate-of-return constraint. Without the expectation of earning a competitive rate of return, investors would not be willing to commit funds for establishing and operating the utility.... Once the utility invests these funds, the long depreciation schedules typical in electricity and telecommunications regulation credibly commit the utility to performing its obligations under the regulatory contract by denying it the opportunity to recover its capital before the end of its useful life.[1]

Sidak and Spulber's argument for deregulatory takings represents a modern application of the legalistic regulatory contract (see Chapter 1). On this account, the state presumptively bears legal liability when the regulatory contract is breached by a regulatory transition. As a matter of legal doctrine, governmental liability for regulatory change potentially arises due to the Takings Clause of the United States Constitution or breach of contract claims against the state (Sidak & Spulber, 1997).[2] In terms of efficiency, deregulatory takings proponents see the Takings Clause and contract law as designed primarily to protect regulatory commitments. A credible threat of litigation and damage awards against state actors for upsetting regulatory commitments is intended to promote certainty in investments by working to deter the kind of predatory conduct on the

[1] Sidak & Spulber, 1997: 109.

[2] Apart from financial liability or prohibitions on legal change due to constitutional takings or breach of contracts claims, legal constraints on regulatory transitions may also arise pursuant to ordinary judicial review of a regulatory agency's policy decisions (Pierce, 1991; Rossi, 1994). Such judicial review differs fundamentally in the remedy (typically, administrative law review results in a remand to the agency) and in the standard of review (typically, an agency would be afforded deference, although there may be some obligation for it to explain the reasoning behind its decision).

part of the state that would upset investor-backed expectations and lead to inefficiently low levels of investment.

In contract law, one of the most important scholarly debates in recent decades focuses on default rules – the rules of thumb courts might look to fill in gaps in incomplete contracts. Incompleteness in contracting gives rise to some demand for judicial gap-filling measures, including remedies for conduct that is deemed wrongful (Ayres & Gertner, 1992). Where the actor whose conduct is under scrutiny is the state, an incomplete contracts analysis focuses on the default rules for fundamental issues of public governance, including the obligations of the state in changing the rules of the game. According to advocates of deregulatory takings, who implicitly adopt a presumption in favor of compensation, courts reviewing regulatory transitions are to adopt a gap-filling measure that reflects the preferences of a majority of the firms that contract with the government for compensation for legal transitions.

In this sense, the case for deregulatory takings envisions that courts invoke what contract law scholars might refer to as a substantive "majoritarian" default rule in considering the harms associated with regulatory transitions. Majoritarian default rules are a natural starting place in evaluating the judicial role in assessing gap-filling alternatives for regulatory bargains. Contract law scholars look to "majoritarian" default rules for incomplete bargains as gap-filling measures that mimic what most participants in the regulatory system – consumers, firms, and so on – would prefer (Posner, 2003). A majoritarian default rule has the advantage of reducing transaction costs in the bargaining process; if the parties to a bargain expect courts to fill in the gap with a term they would likely select in bargaining, there is little need to bargain over this term and private transaction costs are lower. Courts could best promote efficiency by choosing the gap-filling term that is expected to lower transaction costs in most cases. In this sense, majoritarian default rules converge with efficient contract terms, although the efficient term is case specific, whereas the majoritarian term applies across a general class of similar cases (Posner, 2003: 840). In the context of regulatory transitions, a substantive majoritarian default rule for breach of the regulatory bargain would presumptively favor compensation for regulatory changes that upset investor-baked expectations. This is precisely the result that deregulatory takings advocates envision.

Most discussion of regulation focuses on substantive majoritarian default rules. For example, a leading treatise on the economics of regulation emphasizes the balancing of substantive fairness and efficiency in the content of regulatory policy decisions (Zajac, 1995). If courts envision their role as gap filling with substantive majoritarian default rules, their primary task would be to structure substantive rules to promote the most fair or efficient result in most cases. However, understanding regulation as a bargain does not necessarily commit courts to this role. Even if it is the case that default rules are most efficiently designed with an eye to respecting the preferences of most stakeholders, a majoritarian default rule need not answer every substantive question about a regulatory bargain. A majoritarian default rule might, for instance, favor a nonjudicial process for the resolution of disputes (e.g., a private negotiation) that a majority of contracting parties would prefer. In the context of economic regulation, for instance, process-based majoritarian defaults, such as a standard principle of judicial deference to agency regulators, can play an important role in ensuring sound and legitimate policy decisions (Pierce, 1991). A process-based majoritarian default might look to institutions that a majority of bargaining parties would prefer to have resolve a problem, rather than attempt to discern the substantive result a majority would prefer. If the analysis is framed this way, the fundamental focus is on institutions. Courts, legislatures, or agencies may have distinct comparative advantages in addressing the harms presented by regulatory transitions. An institutionally informed, process-based approach to default rules is preferable where there are high error costs to picking a substantive majoritarian default rule (Pierce, 1984).

Further, in many regulatory contexts, a substantive majoritarian default rule will have significant costs associated with it (Chen, 1999; Rossi, 1998b). More than in the context of private bargains, in the context of regulatory bargains in which one or more stakeholders is a government body, ex ante incentives for private firms in the regulatory process (defined broadly, to include courts and the legislature, as well as federal and state agencies) can have ex post consequences for social welfare. Looking at the regulatory bargain as a type of incomplete contract provides a counterjuxtaposition to other accounts of regulation, which discourage renegotiation, downplay the role of the political process, and largely ignore ex ante incentives. Judicially applied doctrines of constitutional, regulatory, and administrative law shape these interactions, but little serious attention has been paid to their role in the deregulatory environment. Deregulation provides an opportunity to evaluate the relevance of firm–government interaction to these doctrines in the new environment facing traditionally regulated industries. The optimal default rule may well diverge from majoritarian defaults when incentive effects are taken into account. For example, clear statement rules, which limit judicial intervention to expressly bargained-for language, may encourage more politically accountable decision making in the public law context, while also respecting the voluntary nature of the bargaining process.

Sometimes, it may even be appropriate for a regulator or court to impose a "penalty" default: selecting a term that one or more parties to a bargain – perhaps even a majority – may not necessarily prefer in order to improve the bargaining process in the future (Posner, 2003). Law and economics scholars see penalty defaults as desirable for two reasons. First, they discourage the parties to a bargain from externalizing the costs of enforcement on courts. Second, they discourage parties from opportunistically withholding information from each other and from enforcement officials (Ayres & Gertner, 1992). Nonmajoritarian defaults, such as penalty default rules, can also play an important role in regulatory law.

Presumably, majoritarian defaults – such as the presumption favoring compensation urged by deregulatory takings advocates – are desirable because of their legitimacy and predictability among members of the contracting community. Yet, a decade after deregulatory takings theories first appeared in the literature, no court has clearly adopted the theory behind deregulatory takings. Rather, it seems that courts evaluating the types of conflicts that arise from changes to the regulatory bargain do not envision their role as adopting substantive majoritarian gap-filling measures. Conventional constitutional takings doctrine developed by United States Courts does not provide a settled basis for governmental liability for regulatory transitions. The constitutional deregulatory takings arguments in favor of compensation borrow from an interpretation of land use takings cases as focusing primarily on protecting investor-backed expectations. This reading of the takings case law, however, is descriptively flawed. Its unpredictability makes it incapable of achieving its stated goals of deterrence and promoting efficient investment. In contrast to the land use regulation setting, in the infrastructure context – including regulation of electric and telecommunications utilities – courts have taken a different approach. The outcomes of takings cases in the infrastructure context are much more predictable in their consistently deferential stance toward government regulation. In the economic regulation context, courts generally defer to government regulators, largely out of institutional concerns with promoting expertise and political accountability in public decision making.

The view of contract underlying many of the arguments for deregulatory takings is overly formalistic in the way it addresses the problem of regulatory change. At its extreme, it results in sweeping governmental liability for regulatory change, including liability for transitioning to competitive markets. An incomplete contracts informed approach would look beyond substantive majoritarian default rules to provide a more balanced, accurate, and nuanced picture of the relationship between the firm and governmental regulators. The bargaining approach also opens up a new series of inquiries for regulatory law – inquiries that are often ignored in the literature that glorifies legalistic contract. A focus on government relations bargaining can illustrate why the emphasis on majoritarian default rules, as deregulatory takings advocates favor in this context, is misplaced. As contract law scholars recognize, the role of contract rules is not to reflect majoritarian substantive commitments in every case. An expectation that a court will come to the rescue could produce adverse incentives in the bargaining process (Posner, 2003). In the private law context, the costs of majoritarian default rules may be small because typically the costs are born only by the contracting parties. In the public law context, however, majoritarian default rules risk imposing significant public costs by ossifying governmental policies or creating significant financial liability for regulatory bodies (and the public fisc). In the public law context, legitimacy and predictability could be provided by alternative types of default rules – focused on institutional actors rather than substantive efficiency – without having an adverse effect on incentives and behavior.

As this chapter argues, given the institutional context of the regulatory process, judicially enforced clear statement rules fit the descriptive approach courts take in reviewing governmental liability for regulatory change better than substantive majoritarian default rules. Critics of deregulatory takings (Chen, 1999; Hovenkamp, 1999b; Rossi, 1998b) stake out a view of the regulatory contract that contrasts with the legalistic enforcement model embraced by deregulatory takings advocates. They would allow regulators to changes the terms and conditions of the regulatory contract with little or no attention to the costs this may impose on incumbent firms. On this view courts only intervene to enforce a regulatory contract where the terms of the bargain are explicit, or where there is a clear statement to make a binding commitment on the part of the state.

II. THE REGULATORY CONTRACT, STRANDED COSTS, AND THE NOVEL ARGUMENT FOR DEREGULATORY TAKINGS

As competitive restructuring and deregulation present new pressures for incumbents in formerly regulated industries, firms routinely look to courts to preserve the status quo or hold them harmless based on the regulatory contract. In the electric power and telecommunications industries, for instance, utilities have routinely claimed that various deregulation policies produce "stranded costs." The definition of stranded costs is by no means settled because it is a term with both legal and political implications for utilities and governments. Indeed, the term itself has a normative loading that hinders an objective assessment of the problem in the policy-making process. By calling costs "stranded," those who argue for compensation imply that the costs are "shipwrecked" – that is, investors are the innocent victims of misadventure brought about by government action. It is not at all clear, however, that government action is the source of all losses firms claim as deregulatory takings.

Economically, stranded costs occur when the costs to the incumbent exceed the costs to new entrants because of the actions of the state, not because of changes in technology or other exogenous economic shocks. These costs reflect the fact that some investments cannot earn a fair rate of return in the deregulated marketplace. However, the consensus ends there. Sidak and Spulber (1997), the leading proponents of stranded cost recovery, define stranded costs in a broad conceptual manner as the "inability of utility shareholders to secure the return of, and a competitive rate of return on, their investment" (27). This definition includes operating expenditures required by regulators and capital investments. In the electric power context, economists have identified four types of stranded costs: "(1) Undepreciated investments in power plants that are more expensive than generators available today. (2) Long-term contracts – most if not all mandated by the 1978 Public Utility Regulatory Policies Act (PURPA). (3) Generators built but not used, primarily nuclear. (4) Expenses related to 'demand-side management' (DSM) and other conservation programs that, as substitutes for new plant construction, were charged to the generation side of the business" (Brennan & Boyd, 1997: 45). Other practical definitions of stranded costs are more limiting, focusing primarily on durable capital asset outlays but not necessarily including other expenses mandated or allowed by regulators (Hovenkamp, 1999b; Rossi, 1998b).

More than a decade ago, estimates of stranded costs from deregulating the United States electric power industry ranged from $34 billion to $210 billion, according to one frequently cited report.[3] Given this large amount, the pressures for regulators to compensate firms in the industry

[3] These estimates represent the after-tax discounted present value of the reduced contributions to cost recovery (Hirst & Baxter, 1995, cited in Brennan & Boyd, 1997).

for some, if not all, of these costs are obvious. The Energy Information Administration (1997) estimates that stranded costs could lead to an increase in bankruptcies in the industry if regulators do not address them. Not surprisingly, in the 1990s, many utilities made vigorous policy arguments in favor of full or near-full recovery of stranded costs before federal and state regulators. In the realm of politics and agency regulatory processes, firms have been fairly successful in their efforts to secure compensation from state legislators and state and federal regulators. For instance, the FERC allowed transmitting utilities stranded cost recovery in its Order No. 888, which implemented wholesale competition for the electric power industry.[4] Many state deregulation plans, such as the initial California, Illinois, and Texas competition plans, provide for full or partial stranded cost recovery.[5] By the late 1990s, however, industry estimates of stranded costs had drastically changed. A 1999 Moody's Investors Service estimated that stranded costs in the electric power industry would total $10 billion; this is a substantial downward revision from their 1995 estimate of $130 billion. According to their estimates, $102 billion of the reduction in the total was due to regulatory and legislative relief by federal and state governments.[6]

[4] The FERC's decision was upheld on appeal to the D.C. Circuit. *Transmission Access Policy Study Group v. FERC*, 225 F.3d 667 (D.C. Cir. 2000), aff'd in part sub nom, *New York v. FERC*, 535 U.S. 1 (2002).

[5] In 2004, a Texas electric utility claimed stranded costs in excess of $4 billion due to investments in nuclear power. Jane Elliott, *Electricity Power Squabble Powers Up*, Houston Chronicle, June 21, 2004, at 1 (Business) (describing request by CenterPoint Energy for $4.4 billion in stranded cost recovery).

[6] The study is summarized in Andrew Taylor, *Debate on U.S. Deregulation Heats Up*, Financial Times, Survey: World Energy (London Ed.), Dec. 8, 1999, at 1. Some states are allowing for stranded cost recovery even though they have not implemented retail competition in electricity. The state of Florida, for example, has adopted a wait-and-see approach to retail deregulation of the electric utility industry. See *Electric Utility Restructuring: Before, During and After*, Public Utilities Fortnightly, Nov. 15, 1999, at 26 (comments of Florida Public Service Commission Chairman Joe Garcia). Although postponement of deregulation has kept the stranded cost issue off the public political agenda, regulators have quietly allowed utilities to accelerate depreciation and recovery of power plants. By the time Florida deregulates the industry, some utilities will have recovered the costs of their plants, so the stranded cost issue may not materialize. For example, Florida Power and Light has struck a deal with state regulators that allow it to accelerate $100 million per year in depreciation expenses for plants during the next 3 years. See *Rate Deal Brightens Outlook for FPL; Utility Has Better Deal Against Competition*, Sun-Sentinel, Mar. 28, 1999, at 1F (noting that "FPL has been able to speed up these reported reductions of its plants through a special agreement with state regulators that was set to expire at the end of the year. The idea behind this was to reduce the company's exposure to 'stranded costs,' or money spent on power plants that won't be recovered when greater competition leaves

If merely a policy or political argument, stranded cost recovery might be ignored (if not forgotten) along with other regulatory bailouts, such as federal efforts to compensate the savings and loan industry, passenger railroads, or airlines. Yet, in the late 1990s, fueled by predictions of financial ruin, the argument for stranded cost recovery moved beyond the political realm. It took on the rhetoric of legal entitlement, in which firms routinely invoke the Contracts Clause and the Takings Clause of the United States Constitution as a basis for enforcing purported regulatory commitments. In contrast to rate regulation, which provided a relatively predictable regulatory forum for firms and investors, deregulation of a formerly regulated industry where a competitive market will displace the regulator in setting prices produces substantial uncertainty regarding the firms' revenues and profits. In such contexts, "deregulatory takings" challenges asserting interference with "investment-backed expectations" – one of the factors deemed relevant by courts in assessing a regulatory taking – may arise. According to Sidak and Spulber (1997), who advocate a legal entitlement to recovery of stranded costs in the United States,

> The competitive transformation of local exchange telecommunications and the electric power industry raises significant questions about whether regulators should give a public utility the opportunity to recover its stranded costs. As regulators mandate the unbundling of basic network elements in local telephony or mandate wholesale and retail wheeling in the electricity industry, they introduce competitive rules that potentially deny utilities the opportunity to recover the cost of service. While competition presents incumbents with opportunities to serve customers in new ways, utilities often leave untouched the utility's preexisting incumbent burdens. Such regulatory action threatens to confiscate private property – shareholder value – for the promotion of competition, without just compensation.[7]

On this view, cost-of-service regulation represents a regulatory commitment that ought to be enforced by courts, just as courts provide legal remedies for breach of other contracts.

Deregulatory takings depends on an account of regulation as contract. Those arguing for widespread compensation claim both that the government has made an implicit (if not explicit) contract with the utilities to guarantee them a competitive rate of return on their capital and has induced them to invest in infrastructure and to make long-term contractual

the older assets obsolete."); see also *Florida P&L Dodges a Rate Case With a Deal to Cut Rates $1 Billion Over Three Years,* Electric Utility Week, Mar. 15, 1999, at 13.

[7] Sidak & Spulber, 1997: 19.

commitments on those terms. If deregulation lowers the expected value of the firm's assets, these commentators claim that a breach of contract has occurred, implicating contractual and constitutional remedies for the harm the firm incurs. To the extent regulation is a contract between the firm and the state, akin to other legally enforced contracts, advocates of this position argue that changes to the terms of the contract that impose financial harm may give rise to remedies for breach. Those arguing for widespread compensation claim both that the government has made an implicit (if not explicit) contract with the utilities to guarantee them a competitive rate of return on their capital and has induced them to invest on those terms. If deregulation lowers the expected value of the firm's assets, these commentators claim that a breach of contract has occurred that both violates the Contracts Clause of the Constitution and may also amount to an unconstitutional taking of property, entitled to "just compensation" under the Takings Clause.

Such liability is particularly an issue in deregulated industries, as regulators abandon or modify old regulatory structures and increasingly experiment with new ones. The less stable a regulatory structure, the more likely that firms will complain about regulatory change and seek redress for its occurrence. At the extreme, instability may cause investors to move their resources away from infrastructure industries and may lead to underinvestment in important network infrastructure facilities. At the same time, large-scale liability, whether actual or threatened, poses a serious problem for regulatory law because it may impose costs on regulators that lead to ossifications of existing regulatory approaches. Even if government is not found liable for regulatory change, the prospect of regulatory takings lawsuits may influence how regulators set access charges for network facilities, such as electric power transmission or telecommunications wires (Spulber & Yoo, 2003). Deregulatory takings advocates see "just compensation" as requiring regulators to include within the definition of costs all opportunity costs to the firm, including the private opportunity costs for the incumbent monopolist. For example, in the telecommunications context, deregulatory takings proponents have advocated that the FCC set network access charges in deregulated markets to include not only historical costs, but also the opportunity costs incurred by incumbent firms (Sidak & Spluber, 1997; Spulber & Yoo, 2003).

Deregulatory takings is a novel legal claim, based on a clever doctrinal argument. The term "deregulatory takings" does not appear in any federal judicial opinion published prior to 1998 and, after 1998, it only appears to arise in the case law through citation to Sidak and Spulber's work (Chen, 2000; 931, n. 48). Yet, deregulatory takings threatens to turn the status quo of regulation into a constitutionally or contractually protected entitlement – a property or contract argument that allows individual firms to benefit from the exiting regulatory order. The new property or contractual entitlements associated with regulation might have profound implications for economic regulation, as well as regulation more generally. Like many novel legal claims and like many clever legal arguments, the argument for deregulatory takings requires careful assessment and analysis.

III. THE UNPREDICTABLE NATURE OF LAND USE TAKINGS

The Fifth Amendment to the United States Constitution provides that private property will not be taken for public use without just compensation.[8] As Justice Hugo Black famously noted, the "Fifth Amendment's guarantee . . . [i]s designed to bar Government from forcing some people alone to bear public burdens which, in all fairness and justice, should be borne by the public as a whole."[9] In implementing this design, the Supreme Court has required compensation when tangible things are taken directly by the government, but has often refused compensation where the owner merely suffers a diminution in the value of its property. For example, if the government physically invades a farmer's land by building a highway through his cornfield or condemning a private individual's house site for use as a public swimming pool, compensation is required. It is far more difficult to determine whether compensation is required when a road is moved, changing traffic access to a gas station or providing traffic and noise disturbances to homeowners in a quiet, secluded neighborhood.

The Supreme Court has had several opportunities to address the regulatory takings issue in the land use context in more recent years. In applying the Takings Clause to land use regulations, some commentators purport to find a pattern in the cases. For instance, Frank Michelman's (1968, 1988) view that the Takings Clause should preserve "investment-backed expectations" finds some support in *Penn Central Transportation Co. v. City of New York*, where the Supreme Court endorsed "interference

[8] "[N]or shall private property be taken for public use, without just compensation." U.S. Const. amend. V. See *Dolan v. City of Tigard*, 512 U.S. 374, 383–84, n. 5 (1994) [citing *Chicago B & Q R.R. v. City of Chicago*, 166 U.S. 226 (1897)] (extending Takings Clause to the states). Under the Fourteenth Amendment, the clause applies to state governments, as well as the federal government.

[9] *Armstrong v. United States*, 364 U.S. 40, 49 (1960).

with distinct investment-backed expectations" as one factor in its ad hoc assessment of regulatory takings.[10] Under this approach, takings law should be predictable so private individuals can confidently commit resources to capital projects. This view also serves as the theoretical basis for arguments in favor of recovery for stranded costs, advanced by commentators such as Sidak and Spulber.

Many commentators writing in the law and economics tradition, such as Michelman, argue that the Supreme Court has developed a model of takings jurisprudence designed primarily to promote certainty among investors for the purpose of deterring predatory actions by the state against property owners. Once a "taking" is found, the level of compensation is to be set at "fair market value," but if the owner disputes the state's judgment on this matter it is a court, not the market, that sets the price.[11] In some cases, injunctive relief may be appropriate. Judicial remedies for predatory governmental actions occurring in the regulatory process may serve to deter the state from overreaching against private landholders, promoting greater certainty and attracting investment.

On inspection, however, land use takings case law is hardly a model for certainty. Instead, it is frequently described as ad hoc and unpredictable (Rose-Ackerman, 1988, 1992; Rose-Ackerman & Rossi, 2000). Since the Supreme Court's 1978 decision in *Penn Central Transportation Co. v. City of New York*, the Court has characterized its approach to regulatory takings as "essentially ad hoc, factual inquiries."[12] In deciding whether a regulatory taking has occurred, the Court has focused on balancing three factors: the "character of the governmental action"; the extent to which the action interferes with "distinct investment back expectations"; and the degree of diminution in value.[13] According to one commentator, "[I]t is difficult to imagine a body of case law in greater doctrinal and conceptual disarray." (Peterson, 1989: 1304). Even Richard Epstein (1997b), one of the strongest advocates for constitutional protection of private property, believes that takings jurisprudence is "a sprawling affair with little intellectual coherence" (22).

[10] 438 U.S. 104, 124 (1978). In addition to *Penn Central*, Michelman's position has been picked up by the Supreme Court in *Kaiser Aetna v. United States*, 444 U.S. 164, 175 (1979); *Keystone Bituminous Coal Assn. v. DeBenedictis*, 480 U.S. 470, 493, 499 (1987).

[11] See *United States v. Miller*, 317 U.S. 369 (1943). Some states depart from this approach, allowing property owners to recover a portion of the gain in value attributable to a public project. See, e.g., *Dep't of Transportation v. Nalven*, 455 So.2d 301 (Fla. 1984); *Calhoun v. State Highway Dep't*, 153 S.E.2d 418 (Ga. 1987).

[12] 438 U.S. 104 (1978).

[13] Id. at 124.

The most recent crop of cases continues the trend of ad hoc balancing in the broad range of regulatory takings cases. In 1992, the Supreme Court attempted to bring formalism and predictability to its takings jurisprudence with its decision in *Lucas v. South Carolina Coastal Council*.[14] This decision holds that there is a presumption that regulatory action that totally eliminates the economic value of private property is a taking. It does not, however, articulate a per se rule for partial regulatory takings cases and leaves a broad gray area where courts must struggle to adjudicate. Even in total deprivation cases, the *Lucas* majority left open two broad categories of exceptions: uses of private property that contravene "existing rules or understandings," as defined in state law;[15] and the "nuisance exception," allowing for deference to government action intended to address key public health safety and welfare concerns.[16] Inquiries regarding "existing rules and understandings," as well as the definition of "nuisance,"[17] lead litigants to face substantial uncertainty in lower courts, which grapple to define the scope of these exceptions on a case-by-case basis.

In 1994, the Court handed down its decision in *Dolan v. City of Tigard*, another substantial victory for the property rights movement.[18] *Dolan* continues and expands on the Court's application of a due process test that would invalidate land use regulations "not substantially advancing legitimate government interests."[19] Although an earlier case had required an "essential nexus" between the dedication of property and a legitimate state interest,[20] *Dolan* demands only "rough proportionality" between the dedication and the impact of the proposed development.[21] Taken

[14] 505 U.S. 1003 (1992).
[15] Id. at 1027–28, 1030.
[16] Id. at 1027.
[17] In his majority opinion for the Court, Justice Scalia noted that relevant factors in assessing a nuisance include

> the degree of harm to public lands and resources, or adjacent private property, posed by the claimant's proposed activities, the social value of the claimant's activities and their suitability to the locality in question, and the relative ease with which the harm can be avoided through measures taken by the government (or adjacent landowners) alike.... (505 U.S. at 1030–31)

Such nuisances must be recognized under preexisting state law (Id. at 1029) and the application of nuisance principles must be "objectively reasonable." (Id. at 1032, n. 18)
[18] 512 U.S. 374 (1994).
[19] See *Agins v. City of Tiburon*, 447 U.S. 255, 260 (1980).
[20] *Nollan v. California Coastal Comm'n*, 483 U.S. 825, 837 (1987).
[21] As Justice Rehnquist stated, the *Dolan* test goes beyond the nexus required by *Nollan*, focusing on "whether the degree of the exaction demanded... bear the required relationship to the projected impact" from the proposed development (512 U.S. at 388).

together, *Lucas* and *Dolan* might be seen as the Court responding to prior requests for "a good dose of formalism" (Rose-Ackerman, 1988: 1700), but the application of the cases is narrow, and both leave substantial issues to be adjudicated. Thus, it is questionable whether the post-1987 cases have changed much in the court's ad hoc approach; at best, they stand for a symbolic formalism of limited applicability (Alexander, 1996).

By bolstering the perceived legal status of property rights to invite additional takings claims,[22] the Supreme Court has ensured its ad hoc approach will continue. In fact, the Court seems to be inordinately proud of the ad hoc nature of its takings opinions and has reiterated its support of case-by-case balancing in more recent opinions. For example, Chief Justice Rehnquist argues that "questions arising under the Just Compensation Clause rest on ad hoc factual inquiries, and must be decided on the facts and circumstances in each case."[23]

Some authors have argued that the unpredictable nature of takings jurisprudence is functional and appropriate, given the ongoing social process of creating and revising property rights (Poirier, 2002). Yet, while consistent with a property right rhetoric, it is doubtful that this ad hoc balancing approach can protect investor-backed expectations or promote efficiency in infrastructure investment. Where, as in the case of infrastructure investments, investments are long lived and special purpose, certainty in doctrine is more important than in other contexts. To preserve investment-backed expectations, takings law should be predictable so private individuals can confidently commit resources to capital projects. This would not require compensation in all cases. It would only require that investors be able to predict what might or might not happen. No taking can legitimately be claimed if the property owner anticipated that an uncompensated state action was possible and this belief is reflected in the price paid for the asset. Property values "are enjoyed under an implied limitation and must yield to the police power," according to Justice Holmes.[24] No government could or should indemnify investors against the hazards of business life.

[22] In *Dolan* it was stated, "We see no reason why the Takings Clause of the Fifth Amendment, as much a part of the Bill of Rights as the First Amendment or Fourth Amendment, should be relegated to the status of a poor relation..." (512 U.S. at 392).

[23] 480 U.S. at 508 (J. Rehnquist, dissenting). Similar language is found in Brennan's majority opinion in *Andrus v. Allard*, 444 U.S. 51, 65 (1979): "There is no abstract or fixed point at which judicial intervention under the Takings Clause becomes appropriate. Formulas and factors have been developed in a variety of settings. Resolution of each case, however, ultimately calls as much for the exercise of judgment as for the application of logic."

[24] *Pennsylvania Coal Co. v. Mahon*, 260 U.S. 393, 413 (1922).

If takings jurisprudence is both ad hoc and ex post, as the land use takings cases indicate it is, investors may have a difficult time knowing whether a particular state action will or will not be judged to be a taking. Therefore, even if the menu of possible state actions is known and probabilities can be assigned to each policy, investors cannot make informed choices because the Court has not given them clear standards to determine when compensation will be paid. The shifting doctrines of takings law introduce an element of uncertainty into investors' choices that has nothing to do with the underlying economics of the situation. This uncertainty creates two problems. First, investors do not know whether damages will be paid. Second, in the event damages are not paid, investors may be left bearing the costs of an uninsurable risk. To the extent that investors are risk averse, the very incoherence of the doctrine produces inefficient choices.

The problem of judicially created uncertainty is exacerbated by the ex post nature of court decisions. Federal judges are reluctant to decide cases until someone has "actually" been harmed. Not only are they reluctant to articulate general principles of takings law, but judges are also unwilling to make general rulings on the status of state actions under individual statutes.[25] In the field of regulatory takings, where the future direction of the law is unclear, economic actors cannot obtain a prospective ruling from the court on whether a particular law will cause a taking. They must wait until a concrete harm has occurred before the statute can be tested. In the face of this uncertainty, investors may forgo otherwise profitable activities, and thus, the current state of the law may produce an inefficiently low level of investment.

Investors are not the only ones adversely affected by the incoherence and unpredictability of takings law. Government officials may also

[25] Thus, in *Keystone*, Justice Stevens, in discussing *Pennsylvania Coal Co. v. Mahon*, dismisses Justice Holmes' analysis of the general validity of the act as an uncharacteristic "advisory opinion" (480 U.S. at 484). Stevens then goes on to argue that no taking has occurred under the similar Pennsylvania law at issue in *Keystone* because at the time of the lawsuit no company could actually demonstrate that it had been harmed. The companies were asking the Court to pass on the general legitimacy of the statute, and this the majority declined to do. Rehnquist in dissent would have been willing to do this. He argues that in *Pennsylvania Coal* the general validity of the act "was properly drawn into question" (480 U.S. at 507). Similarly, in *Pennell* an association of landlords was given standing to challenge a portion of San Jose's rent control ordinance, but their claim that a taking had occurred was dismissed as "premature" because no landlord had actually suffered harm from the disputed provision [*Pennell v. City of San Jose*, 485 U.S. 1, 5–7 (1988)]. The partial dissent, in contrast, would have reached the merits of the takings claim (Id. at 16–19).

be affected because the vagueness of the doctrine may act as a force for conservatism among public officials. Risk-averse officials facing the possibility of compensation suits against their jurisdictions may restrict their activities simply because they dislike uncertainty. As Justice Stevens notes: "It is no answer to say that '[a]fter all, if a policeman must know the Constitution, then why not a planner?' To begin with, the Court has repeatedly recognized that it, itself cannot establish any objective rules to assess when a regulation becomes a taking. How then can it demand that land planners do any better?"[26]

The ad hoc nature of the Court's opinions is itself troubling and is impossible to reconcile with a belief in the importance of preserving investors' expectations, especially for infrastructure investments that are long lived and special purpose. The shifting doctrines of regulatory takings law themselves introduce an element of uncertainty into investors' choices. To the extent that investors are risk averse, the very incoherence of judicial doctrine may produce inefficient choices.

IV. TAKINGS JURISPRUDENCE IN INFRASTRUCTURE INDUSTRIES

In contrast to land use and regulatory takings cases, which have undergone a transformation favoring the property owner, in the case of infrastructure regulation, particularly of regulated utilities, takings law challenges have produced a distinct line of opinions – in terms of both precedential value and reasoning. The courts treat these cases separately from other takings cases because most regulated utilities are subject to government regulation of prices. Since the New Deal, takings cases addressing utility price regulation have been much clearer – and better justified in light of institutional concerns – than the ad hoc line of opinions addressing takings in the land use regulation context.

In the early days of utility regulation at the end of the nineteenth century, the Supreme Court endorsed a "fair value" test, an approach that thrust courts into the business of valuing utility rates on substantive due process grounds.[27] Much like the current line of land use cases, these early rate-making cases, decided largely during the *Lochner* era (in which courts looked with disfavor on state regulation of economic activity),[28]

[26] *First English Evangelical Lutheran Church of Glendale v. Los Angeles*, 482 U.S. 304, 341 n. 17 (1987) (J. Stevens, dissenting).
[27] See *Smyth v. Ames*, 169 U.S. 466 (1898).
[28] See *Lochner v. New York*, 198 U.S. 45 (1905).

take an ad hoc approach to adjudicating whether government-set rates are constitutional. The inquiry into fair value required courts to consider a range of facts – "to be given such weight as may be just and right in each case"[29] – in determining whether fair value was provided. During this era, rate-making controversies were arguably "[t]he most significant cases in the Court's campaign to expand the definition of property and takings" (McUsic, 1996: 616). The cases of the period have been described as ad hoc and unpredictable, leading to "endless litigation" and calling into question the role of courts in reviewing economic matters (Chen, 1999). Justice Brandeis, joined by Justice Holmes, famously criticized the substantive judicial inquiry into fair value for requiring courts to invest substantial resources into determining utility rates without producing a very useful economic rate structure.[30]

Eventually, following the advice of Brandeis, the Court repudiated this activist position in the 1940s, adopting instead an "end results" test. In *Federal Power Commission v. Hope Natural Gas Co.*,[31] the Court indicated that it will focus on the result rather than the method of rate making. According to Justice Douglas, "It is not the theory but the impact of the rate order which counts. If the total effect of the rate order cannot be said to be unreasonable, judicial inquiry . . . is at an end."[32] This approach is consistent with the Court's repudiation of *Lochner* and its generally deferential judicial review of economic regulation in the New Deal era.

The Supreme Court has reaffirmed this deferential approach to reviewing utility price regulation in every case decided since 1944. In *Market Street Railway v. Railroad Commission*, the Court refused to require compensation when the government did not authorize full recovery of the costs of obsolete technology.[33] Later, in the *Permian Basin Rate Cases*, the Court rejected a challenge to the Federal Power Commission's ability to set areawide rates, reasoning that there is no constitutional obligation to determine individual rates on a cost-of-service basis.[34] The most recent rate-making case considered by the Court, *Duquesne Light Co. v.*

[29] 169 U.S. at 546–47.

[30] See also Missouri ex rel. *Southwestern Bell Tel. Co. v. Public Serv. Comm'n*, 262 U.S. 276, 299–301 (1923) (J. Brandeis, dissenting).

[31] 320 U.S. 591 (1944).

[32] Id. at 602.

[33] 324 U.S. 528, 557, 564–65 (1945) (deferring to regulators decision not to allow recovery of San Francisco street cars and bus lines valued by regulators at less than one-third the amount at which they would have been valued using historical or reproduction costs).

[34] 390 U.S. 747 (1968).

Barasch,[35] upheld a lower court's disallowance of non-"used and useful" nuclear assets and expressly reaffirmed *Hope*: "[T]oday we reaffirm these teachings of *Hope Natural Gas*."[36] Although the Court frequently does review the procedures used by regulatory bodies, it continues its reluctance to review the economic reasoning of regulatory decisions involving public utilities.

Two rationales, not as prominent in the land use context, explain the Court's deferential approach to utility rate-making cases. First, the rate-making process is self-correcting (see Chapter 2). Regulators may underestimate the cost of capital in one year, but in a later year, through modifications, they can correct any deficiency in utility earnings and revenues by adjusting cost of capital. Hence, there is little in terms of increased accuracy to be gained from judicial review.

Second, the political process provides adequate protections for utilities and their investors. Utility rate-making and other regulatory processes, which tend to be transparent and well-developed, provide a forum for regulators to balance the interests of investors, firms, consumers, and the state. According to Richard Pierce (1989),

> Detailed judicial review of ratemaking has little, if any, effect in constraining the political process. Moreover, the judicial review process imposes high error costs and high judicial resource costs. Thus, the "end result" test announced in *Hope* can be seen as a decision to allocate to the political institutions of government near total power to protect the constitutional values underlying the takings clause in the ratemaking context. This is required by the severe institutional limitations of the judiciary as a potential source of protection for these values.[37]

In utility regulation controversies, courts use the deferential approach of cases like *Hope, Market Street Railway*, *Permian Basin*, and *Duquesne* over the more activist review approach of the recent land use takings cases. Justice Black's articulation of the purpose of regulatory takings – "to bar Government from forcing some people alone to bear public burdens which, in all fairness and justice, should be borne by the public as a whole"[38] – is not a central concern in utility regulation. As Richard Goldsmith (1989) argues: "Rate regulators do not allocate burdens between the 'public' on the one hand and the 'few' on the other" but balance

35 488 U.S. 299 (1989).
36 Id. at 310.
37 Pierce, 1989: 2062.
38 *Armstrong v. United States*, 364 U.S. 40, 49 (1960).

"the cost of utility service between large classes of investors and consumers" (255) It would be particularly odd to invoke takings protections to the advantage of investors and the utility industry because here (unlike in the land use context) they have an overwhelming advantage in information, wealth, and political power and "boast a superior ability to bear risk and to mitigate damage from unforeseen contingencies – the precise economic attributes that justify the imposition of liability in virtually every other legal context" (Chen, 1999: 1558–59). In fact, given their institutional disadvantage in making politically accountable decisions, courts generally defer to regulators and avoid involving themselves actively in the policing of utility rate regulation (Pierce, 1989).

This is not to suggest that the Takings Clause is without *any* application to utility price regulation. In *Duquesne*, the Court expressly recognized that there is a constitutional limit in setting utility prices: If regulators threaten the financial integrity of a utility or provide inadequate compensation to current equity owners for the risks associated with their investments, they may effectuate a taking.[39] Although lower courts occasionally raise such concerns,[40] the Supreme Court has not applied these limits in the utility rate-setting context and its cases during the past 50 years do not suggest any eagerness to engage in a more activist review of utility price setting. In fact, despite *Duquesne*'s anticipation that takings claims may legitimately be asserted against regulators' price setting, some lower courts interpret the cases as allowing a significant public interest to justify the financial destruction of a regulated utility.[41]

[39] *Duquesne Light Co. v. Barasch*, 488 U.S. 299. As the Supreme Court stated: "No argument has been made that these slightly reduced rates jeopardize the financial integrity of the companies, either by leaving them insufficient operating capital or impeding their ability to raise future capital. Nor has it been demonstrated that these rates are inadequate to compensate current equity owners for the risk associated with their investments under a modified prudent investment scheme. . . . " Id. at 312–14.

[40] See, e.g., *Jersey Central Power & Light c. v. FERC*, 810 F.2d 1168, 1181–82 (D.C. Cir. 1987) (reversing and remanding the FERC's disallowance of unamortized nuclear investment from rate base for failure to provide an explanation); Id. at 1188 (Starr, concurrence) (arguing that a "reasoned consideration" of investor interests requires more than a mechanical application of rules but consideration of what expectations exist under a regulatory compact).

[41] See *Gulf State Utils. Co. v. Louisiana Pub. Serv. Comm'n*, 578 So.2d 71, 116 (La. 1991) (holding that a taking will be found only when the state "failed to consider the legitimate interests of the utility and its investors in a higher rate of return, and to weigh those interests against the competing concerns of ratepayers"); *Ohio Edison Co. v. Public Utils. Comm'n*, 589 N.E.2d 1292, 1300 (Ohio, 1992) (bolding asserting the "Constitution no longer provides any special protection for the utility investor.").

In the Supreme Court's most recent case to address the topic of infrastructure takings, the Court more directly struggled with a deregulatory takings claim. In reviewing the FCC's network access pricing rules under the Administrative Procedure Act, the Court seemed to clearly reject that the FCC's pricing mechanism, widely criticized by deregulatory takings advocates, presents an unconstitutional taking.[42] Even after this decision, however, deregulatory takings advocates continue to assert that *Duquesne* and other cases constrain how the government can set competition policy and, specifically, how it can price access to essential network facilities. Deregulatory takings proponents continue to advocate constitutional protections for the precompetition expectations of incumbent firms, arguing that these expectations must be reflected in the measure of costs used by regulators in adopting interconnection and network access pricing mechanisms (Spulber & Yoo, 2003).

V. INCOMPLETE CONTRACTS AND DEREGULATORY TAKINGS

To the extent regulation is analogized to a contract, many commentators have observed that this creates binding legal obligations on the part of governmental actors. These legal obligations may flow from a contract itself, rather than some constitutionally protected property right.[43] Once this obligation is deemed property, a legal claim for deregulatory taking becomes an obvious way to protect it, particularly given more recent judicial trends toward strong protection of private property.

Although intuitively attractive, this argument for deregulatory takings relies on simplistic understanding of contracts. It echoes a view of the regulatory contract that the Supreme Court rejected more than 150 years ago. The classic Charles River Bridge case, decided in 1836, provided American courts one of the first opportunities to elaborate on the legal implications of the regulatory contract. The case rejected a claim that the proprietors of the Charles River Bridge were entitled to compensation by the Commonwealth of Massachusetts. The Charles River Bridge

[42] *Verizon Communications, Inc. v. FCC*, 525 U.S. 467 (2002).

[43] The arguments are closely interrelated, in that constitutional takings jurisprudence recognizes that a contractual obligation can, in certain instances, give rise to a property right protected by the U.S. Constitution. See *Armstrong v. U.S.*, 364 U.S. 40 (1960) (observing that contractual liens against the government can give rise to constitutionally protected property interest); *Lynch v. U.S.*, 292 U.S. 571 (1974) (valid contracts are property within the meaning of the Takings Clause). See also *Ruckelshaus v. Monsanto*, 467 U.S. 986 (1984) (finding a constitutionally protected property interest in an intangible trade secret).

Proprietors were given a grant by the Commonwealth to operate a toll bridge, but the Commonwealth later approved a competitor, the Warren Bridge, which was obligated by law to become free once its proprietors had recouped their investment and a return. The Charles River Bridge lost three-fourths of its tolls when the Warren Bridge opened for traffic (Hovenkamp, 1991), and its proprietors sued to recover some of its losses. In the words of Chief Justice Taney, who wrote for the majority rejecting the proprietors' claim for compensation, "in grants by the public, nothing passes by implication."[44] Because the Charles River Bridge charter did not contain a specific and express provision granting a monopoly that protected against competing bridges – let alone any provision that would have promised compensation if operation of the bridge were to become unprofitable – a breach of contracts claim against the Commonwealth could not be sustained.

Justice Taney's majority opinion reflects a view of the regulatory contract that has had an impact, if only a subtle one, on regulatory law. In Justice Taney's view, a regulatory contract between a firm and the state is only enforceable to the extent its terms are expressly negotiated. This classical approach envisions courts enforcing regulatory contracts only where terms are clear – a judicial approach that reverberates in modern arguments that courts ought to limit contractual enforcement to plain meaning or ought to use "clear statement rules" in complex regulatory cases.[45] The main role of courts under the classical approach is to enforce clear statements in regulatory law, but beyond this Justice Story's regulatory contract does not envision much role for the judiciary in the regulatory process. In contrast, the express regulatory contract approach gives enormous discretion in bargaining to the state, leaving private firms and other stakeholders without any judicially enforceable remedy unless they have successfully negotiated for express terms (Hovenkamp, 1991).

In a famous dissent to the Charles River Bridge case, Justice Story invoked an alternative view. He used memories of the financial ruin of the Confederacy, and ensuing drafting of the United States Constitution, to lay down the premise for an alternative account of regulation. Justice Story wrote:

> I maintain, that, upon the principles of common reason and legal interpretation, the present grant carries with it a necessary implication, that the

[44] *The Proprietors of the Charles River Bridge v. The Proprietors of the Warren Bridge*, 36 U.S. 420, 465 (1837).

[45] For reference to this literature, see Eskridge and Frickey (1992).

> legislature shall do no act to destroy or essentially to impair the franchise; that (as one of the learned judges of the state court expressed it) there is an implied agreement that the state will not grant another bridge between Boston and Charleston, so near as to draw away the custom from the old one; and (as another judge expressed it) that there is an implied agreement of the state to grant the undisturbed use of the bridge and its tolls, so far as respects any acts of its own, or any persons acting under its authority....[46]

Consistent with this concept, in a concurrence, Justice McLean stated that there is no reason charters granted by the state "should not be construed by the same rule that governs contracts between individuals...."[47] Although perhaps born of Justice Story's dissent or Justice McLean's concurrence, the regulatory contract has had staying power in American courts for more than 150 years, as is illustrated by the contract on which deregulatory takings advocates rely.

Like the Charles River Bridge case, however, deregulatory takings does not present a clear contractual case for compensation because many terms of the regulatory deal are missing or unclear. For example, at the outset of a government regulator's interactions with a firm, it is rare for the regulators to explicitly promise to provide compensation for changes to regulation in the future. Historically, express indemnification on the part of the regulator is rare; in fact, many agency regulators may lack the authority to make such commitments without legislative authorization. An incomplete contracts account, in contrast, recognizes that regulation, analogized to a contract between the regulator and private firms, will often fail to address these types of concerns. Because regulation is subject to constant renegotiation, terms that are outside the express provisions of the contract may be renegotiated as a part of the regulatory process in the future. Courts are not necessarily the ideal institution for completing the terms of the contract because a future political or regulatory process may just as well have been an anticipated condition of the original bargain. For this reason, judicial deference to the political and regulatory process is important to an incomplete contracts account of regulation.

Implicit to the argument for deregulatory takings is the suggestion that courts should turn away from the deferential review of *Hope*, *Market Street Railway*, and *Duquesne* and move toward the more rigorous review seen in recent land use decisions – if not a complete return to the *Lochner*-era approach of *Smyth v. Ames* (Chen, 1999). For instance, Sidak and

[46] 36 U.S. at 646.
[47] Id. at 557 (J. McLean, concurring).

Spulber's approach gives central importance to the investment-backed expectations variable in the ad hoc *Penn Central* calculus. According to them, investment-backed expectations do "all the heavy lifting in a regulatory takings case" (Sidak & Spulber, 1997: 224). In addition, in support of their argument, Sidak and Spulber cite many of the Court's more recent land use takings cases, including *Lucas* and *Dolan*. In this sense, advocates of deregulatory takings are urging a major change in the approach of takings jurisprudence for infrastructure industry, one that would routinely require courts to award compensation for changes in regulation, rather than adopt the deferential approach they currently use.

An incomplete contract approach to this problem, however, would not routinely require compensation for changes to regulation, as advocates of deregulatory takings suggest to be necessary. Instead, if anything, an incomplete contracts analysis advises against compensation in most cases, as the deferential approach in the infrastructure takings case law would suggest. An incomplete contracts account does not suggest that the government is never liable for a taking. Governmental liability, however, is very narrow and will most likely be in contexts where the state has clearly indemnified private firms for the costs they will incur due to changes in regulation.

A. The Limits of Contractual Liability

Deregulatory takings advocates envision both breach of contracts and takings claims against the government for regulatory change. To the extent that a firm and the state have entered into an express agreement against regulatory change and in favor of indemnification for modification, the breach of contract claim for liability has considerable merit. The Contacts Clause of the United States Constitution reads: "No State shall ... pass any ... Law impairing the Obligations of Contracts. ..."[48] Although this clause of the Constitution is sometimes read to apply only to private contracts, a considerable body of case law and academic commentary applies the clause in some fashion to contracts between the state and private individuals and firms (Epstein, 1984; Sidak & Spulber, 1997).

For instance, Richard Epstein, the strongest advocate for this view in the legal literature, views both the Takings Clause and the Contracts Clause as protections against rent seeking and political intrigue.

[48] U.S. Const. art. I, § 10, cl. 1.

According to him, if government wants to take action, it must compensate the losers unless it can justifiably invoke the police power (Epstein, 1985). There are two problems with this libertarian view. First, even in Epstein's own terms, it ignores the possibility that the original contract may itself have been the result of a rent-seeking deal. Perhaps a person with powerful political connections or a willingness to bribe obtained the contract from compliant officials. "White elephant" infrastructure projects are archetypal examples of rent seeking by politicians and private investors. Epstein's "police power" exception may be designed to cover this case, but he does not develop the argument fully (Rose-Ackerman & Rossi, 2000). Second, Epstein takes an overly narrow view of legitimate government. He wants a broad range for compensation and complains that one important case is "far too muddy in leaving open the possibility that contracts could be impaired if the impairment were 'reasonable and necessary' to accomplish some important public purpose" (Epstein, 1984: 720, n. 45). His skepticism of government actions leads him to be *more* protective of private parties who contract with government compared with those involved in private contracts (Rose-Ackerman & Rossi, 2000).

Even if these arguments are not given constitutional status, advocates of deregulatory takings argue that simple breach of contract claims may be brought against the state. Judge Kenneth Starr wrote in a concurrence to a D.C. Circuit case:

> The utility business represents a compact of sorts; a monopoly on service in a particular geographical area (coupled with state-conferred rights of eminent domain or condemnation) is granted to the utility in exchange for a regime of intensive regulation, including price regulation, quite alien to the free market. Each party to the compact gets something in the bargain. As a general rule, utility investors are provided a level of stability in earnings and value less likely to be attained in the unregulated or moderately regulated sector; in turn ratepayers are afforded universal, nondiscriminatory service and protection from monopolistic profits through political control over an economic enterprise.[49]

Borrowing from this notion, Sidak and Spulber see failure to compensate utilities for stranded costs as analogous to a breach of contract against the industry. According to them, "Given that the utility incurred its costs under the regulatory contract, the opening of the utility's market to competition – that is, the termination of the utility's exclusive franchise – is

[49] *Jersey Central Power & Light v. FERC*, 810 F.2d 1168, 1189 (D.C. Cir. 1989) (J. Starr, J. concurring).

a breach of a material term of that contract if not accompanied by an offsetting removal of incumbent burdens" (Sidak & Spulber, 1997: 179).

Apart from Justice McLean's concurrence in *Charles River Bridge*, the strongest precedent supporting this position – that a contract could give rise to a nonconstitutional claim for recovery against the government – is the Supreme Court's 1996 *Winstar* case.[50] There the Supreme Court allowed savings and loans to pursue a breach of contract case against the federal government for failure to provide compensation pursuant to an earlier promised bailout plan. Each agreement between individual firms and the government specifically incorporated existing accounting regulations. When these regulations were changed, claims for liability for breach were filed against the federal government.

Rarely, however, do such explicit agreements between an individual firm and the state exist. In most instances involving regulated industries, such as electric and telecommunications utilities, agreements against changes and in favor of indemnification are implied, not expressed. These bargains are more accurately described as incomplete, relational contracts that the government would not be liable for breaching. In the Charles River Bridge case,[51] the charter did not contain a specific and express provision granting a monopoly to protect against competing bridges (Hovenkamp, 1991; Kutler, 1971). Nor did it contain a provision that would have promised compensation if the bridge were to become unprofitable. As the legal historian Herbert Hovenkamp observes, "The real effect of the Charles River Bridge case was to give entrepreneurs what they bargained for" (Hovenkamp, 1991: 112). The Charles River Bridge lost its case before the Supreme Court because, in the words of Chief Justice Taney, "in grants by the public, nothing passes by implication."[52]

Winstar does not change this (Chen, 2000), although in the case Justice Souter did propose an interesting (and arguably far-reaching) exception to the traditional unmistakability doctrine defense to breach of government contracts. Apart from Souter's plurality opinion, which was not endorsed by a majority, *Winstar* did not endorse a new substantive rule favoring compensation. Instead, read carefully the case merely reaffirmed, by a 5 to 4 vote, the traditional unmistakability doctrine – that promises by the government to forbear from certain types of regulatory action will be enforced by courts only if these are set forth in unmistakably

[50] *United States v. Winstar Corp.*, 518 U.S. 839 (1996).

[51] 36 U.S. 420 (1837).

[52] Id. at 546.

unambiguous language, which the plaintiff bears the burden of proving (Baumol & Merrill, 1996).[53] Since *Charles River Bridge*, however, courts have consistently held that there is a presumption that general language in statutes (and regulations) "is not intended to create private contractual or vested rights but merely declares a policy to be pursued until the legislature shall ordain otherwise."[54]

Ultimately, what an incomplete contracts approach favors in this context is a presumption against compensation for regulatory transitions that can be rebutted only with proof of a clear statement in the initial regulatory instrument that is specific to a firm, not industrywide. "Clear statement rules," valued in many other contexts for enhancing transparency and legislative or electoral accountability (Eskridge & Frickey, 1992), may be an important gap-filling measure in the context of firm-specific governmental liability. In the breach of contracts scenario, clear and unmistakable agreements – clear statements of a sort by the regulator – are necessary as a predicate to finding governmental liability for breach of contract. If the law-making process is viewed as contractual bargaining, the approach of giving private parties what they bargain for – and nothing more – has some important implications. If the bargain is required to be explicit in order to be enforced, this encourages more transparency, and hence accountability, in the law-making process. When an industry has bargained with the state for benefits, these would be required to be revealed to the public (and other branches of government) in language that everyone can see and understand before a bailout for industry transition materializes. In addition, a default clear statement rule in this context would encourage more responsible participation by private parties in the law-making process. Private parties will always seek to advance their interests by seeking rents or other benefits from the state, but parties who otherwise might make backroom deals with the state will be forced to do so openly. Clear statement rules have been harshly criticized for not really

[53] *Winstar* can hardly be said to represent a judicial consensus on the issue. Although Justices Steven, O'Connor, and Breyer joined the portion of Justice Souter's plurality opinion that recognizes a general exception to the unmistakability doctrine for government indemnification agreements (518 U.S. at 871–87), five justices rejected this exception (and thus reaffirm the unmistakability defense). Justices Kennedy and Thomas joined in a concurrence by Justice Scalia (Id. at 920–24), and Justice Ginsburg joined in Chief Justice Rehnquist's dissent (Id. at 924–31). For further discussion of *Winstar* and its implications for government contract defenses, see Gilliam (1997), Hadfield (1999), Malloy (1998), and Schwartz (1997).

[54] *National R.R. Passenger Corp. v. Atchison Topeka & Sante Fe Ry. Co.*, 470 U.S. 451, 466 (1985), quoting *Dodge v. Dept. of Educ.*, 302 U.S. 74, 79 (1937).

requiring clear statements but obfuscating judicial endorsement of substantive values (Eskridge & Frickey, 1992; Nagle, 1995); however, when liability for regulatory change is at issue, a default rule, or a strong presumption, against governmental liability has benefits for the lawmaking process with little risk of judicial overreaching.

B. Problems with Constitutional Takings as a Gap-Filling Measure

When no such agreement exists, the Takings Clause of the Constitution might be said to serve as a gap-filling measure, in which the state assumes liability for certain regulatory changes. The Takings Clause, however, is not a mere default rule, around which parties can readily bargain in the contracting process. It is a mandatory rule, supplied by the Constitution – perhaps even if, for example, parties have clearly specified a preference for no liability. Given the rigidity of resorting to constitutional remedies, and the cost to the public associated with paying "just compensation," such mandatory rules ought to be relegated a minor role in regulatory law – invoked only if necessary and as a last resort.

Although the analogy is not perfect, a default rule bargaining perspective illustrates the problem with resorting to constitutional takings doctrine as indemnification for regulatory transitions. Even if we are to treat the takings claim as a type of default rule, which parties may contract around, it still is not clear that a default rule favoring liability for regulatory change is the best approach. The incomplete contracts literature recognizes that incompleteness in relationships is inevitable due to transaction costs. Not all incompleteness, though, will necessarily arise for this reason. Another important insight in the incomplete contracts literature is that in many circumstances incompleteness exists for strategic reasons. For instance, if two contracting parties are bargaining for terms and one party has information regarding the performance of the contract (e.g., a manufacturer possessing information regarding a labor strike that could influence whether goods are actually produced and delivered), this may influence whether such terms are addressed in a contract. Asymmetric information may encourage strategic nondisclosure on the part of one, or perhaps even both, contracting parties.

Further, even when incompleteness does exist for neutral – transaction cost related – reasons at the time of performance, incompleteness may invite inefficient behavior on the part of one, or both, parties. If one party is in a better position to avoid a breach and minimize the concomitant loss, contractual incompleteness regarding this issue would not discourage such behavior. For instance, once a manufacturer has contracted for the sale of goods, it may face little incentive to bargain in good faith with its labor union, as opposed to inviting a strike and paying damages of seeking an alternative supplier for its contractual obligations. Similarly, one party may be in a better position than the other to insure for losses in the event of a breach.

Because of such strategic nondisclosure, an incomplete contracts analysis of the problem requires an inquiry into the reasons for incomplete regulatory bargains. Where one party in the regulatory process possesses superior information, an information-forcing default rule might be structured to require that party to divulge this information in the bargaining process (Posner, 2003). Similarly, where one party is in a better position to minimize a loss and stands to gain by the discretion that incompleteness provides at the time of performance, a loss-avoidance default rule might be appropriate. In contract law, the phenomenon of incompleteness gives rise to default rules designed to address defects in the bargaining process, to encourage more efficient bargains in the future, and to minimize the losses associated with strategic behavior on the part of one or both parties.

In the deregulatory takings context, this view has important implications for how we determine the appropriateness and level of compensation. The incomplete contracts account rejects that the Takings Clause is exclusively concerned with protecting property rights against majoritarian intrusions (Epstein, 1985). In addition, the incomplete contracts account rejects the view that takings jurisprudence is exclusively, or even primarily, concerned with deterring governmental predation by protecting investor-backed expectations (Michelman, 1968, 1988). In fact, there is some reason to believe that deterrence in this context is not very effective. A focus on deterrence assumes the democratic process provides strong accountability for budget management by governmental officials (holding the primary decision maker to account for all wrongdoing), but principal agent problems make this unrealistic, and often governmental officials are more influenced by political as opposed to monetary factors in making their decisions (Levinson, 2000). Instead, an incomplete contracts approach advises caution before invoking governmental liability, given its implications for future contracting behavior. Specifically, legal liability should, as much as possible, leave private investors indifferent between the government and other potential purchasers of their property. In fashioning legal remedies, an incomplete contracts approach would recommend that courts focus their attention on private investment decisions, particularly in contexts where private decisions are likely to be responsive (or elastic) to the likelihood and level of government compensation. Compensation can have some seriously adverse implications for future private conduct in the regulatory process. Even when there is not a legal entitlement to compensation, the incomplete contracts account also has important implications for how we set fees for network access in a deregulatory environment.

Since the New Deal, takings jurisprudence has not found that regulatory actions in infrastructure industries demand compensation. Procedural guarantees and political accountability are sufficient, although those pressing for deregulatory takings also argue that this approach is in need of reform. Supporters of a legal entitlement to compensation would take deregulatory takings cases outside the traditional deferential approach of *Hope*, *Market Street Railway*, *Permian Basin*, and *Duquesne*, treating them in a manner similar to the Supreme Court's land use takings cases. However, the land use cases are weak precedents for compensation in economic regulation transitions for two reasons. First, it is not clear whether the regulatory contract gives rise to a constitutionally protected property right. As Justice Holmes once remarked in dissent, "When an uncopyrighted combination of words is published there is no general right to forbid other people repeating them – in other words there is no property in the combination or in the thoughts or facts that the words express. Property, a creation of law, does not arise from value, although exchangeable – a matter of fact. Many exchangeable values may be destroyed intentionally without compensation."[55] In other words, property does not exist in the abstract, independent of government actions. Courts need to carefully assess whether contractual bargaining gives rise to something akin to property, but property does not precede the existence of regulatory law. Second, unlike individual property owners, utility investors appear to be adequately protected in the political and regulatory process – the process under which contracting with the state ordinarily occurs. Deregulation has not challenged this rationale, as with deregulation a significant ongoing relationship between firms and the government continues. The Takings Clause should not be used to protect those who already have a chance to influence policy or who are in a position to anticipate future changes in policy and take them into account at the time of contracting in their investment prices and actions.

Firms seldom have explicit contracts guaranteeing regulated firms a certain rate of return on their assets or promising to indemnify them against future changes in policy (Hovenkamp, 1999b; Rossi, 1998b).

[55] *International News Service v. Associated Press*, 248 U.S. 215, 246 (1918) (J. Holmes, dissenting).

Normally, the firm will have internalized these risks in making their investment choices. The deferential approach of the Supreme Court's opinions in rate-making cases generally requires utility owners to accept the risks of unsuccessful investments in contracting with the state. In contrast, when investors are well diversified and knowledgeable of risks, compensation may reduce incentives for self-insurance. For example, in *Shanghai Power v. United States*, an American Corporation sought compensation against the United States government for its lost claim against China due to China's compensation of the company's power plant in Shanghai.[56] In making diplomatic policy that reestablished relationships with China after the actual confiscation occurred, President Carter extinguished all outstanding claims against China and Shaghai Power received about $20 million – far less than the $144 million the company claimed in the plant. The court of claims found that no taking existed: notwithstanding a disproportionate loss to the company in the short tem, Judge Kozinski cited long-term incentives for the company to diversify in its investments and benefit elsewhere as reasons against compensation. Similarly, a default rule against compensation for regulatory changes creates incentives for firms to diversify and self-insure against regulatory change.

Some commentators argue that utilities were not induced to invest by eager regulators but instead pushed the regulators to permit high levels of investment (Hovenkamp, 1999b; Rossi, 1998b). If firms anticipate that their costs will be reimbursed regardles of the competitive environment, they have an incentive to overinvest. Assured compensation affects the incentives for strategic behavior inherent in the relationship between the regulated firm and the regulatory agency officials (Williamson, 1996b). One adverse result may be to exaggerate the Averch-Johnson effect under which firms select inefficiently high capital–labor ratios (Averch & Johnson, 1962; Michaels, 1996; Williamson, 1996b; see also Chapter 3).

To date, not a single court has accepted the deregulatory taking argument advocated by the industry. When the breach of contract claim has been raised, courts have uniformly required clear and explicit contracts as a basis for protection of the utility's interest in stranded cost recovery.[57]

[56] 4 Cl. Ct. 237 (1983).

[57] In *Energy Ass'n of New York v. Public Serv. Comm'n of New York*, the court rejected a utility's argument that the "failure to guarantee full recovery of stranded costs constitutes breach of contract" [653 N.Y.S.2d 502, 513–14 (1996)]. Instead, the court held "just and reasonable rates do not necessarily... immunize utilities from the effects of competition" (Id.). Thus, only those utilities expressly contracting for monopolies will probably be

Outside cases involving physical invasion for access to network wires,[58] the takings claims have also been rejected by the courts.[59] Although

able to have such monopolies recognized and enforced. See also Hovenkamp, 1999b: 811 [citing *In re Binghamton Bridge*, 70 U.S. (3 Wall.) 51, 82 (1865)] ("enforcing an explicit monopoly provision in a corporate charter"). In another case, the Public Service Company of New Hampshire (PSCH) had been promised by the State of New Hampshire recovery of a specific investment of $2.3 billion in a bankruptcy proceeding. PSCH successfully obtained an injunction against a New Hampshire restructuring plan that did not guarantee recovery of the costs of this investment. In reviewing the district court injunction, the U.S. Court of Appeals for the First Circuit determined that there was a likelihood of success on the merits, given the specific agreements between the utility and state and federal regulators. The court also noted that the possibility of irreparable harm from bankruptcy made issuance of a preliminary injunction appropriate. See *Public Service Co. of New Hampshire v. Patch*, 167 F.3d 15 (1st Cir. 1998). However, the First Circuit held that the district court was incorrect in its decision to issue an injunction against implementation of New Hampshire's plan for all New Hampshire utilities:

> The district court's extension of the injunction to protect all other New Hampshire electric utilities is more troublesome. Although the other utilities have joined in attacks on the Final Plan similar to those made by PSNH, it is not clear that they can assert the Contracts Clause or bankruptcy reorganization arguments that made PSNH's case so appealing to the district court. Nor is it evident that utilities are constitutionally insulated against losses that result merely from a change in rate regulation that introduces competition.

Id. at 28. See also *Public Service Co. of New Hampshire v. Patch*, 167 F.3d 29 (1st Cir. 1998) (rejecting federal preemption claim based on the "filed rate doctrine," arguing that tariffs filed with the FERC preclude New Hampshire from denying stranded cost recovery, and rejecting injunction claim by utilities that lack clear contract guaranteeing recovery from previous bankruptcy reorganization).

58 Notions of physical invasion hold a grip on the definition of what constitutes a taking in the American legal mind. In *Loretto v. Teleprompter Corp.*, 458 U.S. 419 (1982), the Supreme Court found that the use of a few square inches of property on the outside of a building for a cable television cable connection constituted a taking. The smallest physical invasion, according to *Loretto*, can constitute a taking. Thus, mandated open access of network facilities, such as power transmission lines, without compensation may be held to be a taking. In the context of a physical occupation, courts have not had the same reluctance they seem to have in finding a taking for failure to compensate stranded costs. See *Gulf Power Co. v. United States*, 998 F. Supp. 1386, 1394–95 (N.D. Fla. 1998) (relying on Sidak and Spulber to support the proposition that a permanent physical occupation of property constitutes a per se taking); *GTE Southwest, Inc. v. Public Utility Commission of Texas*, No. 03-97-00148-CV (Ct. of App., Austin, July 15, 1999) (finding a taking based on *Loretto* where the Commission ordered GTE to revise its tariff to ensure reasonable, nondiscriminatory bases for decisions affecting access to customers by alternate service providers, including "the relocation of multiple demarcation points to a single point of demarcation on multi-unit premises").

59 See, e.g., *In the Matter of Energy Association of New York State v. Public Service Commission*, 653 N.Y.S.2d 502, 515 (Sup. Crt., Albany Cty. 1996) (rejecting deregulatory takings argument against stranded cost recovery, stating "The rule of *Smyth v. Ames* . . . does not prevail today.").

the courts routinely reject deregulatory takings claims, the threat of deregulatory takings lawsuits have resulted in many settlements – for example, in Pennsylvania, a settlement resulted in transition surcharges that cost consumers billions (Isser & Mitnick, 1998) – and have influenced the adoption of consumer surcharges and access charges by regulators and legislators at the federal and state levels (Chen, 1999). The very success of public utilities in having their interests heard at both the federal and state levels is an argument against applying the Constitution's Taking Clause to require compensation. Although the firms will not always win all the compensation they want, utilities are clearly an important force in state politics well able to raise their concerns within the institutions and procedures that exist. Consistent with its deferential approach in infrastructure cases, the United States Supreme Court recently refused a deregulatory takings challenge to an FCC rule setting a general formula for the determination of access rates. The Court left open the possibility of future challenges to particular access rates as "so unjust as to be confiscatory" to the extent it threatens an incumbent's "financial integrity" but refused to reread its infrastructure takings cases as providing for the same rigorous review of takings the Court has recently afforded in the land use context.[60]

Although an incomplete contracts account of regulation advises a deferential approach to takings and breach of contracts jurisprudence claims, it also has implications for how regulators might approach network access more generally. Daniel Spulber and Christopher Yoo argue that the Supreme Court's takings jurisprudence mandate that regulators set access prices based on market-based, rather than cost-based, factors (Spulber & Yoo, 2003). To the extent that a taking is found – as may be most likely under the Supreme Court's physical occupation cases where mandated access requires interconnection or access to telecommunications or electric transmission or distribution wires[61] – regulators must determine how to set access prices in order to avoid a "just compensation" challenge. Cost-based pricing (based solely on historical determinations of cost) may not, as a matter of policy, always provide an adequate incentive for companies who own network facilities to expand capacity to meet demand. In

[60] *Verizon Communications, Inc. v. FCC*, 535 U.S. 467, 523–24 (2002) (citing Duquesne Light Company, 487 U.S. at 307, 312).

[61] Even this, however, is not necessarily an unconstitutional taking for which just compensation is constitutionally necessary. As other have noted, common carrier interconnection does not always constitute a physical invasion of private property under takings jurisprudence, especially given the rich tradition of regulatory intervention in this context (Candeub, 2004; Chen, 2004).

contrast, a general presumption of market-based prices could provide important signals and holds promise to create incentives for investment in network facilities. In many instances, such as in the case of electric power transmission, the correct economic signals for facility expansion are crucial to avoiding bottlenecks and allowing deregulated markets to succeed.

Although economic incentives are important for network industries, it would not be efficient to include in compensable costs all private opportunity costs. Deregulatory takings advocates argue that new entrants should pay a price for interconnection and network use based on the monopoly profits of the incumbent, including its private opportunity costs. However, this confuses private and public opportunity costs. As Nicholas Economides explains,

> Suppose that two companies, X and Y, are competing for the business of customer C, which is worth $C to each of them. Assume that X and Y are equally cost efficient in serving C. If customer C used to buy from X and now buys from Y, firm X's private opportunity cost is $C. However, the social opportunity cost of the switch of customer C from X to Y is exactly zero, since society does not gain or lose from customer C's change of carrier. Essentially, since firm X's loss was firm Y's gain, private opportunity costs and gains cancelled each other, and the social cost of customer C's change of carrier is zero.[62]

Jim Chen (2000) also observes that such a pricing mechanism has serious intergenerational costs. Although a market-based pricing rule of thumb is unassailable in a competitive industry (Candeub, 2004), it should not be invoked as a backdoor way to tax the public in order to compensate an incumbent's private opportunity costs. The incomplete contracts account of regulation certainly does not make the finding of an unconstitutional taking automatic, but if a breach of contract giving rise to liability is found, a limited presumption of market-based pricing (not including private opportunity costs based on the old regulatory regime) should apply. The best measure of market prices should reflect the current competitive industry – not idiosyncratic expectations associated with the old regulatory structure.

* * *

All in all, despite the strong entitlement-oriented rhetoric of deregulatory takings, contractual concepts have had little purchase as a basis for

[62] Economides, 2003: 142–43.

governmental liability in the context of deregulation and other transitions. This does not make bargaining a worthless area of analysis for regulatory law. It only limits its practical application to judicial review as a mechanism that leads to compensation for adverse governmental decisions. If we can move beyond the legalistic enforcement model on which deregulatory taking advocates rely, bargaining approaches to understanding regulation have far more extensive implications for regulatory law. A bargaining-centered approach to regulation makes explicit the focus on bargaining as an activity, a worthwhile area of inquiry for regulatory law, without necessarily committing courts to the role of enforcing contracts. Instead of focusing on contract as a liability mechanism, a bargaining analysis can frame how regulatory law approaches issues of institutional governance, such as the standard of review courts should apply in reviewing changes to the regulatory order and the implications of the standard for incentives and behavior.

6

Incomplete Regulatory Tariffs and Judicial Enforcement

Analyzing deregulatory takings through a bargaining lens does not commit courts to an activist role in deregulated markets. Instead, an incomplete bargaining assessment of deregulatory takings suggests that in most instances courts will best promote accountability and transparency, as well as predictability, by deferring to the decisions of regulatory agencies. If anything, clear statement rules are the appropriate default mechanism for courts to invoke in evaluating the availability of compensation against governmental bodies that skirt their regulatory commitments. Absent an express, bargained-for statement of commitment to compensation on behalf of a political institution, courts will not interfere with regulatory transitions. Instead, deference to an otherwise legitimate political process is appropriate. As in other agency regulatory contexts, where judicial deference is the norm, to the extent the political process and expertise of agency regulators is more capable than courts of tackling complex regulatory issues of economic regulation, judicial deference is the most desirable initial stance for courts to take in evaluating the decisions of political institutions in the deregulatory era.

However, courts are also not limited to clear statements and deference in evaluating all issues of public law in a deregulatory environment. Rather, approaching regulation through a bargaining lens provides the foundation for a much more nuanced account of the role of courts in market transitions. Although deregulatory takings address incompleteness in the degree of regulatory commitment, the regulatory process also presents other types of incompleteness, creating need for the judicial response to adapt to the institutional problem at hand. The optimal institutional response to incompleteness and bargaining vary, depending primarily on the incentives on private parties in future regulatory bargaining. Not all bargaining occurs under the same conditions, nor does it create similar incentives for private behavior in the future regulatory processes.

For instance, perhaps more than any other activity in economic regulation, regulatory agencies accept, frequently review, and sometimes approve filings by private firms whose activities may be subject to the agency's jurisdiction. Often, these filings are incomplete. Incompleteness may be due to obvious limits on the scope of a private filing (e.g., if a firm filing a tariff fails to address an issue related to the filing). However, private tariff filings will often raise a general issue but leave some ambiguity. For example, to the extent a privately filed tariff depends on a firm's voluntary disclosure, although a tariff will frequently envision a general type of conduct on the part of the firm (e.g., the provision of transmission access and pricing in a certain manner), an agency may lack the enforcement mechanism necessary to make the tariff mandatory or to deter violations. For example, the FERC may lack the statutory authorization to mandate the expansion of transmission, and simply requiring compliance with an access tariff ex post – after competitors have been denied a market opportunity in a time of constrained capacity – may not be sufficient to ensure competitive markets. Put simply, a tariff does not necessarily tell the regulator as much as it needs to know, nor does a tariff necessarily authorize sufficient regulatory authority, in order for the regulator to do its job. Privately filed tariffs alone also may not sufficiently disclose to other firms the information necessary for competition to thrive.

Notwithstanding this widely recognized defect in the filing of regulatory tariffs by private firms, under the long-standing "filed tariff doctrine," courts frequently afford tariff filings a legal effect, presumptively allowing tariffs to determine the institutional mechanism for regulatory enforcement. The filed tariff doctrine precludes a court from adjudicating a claim, such as an antitrust suit, tort, or contract case, if it would result in a judicially imposed damage award that conflicts with an agency filed rate (Rossi, 2003). Although this doctrine presents a simple rule for courts that is consistent with many general goals, including deference to agency regulators, it also presents private firms the opportunity to strategically file and provide information in tariffs – particularly in contexts where tariffs are never reviewed or approved by the government regulator. In this sense, tariff filing decisions by private firms can influence the institutional forum for regulatory enforcement. In other environments, such as liability for medical malpractice or torts, disclosure of risks has proven to be an effective private strategy for forestalling future litigation, although there is also a well-acknowledged need for safeguards to minimize strategic manipulation of disclosure [see Berg (2003) regarding informed consent in medical malpractice, and see Simons (2002) regarding assumption of the risk in tort]. In the regulatory environment, private disclosure in tariff filings could have the same effects, but the literature on economic regulation has completely ignored the need for safeguards. A bargaining perspective sheds light on the problem presented by the filed tariff doctrine in a deregulatory environment, recommending a more nuanced role for courts in considering antitrust, tort, and contract claims against firms that have also made private tariff filings with regulators.

I. THE FILED RATE DOCTRINE AND TARIFFING IN THE COST-OF-SERVICE ENVIRONMENT

Throughout the twentieth century, courts invoked the filed tariff doctrine as an independent legal basis for refusing to modify, or allow modifications to, rates approved by agency regulators. Courts have extended the doctrine to apply not only to rates, but also to terms and conditions approved by regulators, such as service quality terms included in tariffs. The doctrine's original goals focused on consumer protection – in particular, protection against unjust discrimination in service pricing (the "unjust discrimination" strand). At the same time, institutional concerns of federalism (the "federal preemption" strand) and deference to regulators (the "deference" strand) help to justify it. With time, this doctrine that began as a consumer protection sword evolved into a shield – a type of ultraimmunity for regulated firms from lawsuits designed to protect consumers and competition.

A. Basics of the Filed Tariff Doctrine

The filed tariff doctrine affords the contractual rights of a firm-specific tariff the full legal force of other agency regulations. In 1951, for example, the Supreme Court held all tariffs filed with and accepted by the Federal Power Commission, the FERC's predecessor, to be binding on the federal courts. The Court reasoned that a party to the contracts "can claim no rate as a legal right that is other than the filed rate, whether fixed or merely accepted by the Commission, and not even the court can authorize commerce in the commodity on other terms."[1] Thomas Merrill and Henry Smith describe the doctrine as follows:

> Under this doctrine, utilities and common carriers must establish their rates and services in standard form contracts called tariffs, which must be made available on equal and nondiscriminatory terms to all customers. Deviations from the filed tariff are not permitted, but the relevant regulatory agency is authorized to review and adjust the terms to ensure that they are "just and reasonable" to affected customers. In effect, the singular provider of services establishes an in personam right which is made available to a numerous class of customers, and the customers (who remain rationally ignorant of the details of the tariff) are then protected from exploitation by the provider through agency oversight.[2]

The traditional rate regulation process, which set rates based on an evaluation of the cost of providing service, provided a sufficient opportunity to protect the public interest in approved tariffs.

Historically, the nondiscrimination principle is the primary reason cited by courts for requiring adherence to a filed, published rate. As early as 1907, the Supreme Court held that a shipper seeking damages under the Interstate Commerce Act (ICA) based on the alleged unreasonableness of a carrier's rates must do so through the Interstate Commerce Commission (ICC), not the courts, because the agency alone "is vested with the power originally to entertain proceedings for the alteration of an established schedule."[3] Although adherence to the filed rate might, in some cases, create hardship, the Supreme Court has stated that this doctrine "embodies the policy which had been adopted by Congress in the regulation of interstate commerce in order to prohibit unjust discrimination."[4] Thus, in original design, the doctrine was intended to protect against the inefficiencies of monopolistic price discrimination – such as a railroad charging different rates to customers of different states, charging the shipping companies with whom it competes exorbitant prices, or providing kickbacks or gratuities to secure customers – without any justification based on the cost of providing service to the customer.

Unlike other exclusionary practices, price discrimination does not necessarily change the monopolist's output level (although if imperfect it may); however, the practice is generally condemned to the extent it maximizes the monopolist's profits (representing a transfer from consumers

[1] *Mont.-Dakota Utils. Co. v. Northwestern & Pub. Serv. Co.*, 341 U.S. 246, 251–52 (1951).
[2] Merrill & Smith, 2002: 808, n. 112.
[3] *Texas & Pac. Ry. v. Abilene Cotton Oil Co.*, 204 U.S. 426, 448 (1907).
[4] *Louisville & Nashville R. R. v. Maxwell*, 237 U.S. 94, 97 (1915).

to the monopolist), while also encouraging the monopolist to waste resources in maintaining its dominant position. For a price-regulated industry, such as an electric or telecommunications utility, price discrimination can create a more specific problem. Unregulated price discrimination can lead to overcapacity and inefficient use of resources. Absent a prohibition on price discrimination, a utility may preferentially charge some customers, perhaps those who have substitutes for the utility's service (e.g., the large municipal or industrial customer), less than the average cost of providing service to them. To the extent that the utility does so, rate regulation would allow the utility to still recover the cost of providing service to the preferentially treated customers by increasing the rates it charges other customers. For instance, assume an electric utility has three municipal customers. The total cost to the utility of building a plant to serve the three customers is $660,000 annually, with each customer having an equal average cost of service of $220,000. Suppose one of the municipal customers, *X*, also owns hydroelectric plant, which it can operate to displace its demand for the utility's power at a cost of $200,000 annually, saving $20,000 per year over the cost of purchasing power from the utility. The utility can cover its total costs and also maximize its customer base by discriminating in its rates – charging *X*, say, $190,000 annually and charging each of the other customers $235,000 per year.

However, this is not efficient. The lower-cost plant will not be built, but instead the utility will overinvest in its own capital facilities, using price discrimination as a strategy to foreclose competitors from using more efficient alternatives, such as the hydroelectric plant. Because price discrimination provides the utility little incentive to avoid overinvestment in capital, it potentially leads to a higher than optimal capital-to-labor ratio in the industry (Averch & Johnson, 1962; see also discussion in Chapter 3). In contrast, the prohibition on price discrimination would encourage the utility to more carefully expand capital to serve individual customers based on the cost of providing service to them individually, increasing efficiency in the use of capital resources.[5]

At the same time, because perfect price discrimination would allow the monopolist to expand output to include customers who otherwise would be priced out of the market, as a matter of economic theory this principle against nondiscrimination in rates is hardly uncontroversial. Ramsey

[5] A related, and more general, criticism of price discrimination in antitrust regulation is that it encourages the monopolist to leverage its primary market into a second market (Kaplow, 1985; Sullivan, 1992).

pricing, or raising prices in inverse proportion to customer demand elasticity, provides a theory of value-based pricing that can minimize the deadweight loss associated with price discrimination (Brown & Sibley, 1986). Ramsey pricing thus provides a regulatory mechanism for mitigating the inefficiencies of the Averch-Johnson effect under cost-of-service regulation. In addition, Chicago school theory sees price discrimination as bringing a monopolistic market closer to a competitive one and thus reducing the "misallocative effects of monopoly" (Hovenkamp, 1999a; Posner, 1979).

The price discrimination rationale behind the filed tariff doctrine is hardly unassailable. Nevertheless, twentieth-century courts extended the impact of the filed tariff doctrine far beyond rates to essentially include all terms and conditions in approved tariffs.[6] Because tariffs often regulate not only the price of service, but also its terms and conditions, the filed tariff doctrine's scope would eventually expand to allow the entire regulatory process to produce decisions that have the force and effect of a contract that is even considered binding on courts.

B. The Institutional Context

The unjust price discrimination strand of the filed tariff doctrine is steeped in progressive consumer protection rhetoric. However, given the institutional context of economic regulation in the United States, the filed tariff doctrine has two other strands. In applying the doctrine, courts allow the dual federalist enforcement structure of economic regulation to avoid potential conflicts between national government and state regulators (the federal preemption strand) and promote judicial deference to agency regulators (the deference strand).

1. The Federal Preemption Strand

Given that filed tariff shield evolved as a doctrine in the federal courts, it is not surprising that the federal judiciary has used it to bar state regulatory or common law claims from consideration in federal court. Much as federal regulation may preempt state common law claims (McGreal, 1995) or admiralty law can preempt state common law tort claims (Young, 1999), the filed tariff doctrine has the general effect of precluding any state law claims that might allow departures from the filed rate. Because successful

[6] See *N. Natural Gas Co. v. State Corp. Comm'n*, 372 U.S. 84, 90–91 (1963) ("[O]ur inquiry is not at an end because the orders do not deal in terms of prices or volumes of purchases").

state suits would allow service rates and conditions to vary across jurisdictions, the preclusive effect of the filed tariff doctrine promotes national uniformity in tariff rates, terms, and conditions.

This principle, along with the general prohibition of discrimination in rates, has been broadened to give tariffs a preemptive effect over state law claims even when they do not, in their express terms, limit liability. In 1906, the Supreme Court applied this principle to common carriers, precluding a shipper from seeking damages outside an ICC proceeding.[7] Even when customers had negotiated rates below the tariff price, the filed tariff doctrine was held to bar discounts. In one case, a passenger had negotiated a ticket with a railroad for a rate of $49.50, although the published rate for the route was $78.65.[8] After discovering this error, the railroad sued the passenger for the difference and the Supreme Court upheld an award against the passenger, declining to allow any deviation from the filed rate – even if agreed to under state contract law principles.

More recently, in *AT&T v. Central Office Tel. Co.*, the Supreme Court held that the tariff filing provisions of the Federal Communications Act (FCA), modeled after the nondiscrimination provisions of the ICA, require judicial enforcement of filed rates.[9] AT&T had entered into a contract to sell long-distance service to a reseller, giving the reseller sufficient assurances to procure customers, but AT&T later experienced problems with its network, including delays and mistakes in billing. When the reseller was unable to meet its usage commitments to AT&T, AT&T terminated its service 18 months prior to the end of the contract. The reseller sued AT&T under state law for breach of contract and tortuous interference with contract. AT&T had mistakenly billed the resellers' customers, causing substantial damage to the reseller, but AT&T filed tariffs with the FCC specifically addressing some of the same subjects of the discounts. Writing for the majority, Justice Scalia reasoned, "Regardless of the carrier's motive – whether it seeks to benefit or harm a particular customer – the policy of nondiscriminatory rates is violated when similarly situated customers pay different rates for the same services. It is that antidiscriminatory policy which lies at 'the heart of the common-carrier section of the Communications Act.'"[10] Because Section 203(a) of the FCA required each common carrier to file tariffs with the FCC, the Court was compelled

[7] See *Texas & Pac. Ry., v. Abilene Cotton Oil Co.*, 204 U.S. 426, 448 (1907).

[8] See *Louisville & Nashville Railroad Co. v. Maxwell*, 237 U.S. 94, 96 (1915).

[9] *AT&T v. Cent. Office Tel. Co.*, 524 U.S. 214, 227–28 (1998).

[10] See id. at 223 [quoting *MCI Telecommunications Corp. v. American Telephone & Telegraph Co.*, 512 U.S. 218, 229 (1994)].

to enforce the tariff and "[t]he rights as defined by the tariff cannot be varied or enlarged by either contract or tort of the carrier."[11]

Following the Court's application of the filed tariff shield in *AT&T*, wholesale customers of long-distance service face a serious loss of remedy, providing little deterrence of wrongdoing by long-distance carriers in competitive markets. For example, assume a carrier enters into a contract promising a reseller a rate of 5 cents per minute for nationwide domestic switched terminations.[12] In return for this rate, the reseller commits to purchase 1 million minutes per month over a period of 3 years. The reseller then enters into agreements with third parties to resell service for 6 cents per minute. However, due to the negligence or fraudulent intent of the carrier, the underlying carrier's filed tariffs contain a 10-cent rate, rather than the 5-cent promised rate. By law, the carrier is required to charge the reseller the 10-cent rate, even though this would require the reseller to sell to third parties below cost. If the reseller remains liable to the carrier over the full 3-year contract, its losses could be substantial.

The doctrine not only limits state common law claims, but it also narrows the jurisdiction of state agency regulators. For instance, in *Nantahala Power & Light Company v. Thornburg*, a case addressing the scope of the FERC's authority to regulate wholesale rates, the Supreme Court noted:

> [The] FERC clearly has exclusive jurisdiction over the rates to be charged Nantahala's interstate wholesale customers. Once the FERC sets such a rate, a state may not conclude in setting retail rates that the FERC approved wholesale rates are unreasonable. The state must rather give effect to Congress' desire to give the FERC plenary authority over interstate wholesale rates, and to ensure that the state does not interfere with this authority.[13]

The doctrine, for example, precludes a state from "trapping" costs by exercising its "undoubted jurisdiction over retail rates to prevent the wholesaler-as-seller from recovering the costs of paying the FERC-approved rate."[14] A caveat, known as the Pike County exception, allows a state to deny a utility the opportunity to recover costs incurred as a result of buying power at the FERC-established wholesale rates if the specific

[11] Id. at 227 [quoting *Keogh v. Chicago & Northwestern R.R.*, 260 U.S. 156, 163 (1922)].

[12] See Neil S. Ende, *Unholy Contract: The Legacy and Abuse of the Filed Rate Doctrine*, Phone+ (May 1999), available at http://www.phoneplusmag.com/articles/951feat3.html (last visited Sept. 14, 2003).

[13] 476 U.S. 953, 970 (1986).

[14] Id. at 970.

purchase, apart from the rate that was paid, is deemed imprudent.[15] Although the U.S. Supreme Court has never squarely held that imprudence is an escape hatch from the filed tariff doctrine, many circuit and district courts,[16] as well as the FERC,[17] recognize the exception.

2. *The Agency Deference Strand*

Even where federal law, such as the various doctrines of antitrust law, might provide a workable legal standard for evaluating the conduct of regulated firms, courts may invoke the filed tariff doctrine to bar jurisdiction over a claim. As such, the filed rate doctrine serves a function similar to *Chevron* deference:[18] Out of deference to agency regulators and their expertise, courts sometimes refuse to entertain the legal merits of a dispute related to an agency tariff.

Although the Supreme Court has stated that there is no general across-the-board antitrust immunity for transactions approved by regulators,[19] direct antitrust attacks to regulated rates and other terms and conditions have long been limited by the filed rate doctrine.[20] The classic case on the

[15] *Pike County Light & Power Co. v. Pa. Pub. Util. Comm'n*, 465 A.2d 735, 737–38 (Pa. Commw. Ct. 1983).

[16] See *Public Service Co. of New Hampshire v. Patch*, 167 F.3d 29, 35 (1st Cir. 1998) [citing *Mississippi Power & Light v. FERC*, 487 U.S. 354, 373–74 (1988) and *Nantahala*, 476 U.S. at 972]; *Ky. W. Va. Gas Co. v. Pa. Pub. Util. Comm'n*, 837 F.2d 600, 609 (3d Cir.1988) ("Regarding the states' traditional power to consider the prudence of a retailer's purchasing decision in setting retail rates, we find no reason why utilities must be permitted to recover costs that are imprudently incurred."); however, see *Pacific Gas & Elec. Co. v. Lynch*, 216 F.Supp.2d 1016, 1049–50 (N.D. Cal. 2002) (declining to apply the exception because a decision on the permissibility of a prudence review was not "meaningful" at the time of the decision).

[17] See *Palisades Generating Co.*, 48 FERC ¶ 61,144, at 61,574 n. 10 (1989) [citing *Pennsylvania Power & Light Co.*, 23 FERC 61,325, at 61,716 (1983) and *Monongahela Power Co.*, 39 FERC 61,350, at 62,095–96 (1987)](noting that FERC's action in accepting a tariff filing does not preempt or otherwise effect state jurisdiction to review for prudence).

[18] *Chevron U.S.A., Inc. v. Natural Res. Def. Council, Inc.*, 467 U.S. 837, 844 (1985) (finding that "considerable weight should be accorded to an executive department's construction of a statutory scheme it is entrusted to administer").

[19] See *California. v. Federal Power Comm'n*, 369 U.S. 482, 490 (1962) (holding that the Federal Power Commission could not approve a merger application when an antitrust suit was pending in court regarding the same merger).

[20] See *Square D Co. v. Niagara Frontier Tariff Bureau, Inc.*, 476 U.S. 409, 423–24 (1986) (upholding the *Keogh* rule that a private shipper cannot recover treble damages under the Sherman Act in connection with filed tariffs); *Mississippi Power & Light Co. v. Mississippi*, 487 U.S. 354, 375 (1988) (finding "the reasonableness of rates and agreements regulated by FERC may not be collaterally attacked in state or federal court"); *Nantahala Power & Light Co. v. Thornburg*, 476 U.S. 953, 966 (1986) (holding that "a State may not conclude in setting retail rates that FERC-approved wholesale rates are unreasonable").

issue, *Keogh v. Chicago & Northwestern Railway Co.*, held that a private plaintiff cannot recover treble damages against a carrier based on the claim that a tariff rate filed with the ICC was allegedly monopolistic.[21] Writing for the Court, Justice Brandeis emphasized the nondiscrimination principle, but also grounded his decision in respect for an ongoing agency regulatory process. As he observed, the need for an antitrust remedy is questionable, given that Section 8 of the ICA gave shippers injured by illegal rates actual damages plus attorneys' fees. In addition, because an award of antitrust damages would depend on proof that the rate in fact paid exceeds the rate that would have prevailed in a competitive market (hypothetically, of course), this hypothetical rate would also have been approved by the ICC; thus, Justice Brandeis reasoned, what the agency would have approved is a question better determined by the agency than the courts.[22]

Deference has its limits in this context because agency regulators frequently have limited jurisdiction. Recognizing these limits, courts do not defer to regulators on all tariff matters. For example, in antitrust price squeeze cases, courts are careful to examine the scope of the regulator's jurisdiction. In the typical price squeeze case, a monopolist defendant supplies a plaintiff at wholesale (for resale), yet competes with the plaintiff at the retail level. The typical claim is that the defendant engaged in illegal conduct by setting out to destroy the plaintiff by inflating the wholesale price to the plaintiff while artificially depressing the retail price to shared customers. Some courts have rejected a filed rate defense in the context where a monopolist supplier is subject to federal regulation at the wholesale level but not at the retail level,[23] because federal regulators would not necessarily be responsible for evaluating retail rates. As one commentator explains,

> The most effective way of eliminating all harmful price squeezes would be to place jurisdiction over both retail and wholesale service in a single agency.

[21] *Keogh v. Chicago & Northwestern Railway Co.*, 260 U.S. 156, 163–65 (1922).

[22] Id. at 163–64.

[23] See *City of Kirkwood v. Union Elec. Co.*, 671 F.2d 1173, 1179 (8th Cir. 1982) (finding that "courts may consider a price-squeeze claim without infringing on the regulatory jurisdiction of the FERC and PSC, because the question is not whether the rates themselves are anti-competitive, but whether defendant utility acted illegally in proposing a certain anti-competitive combination of rates"); *City of Mishawaka v. Ind. & Mich. Elec. Co.*, 560 F.2d 1314, 1321–22 (7th Cir. 1977) (holding that the Federal Power Commission does not have exclusive or primary jurisdiction over an antitrust claim). However, see *Town of Concord v. Boston Edison Co.*, 915 F.2d 17 (1st Cir. 1990) (reaching the same result as the filed rate doctrine based on an analysis similar to assessment of state action immunity at the state level).

> Not only is dual regulation directly responsible for those squeezes produced by regulatory inconsistency, it is indirectly responsible for those caused by deliberate utility conduct. The latter variety, in essence, are possible because the utility may be able to manipulate the regulatory process.[24]

When a federal agency regulates both of the rates in question, however, courts have more consistently invoked the filed rate doctrine as a bar to price squeeze antitrust claims brought by consumers.[25] For similar reasons, courts refuse to apply the filed tariff doctrine to claims for injunctive relief when an agency lacks injunctive authority (Note, 1953; Recent Cases, 1953).

The deference strand is also limited by the primary and original purpose of the doctrine – protecting consumers from price discrimination. For example, courts generally refuse to apply the filed tariff doctrine to claims brought by competitors because there is no real consumer to protect (Areeda & Hovenkamp, 2000). For example, in *Otter Tail Power Co. v. U.S.*, the U.S. Supreme Court refused to apply the filed tariff doctrine to bar essential facilities claims by competitors because the court perceived only "a potential conflict" with the FERC's authority over transmission.[26] The Ninth Circuit has more explicitly recognized an exception to the doctrine for cases involving competitors.[27]

Consistent with the doctrine's nondiscrimination strand, some states have adopted their own state-law equivalent to the federal filed tariff shield, even though the filed rate doctrine is predominantly a principle that applies in federal courts. A filed tariff has a preclusive effect on consumer, tort, fraud, and even antitrust litigation in several states.[28] Some

24 Lopatka, 1984: 638–39.

25 See *Town of Norwood v. New England Power Co.*, 202 F.3d 408, 419–20 (1st Cir. 2000) (recognizing the controversial nature of a filed rate bar and applying it to an antitrust claim).

26 410 U.S. 376, 377 (1973).

27 See *Cost Mgmt. Serv. v. Wash. Natural Gas*, 99 F.3d 937, 944–45 (9th Cir. 1996); *Barnes v. Arden Mayfair*, 759 F.2d 676, 684 (9th Cir. 1985). In practice, it is often difficult to distinguish between a competitor and a consumer. For example, wholesale customers of utilities are frequently also competitors. The competitor exception is ambiguous about how courts should treat claims by a competitor who is also a consumer. A Sixth Circuit case rejects the competitor exception to the filed tariff doctrine. See *Pinney Dock & Transp. Co. v. Penn. Cent. Corp.*, 838 F.2d 1445, 1455–57 (6th Cir. 1988).

28 See, e.g., *Satellite Sys., Inc. v. Birch Telecom, Inc.*, 51 P.3d 585, 587–88 (Ok. 2002) (adopting filed rate doctrine as a matter of state law, but recognizing an exception for fraud); *Southwestern Elec. Power Corp. v. Grant*, 73 S.W.3d 211, 216–17 (Tex. 2002) (invoking filed rate doctrine to bar negligence claim against utility); *N.C. Steel, Inc. v. Nat'l Council on Compensation Ins.*, 496 S.E.2d 369, 372–73 (N.C. 1998) (adopting filed rate under North Carolina law to preclude judicial consideration of complaint that insurers withheld information from regulators, thus forcing plaintiffs to pay more for insurance); *Prentice*

state jurisdictions, however, do not recognize the doctrine as a matter of purely state law.[29] Similar to the deference strand of the federal filed tariff doctrine, states that recognize the filed rate doctrine for their own internal court–agency disputes embrace it primarily out of respect for the expertise of state agency regulators.[30]

C. Judge Friendly's Criticism

Where enforcement is not expressly bargained for in a tariff, the filed tariff doctrine fills a gap regarding institutional enforcement by presumptively vesting all enforcement with agency regulators. Although legislators or regulators have not explicitly precluded judicial enforcement proceedings, to pursue goals of nondiscrimination, preemption, and deference courts rely on a default rule that presumptively frowns on judicial enforcement of legal norms. Over the years, many judges have looked with skepticism on this default rule. For example, in one of the more spirited criticisms of the filed tariff doctrine from the bench, Judge Friendly observed that the filed rate doctrine is not necessary to achieve any of its stated purposes.

Allowing tort and contract claims to proceed to the stage of damages does not necessarily result in discounts or adjustments to rates that violate the general principle of nondiscrimination in rates. Modern civil procedure (in particular, the availability of class actions) makes uniform relief more likely. In the Second Circuit's decision in *Square D.*, Judge Friendly observed that, because consumers can (and, given lower net rates if successful in litigation, will face incentives to) band together to bring class actions for breach of contract, tort, or fraud claims, to the extent that they do so, uniform relief among classes is more likely today than it would have been early in the twentieth century.[31] If appropriately

v. Title Ins. Co., 500 N.W.2d 658, 661–63 (Wis. 1993) (applying filed rate doctrine under state law); *Teleconnect Co. v. U.S. W. Communications*, 508 N.W.2d 644, 648–49 (Iowa 1993) (invoking state-created filed rate doctrine).

[29] *Cellular Plus, Inc. v. Superior Court*, 18 Cal. Rptr. 2d 308, 317–18 (Ct. App. 1993) (declining to apply a state equivalent of the filed tariff doctrine under the California Cartwright Act).

[30] See *Satellite Sys., Inc.*, 51 P.3d at 588 (recognizing purposes behind Oklahoma's adoption of doctrine as "to prevent discriminatory rates and to vest an agency with authority to set reasonable rates"); *Amundson & Assocs. Art Studio v. Nat'l Council on Compensation Ins.*, 988 P.2d 1208, 1213 (Kan. Ct. App. 1999) ("The filed rate doctrine stands for the proposition that because an administrative agency is vested with the authority to determine what rate is just and reasonable, courts should not adjudicate what a reasonable rate might be in a collateral lawsuit.").

[31] *Square D. Co. v. Niagara Frontier Tariff Bureau, Inc.*, 760 F.2d 1347, 1352 (2d Cir. 1985), aff'd, 476 U.S. 409 (1986).

structured, these class actions hold promise to minimize monopolistic abuses in pricing, hence dissolving any need for the filed rate doctrine to protect against discrimination in pricing or to preempt state law claims.

Moreover, Justice Friendly observed, the deference strand of the filed tariff doctrine is based on overbroad premises. Reluctantly invoking the doctrine to bar an antitrust claim, in *Square D.* Judge Friendly recognized that an award of antitrust damages (just as money damages in common law claims) does not necessarily force a particular rate on an agency such as the ICC.[32] Instead, even if a court awards judgment to the plaintiff, an agency retains discretion to accept or reject this as a reasonable cost associated with the activity. It may be necessary to make adjustments in a later rate case, but this is a decision for an agency, not a court. Thus, even before widespread availability of consumer class actions, the threat of money damages enforced by courts served the effect of deterring wrongdoing by utilities without necessarily stepping on the toes of regulators. If damages are awarded against a utility for its illegal conduct, then the regulated firm itself needs to decide whether to absorb the loss and pass it on to shareholders, or to attempt to pass it on to customers through regulated rates. However, by assessing monetary damages, courts do not force this determination onto regulators. Instead, under cost-of-service regulation, only once federal regulators find the conduct leading to damages in judicial proceedings "prudent" are utilities allowed to recover the costs associated with the conduct. Prudence remains an independent finding within the expert judgment of regulators, not courts, and regulators retain the complete authority to make adjustments to the regulated firm's rates in future cases, as reasonableness demands. In *Square D.* Judge Friendly also observed that in many contexts treble damage remedies are permitted even where regulatory remedies are already available[33] and that rules of procedure have developed to allow judicial proceedings to be stayed pending the outcome of agency procedures.[34] Because regulators are not coerced by courts to accept changes to the rate and courts have at their disposal other tools for respecting deference, the filed tariff doctrine is hardly necessary to protect agency discretion.

[32] Id. at 1352–53.

[33] See id. at 1354 (noting "[t]he Court has subsequently found that activity could be challenged under the antitrust laws despite the existence of an administrative agency with authority to regulate the activity.").

[34] See id. at 1353 (contrasting "the many later cases in which the Supreme Court has directed the suspension of judicial proceedings pending the referral of similar issues to the ICC" with *Keogh's* concern about the need for the ICC to determine rates).

On appeal of Judge Friendly's *Square D.* decision to the U.S. Supreme Court, Justice Stevens, writing for a majority, acknowledged that the case at hand could be distinguished from *Keogh*, in that the tariffs at issue were not subject to an ICC hearing prior to going into effect, but instead were merely filed with the agency.[35] However, noting the "established guidepost" of the long-standing filed tariff doctrine, the Supreme Court also upheld the filed tariff bar.[36] According to Justice Stevens, the various developments mentioned by Judge Friendly "seem to undermine some of the reasoning in Justice Brandeis *Keogh* opinion." Despite this, in *Square D.* the Court followed *Keogh*, noting that the reasoning of Judge Friendly's "characteristically thoughtful and incisive opinion" did not "overcome the strong presumption of continued validity that adheres in the judicial interpretation of a statute."[37]

II. DEREGULATION AND THE JUDICIAL RESPONSE TO THE FILED TARIFF DOCTRINE

As industries such as electric power and telecommunications are deregulated, courts continue to steadfastly adhere to the filed tariff doctrine, refusing to address the merits of many contract, tort, and antitrust claims against deregulated firms. Absent clear signals from Congress that tariffs carry no legal effect, courts are reluctant to abandon the doctrine.

One of the cases that illustrates the broad scope – and potential cost – of the filed tariff doctrine for deregulated industries involved a price squeeze claim by a municipal utility in Massachusetts against New England Power Company, alleging, among other claims, that the defendant offered the city's affiliates preferential treatment as customers over Norwood.[38] The claim was based on the combined effect of two tariffs – one, imposing a contract termination charge on the municipal customer; the other, a wholesale standard offer rate that was extended to the municipal's affiliates but not to municipalities themselves. The FERC had approved these terms as "just and reasonable" as part of New England Power Company's restructuring plan, which included market-based tariffs. Because both tariffs were on file with the FERC, the U.S. Court of Appeals for the First Circuit invoked the filed rate doctrine as a complete

[35] *Square D. Co. v. Niagara Frontier Tariff Bureau, Inc.*, 476 U.S. 409, 417 (1986).
[36] Id. at 423.
[37] Id. at 423–24.
[38] See *Town of Norwood v. New England Power Co.*, 202 F.3d 408, 418 (1st Cir. 2000).

bar to the price squeeze claim. The court observed that "[h]ere, any meaningful relief as to the price squeeze would require the *alteration* of tariffs – and not merely tariffs subject to regulation but tariffs actually scrutinized repeatedly by FERC...."[39] Because "the rationale for the filed rate doctrine is to protect the exclusive authority of the agency to accept or challenge such tariffs,"[40] in the view of the First Circuit, "this is not a case that calls out for revisiting the filed rate doctrine or for strenuous efforts to carve out exceptions...."[41]

In fact, the First Circuit explicitly refused to revisit the doctrine in light of the emerging deregulated wholesale market for electric power, stating:

> Of course, if New England Power's rates were truly left to the market, with no filing requirement or FERC supervision at all, the filed rate doctrine would by its terms no longer operate. But unlike some other regulatory agencies, FERC is still responsible for ensuring 'just and reasonable' rates and, to that end, wholesale power rates continue to be filed and subject to agency review.[42]

The First Circuit's reluctance to abandon the doctrine in light of deregulation has echoed throughout the federal judiciary, as courts are increasingly asked to intervene in disputes. Federal courts continue to vigorously endorse the filed tariff shield, keeping competitor and consumer claims almost completely out of the hands of both state regulators and federal courts.

For example, the U.S. Court of Appeals for the Ninth Circuit applied the filed tariff doctrine to imply federal preemption of the California Governor's effort to protect consumers against strategic manipulation of its power market. In response to California's electric power deregulation crisis, in January 2001, California Governor Davis declared a state of emergency, finding that "the imminent threat of widespread and prolonged disruption of electrical power... constitutes a condition of extreme peril to the safety of persons and property within the state."[43] Following this declaration, the state obtained a temporary restraining order against the California Power Exchange (CalPX), which managed a market for block forward contracts to deliver electricity through the end of 2001, including contracts between Duke Energy, a wholesale supplier, and utilities,

[39] Id. at 420 (emphasis in original).
[40] Id. [citing *Arkansas-Louisiana Gas Co. v. Hall*, 453 U.S. 571, 577–78 (1981)].
[41] Id. at 421.
[42] Id. at 419 (citations omitted).
[43] *Duke Energy Trading & Mktg., L.L.C. v. Davis*, 267 F.3d 1042, 1047 (9th Cir. 2001).

such as Southern California Edison and Pacific Gas & Electric Company. Later, it was alleged that Duke Energy and other suppliers and marketers, such as Enron, were strategically manipulating the market to reap massive profits.[44] As the state's restraining order expired, Governor Davis, acting pursuant to the California Emergency Services Act, issued two executive orders that purported to "commandeer" block forward contracts "to be held subject to the control and coordination of the State of California."[45]

Duke Energy filed a suit seeking injunctive relief against Governor Davis alleging that his commandeering orders were preempted by federal law. Because the case was for injunctive relief, not monetary damages, it is not at all clear how the filed tariff doctrine would serve to protect customers against unjust discrimination. Nevertheless, after deciding that the case should not be dismissed on sovereign immunity grounds,[46] the Ninth Circuit panel applied the filed rate doctrine, which led the court to an inference of preemption. In the court's view, "interstate power rates filed with FERC must be given binding effect" by state regulators, even when regulating in areas subject to state jurisdiction. Thus, the court stated with a sweeping confidence, "FERC-approved rates preempt conflicting regulations adopted by the states."[47]

Although the case contains broad claims about how a filed rate creates an inference of federal preemption of California Governor Davis' commandeering order, the analysis in the opinion is seriously wanting. The Ninth Circuit observed that "by preventing CalPX from liquidating the IOUs block forward positions to cover their defaults in the CalPX markets, Governor Davis' commandeering orders effectively rewrote the terms of the CTS rate schedule [approved by FERC], depriving wholesale suppliers such as Duke of their bargained-for collateral and mitigation rights."[48] Because the FERC had previously refused to allow CalPX to amend its tariff to lower the short-term credit ratings of market participants and because the effect of Governor Davis' commandeering order

[44] See FERC's *Final Report on Price Manipulation in Western Markets*, 54–55, Docket No. PA02-2-000 (March 2003). In August 2003, however, the FERC's staff cleared Duke Energy of any wrongdoing in manipulating the market. See Staff's *Initial Report on Physical Withholding by Generators Selling into the California Market and Notification to Companies* (August 2003), online at http://www.ferc.gov/industries/electric/indus-act/wem/2003/Withholding Report 8-1-03.pdf.

[45] 267 F.3d at 1047.

[46] The court held that the case did not fall within the exception to *Ex Parte Young* carved out in *Idaho v. Coeur d'Alene Tribe*, 521 U.S. 261 (1997). See *Duke Energy*, 267 F.3d at 1052–55.

[47] Id. at 1056 [citing *Nantahala*, 476 U.S. 953, 962, 966 (1986)].

[48] Id. at 1056–57.

was to deprive wholesale suppliers of this financial protection, the court concluded that governor's actions conflicted with federal law, but provided little analysis to support this conclusion.

In another case related to California's deregulation crisis, municipal utilities in the state seeking an expansion of transmission capacity sued several regional utilities, including Bonneville Power Administration, a federal agency, seeking money damages for breach of contract, tort, conversion trespass and nuisance, and, in one instance, fraud.[49] The basic claim was that, by operating another intertie constructed and operated by the defendants and approved by the FERC, the regional utilities had run afoul of an earlier agreement with the plaintiffs to jointly construct and operate the interconnection of two large electricity interties to which the plaintiffs were parties. Observing that the FERC's jurisdiction over wholesale transmission is exclusive, the Ninth Circuit concluded that the plaintiffs "cannot obtain state law money damages allegedly resulting from the operation of an interstate electricity intertie expressly approved by FERC, where the manner of operation was contemplated at the time of approval."[50] In a sweeping statement, characteristic of other courts invoking the doctrine, the Ninth Circuit analogized "allowing TANC to sue under state law for damage allegedly caused to its transmission system by an interconnected interstate system approved by FERC would be akin to allowing an airline to sue under state law for economic damages caused by another airline's FAA-approved plans."[51] The court could not have been saying that, by the very fact of federal approval of a flight plan, airlines are somehow immune from all state law claims, including negligence; instead, what the court seems to be suggesting is that federal approval of a flight plan supersedes any previous private contractual agreement between airlines that conflict with the plan. The court did not, however, explain why this result is required, particularly because the effect of such a rule is to encourage regulated firms to lobby regulators to indirectly invalidate contracts – a particularly disturbing practice in a deregulatory environment. More troubling, as in the *Duke Energy* case, the court failed to explain why the tort, fraud, and other property claims were preempted as a matter of implied or conflict preemption jurisprudence.[52] Notwithstanding its

49 *Transmission Agency v. Sierra Pac. Power Co.*, 295 F.3d 918, 928 (9th Cir. 2002).

50 Id. at 929.

51 Id.

52 Noting that "the Supreme Court has yet to resolve the issue of whether a claim based upon fraud by an agency can be preempted by the filed rate doctrine," the Ninth Circuit sided with two other circuits that found filed rate preemption under such circumstances.

expansive invocation of the filed rate doctrine, the Ninth Circuit did take the care to mention a more recent U.S. Supreme Court case that clarified the hypothetical reach of the FERC's jurisdiction, using it to potentially narrow the application of the filed tariff doctrine in future cases.[53]

Consistent with the sweeping filed tariff doctrine embraced in these Ninth Circuit cases, a federal district court in California recently invoked the doctrine to bar state regulators from limiting a utility's ability to recover the costs of power in the deregulated wholesale market. California electric utilities have consistently claimed that the refusal of the California Public Utility Commission to increase retail rates as wholesale prices for purchased power skyrocketed during the state's deregulation crisis is illegal under the filed tariff doctrine because the FERC had approved wholesale prices based on deregulated market conditions.[54] In *Pacific Gas & Electric Co. v. Lynch*, a federal district court agreed, holding that the filed tariff doctrine precludes the state of California from setting retail rates below the FERC-authorized wholesale rates and prohibiting the recovery of losses, and setting for hearing issues of fact regarding PG&E's claim for recovery. Like the other Ninth Circuit cases applying the filed tariff doctrine in the deregulatory environment, the court in *Lynch* embraced a preemption analysis, rather than the analysis applied to antitrust claims in *Keogh*. Also, like the other Ninth Circuit cases, the federal district court in *Lynch* made several broad-brush statements regarding the scope of the filed tariff shield. For instance, the court stated: "across all regulated industries to which it pertains, the filed rate doctrine has been strictly and rigidly applied, without concern for the equities of

Id. at 933; see *H.J., Inc. v. Northwestern Bell Tel. Co.*, 954 F.2d 485, 494 (8th Cir. 1992); *Taffet v. S. Co.*, 967 F.2d 1483, 1494–95 (11th Cir. 1992).

[53] As the court stated:

> We have grounded our decision in the filed rate doctrine, despite the existence of separate FERC authority over transmission capacity, because no court has yet determined whether the rule against courts assuming hypothetical allocations of authority did not affect FERC-controlled rates. We note, however, that as the Supreme Court has recently explained, FERC's jurisdiction of electricity transmission, unlike its jurisdiction over sales (i.e., rates) can reach intrastate transmissions. Hence, we reserve for future resolution the question whether federal law preempts claims that assume a hypothetical allocation of intrastate transmission capacity, notwithstanding FERC's lack of authority over intrastate sales.

295 F.3d at 931, n. 9 [citing *New York v. FERC*, 122 S.Ct., 1012, 1027 (2002)].

[54] In one context, the issue was settled (allowing the utility to recover $3.3 billion of its $6.3 billion claimed loss), but the utility's argument, if successful, would have prevented the state of California from limiting recovery in retail rates costs incurred in accordance with the FERC-approved tariffs. See *S. Cal. Edison Co. v. Lynch*, 307 F.3d 794, 801 (9th Cir. 2002).

application."[55] Although the court in *Lynch* was clear that it was applying the federal preemption strand of filed tariff cases – rather than the agency deference strand that can be traced to *Keogh* – it noted that arguments that "the introduction of competition into a regulated industry brings into question the continuing application of the filed rate doctrine" have been "uniformly rejected by courts in the regulatory contexts in which they have been raised."[56]

The filed tariff doctrine has also played an important role in more recent litigation involving the telecommunications industry. Following a long, and eventually successful, quest, the FCC adopted a regulation abandoning the filed rate doctrine in most contexts involving long distance carriers. However, under the Telecom Act of 1996, which provides for FCC review of access disputes, the Seventh Circuit has arguably read antitrust immunity into the federal statute in instances where claims are not properly pled under the statute.[57] The Supreme Court, however, eventually held that the filed tariff doctrine does not serve as an automatic bar to antitrust claims brought under the Telecommunications Act of 1996.[58]

III. STRATEGIC TARIFF FILINGS AND RADICAL DEREGULATION

Although Judge Friendly's criticisms of the filed tariff doctrine have much to commend, a government relations bargaining perspective provides a different rationale for revisiting the doctrine as telecommunications and electric power are deregulated. If tariffs and other regulatory filings are understood as a type of incomplete bargain, courts should approach incompleteness in enforcement with extreme caution before entirely dispensing with judicial consideration of the merits of antitrust, tort, and contract claims. Such incompleteness may be strategic, to the extent private firms have sought to avoid enforcement of a regulatory matter in their regulatory filings. Even if incompleteness in filed tariffs itself is not intentional – it may, for instance, also be due to imperfect information about future problems with regulation – a default rule against judicial intervention, such as that provided by the filed rate doctrine, may encourage

[55] See *Pac. Gas & Elec. v. Lynch*, 216 F. Supp. 2d 1016, 1038–40, 1049 (N.D. Cal. 2002).

[56] Id. at 1039.

[57] *Goldwasser v. Ameritech Corp.*, 222 F.3d 390 (7th Cir. 2000) (refusing antitrust jurisdiction where the FCC has enforcement authority under the 1996 Telecom Act).

[58] *Verizon v. Law Offices of Curtis V. Trinko, L.L.P.*, 124 S.Ct. 872 (2004) (exercising jurisdiction over essential facilities claim but rejecting the claim on its merits).

strategic filings aimed at precluding judicial enforcement of important antitrust, contract, and tort doctrines.

Understood as such, the filed tariff shield not only influences the course of litigation, but it also affects the forum-shopping behavior of private firms and agencies in the regulatory process before actual litigation commences. Institutionally, agencies and courts have never been very effective at monitoring tariffing as a private forum-shopping strategy. This may have been a stable state of affairs with cost-of-service regulation, given routine regulatory proceedings that served as some safeguard for public values. However, with the introduction of competition to formerly regulated industries and other regulatory transitions, market norms are emerging to expose a gap in regulatory agency ability to deter wrongdoing by private firms. To the extent the filed tariff doctrine encourages strategic manipulation of the tariffing process to foreclose judicial enforcement, it widens this gap and may even result in more radical deregulation than either Congress or agencies intend – markets without essential antitrust, contract, and tort protections.

A. Influence of the Legal Doctrine on Behavior and Institutional Choice

In assessing the effects of the filed tariff doctrine, it is important to focus on the behavior of private firms, regulators, and courts. To conceptualize the basic effects of the doctrine, a few simplifying observations about the behavior of these actors are in order: assume a private firm is motivated by its ability to avoid substantial penalties for its market decisions (along with other goals such as maximizing profits); assume an agency is motivated by sustaining and expanding its jurisdiction (among other goals, perhaps even including regulating in the public interest); and assume reviewing courts are concerned with sustaining their independence and institutional posture (along with other goals, perhaps even including promoting sound governance by other branches of government, as deference to an agency might reinforce).

Against the backdrop of these various actors, neoinstitutionalist economists and political scientists recognize that issues of regulation can be evaluated through the lens of behavior of institutional choice (Furubotn & Richter, 1998; Williamson, 1996a). Placing aside the issues associated with federalism (which are further discussed in Chapters 7 and 8), when managing an industry such as electric power or telecommunications, three main institutional fora are available for guiding private choices. First, and most prevalent throughout the twentieth century, regulatory agencies (federal or state) can set prices, structure, and service terms and conditions for firms in an industry. Second, courts, through the application of statutory standards, such as the antitrust laws, and common law doctrines (including the law of fraud and contract) can regulate structure and service terms and conditions in an industry. Third, spontaneous ordering of the market can regulate the prices, structure, and service terms and conditions in an industry. Of course, in most industries, some mixture of these three institutional options regulates the conduct of private firms. For instance, in most unregulated industries, a mix of the second and third options serves to govern private behavior. Prices are determined through the market, but courts also apply antitrust laws and common law doctrines in order to enhance overall social welfare in a competitive marketplace.

In contrast, in the context of twentieth-century natural monopoly regulation, industry governance banked most of its promise on the institutional choice of the regulatory agency. Apart from a few "tools" of regulatory reform, such a price cap regulation, avoided cost pricing, and market-based filings, other approaches – particularly courts and competitive markets – were largely ignored. Courts deferred to regulators, and competitive markets were widely considered unworkable in public utility industries with natural monopoly features. Focusing on how the regulatory agency affects private conduct, public choice theorists (Becker, 1983; Peltzman, 1976; Stigler, 1971) and other economists (Tirole, 2002) have chronicled the potential problems of this approach to managing regulatory problems. Most of this literature, however, cynically attributes any adverse welfare consequence of this regulatory process to regulation itself (Mashaw, 1997; Noll, 1971).

Underacknowledged in the literature is the impact of specific legal rules, such as the filed tariff doctrine, on the successes or failures of the regulatory process. More recently, however, political scientists and economists have begun to analyze how interest groups, including regulated firms, decide to allocate their resources between various types of regulation, congressional, agency, or judicial (de Figueiredo & de Figueiredo, 2002; Rubin et al., 2001). A worthy candidate for similar analysis, the filed tariff doctrine has serious and unique implications for the behavior of regulated firms. Because the doctrine is only available on a widespread basis if a utility has filed its tariff with federal regulators, the doctrine creates a strong ex ante incentive for private firms, such as regulated utilities, to invest more heavily than otherwise in lobbying regulators to accept or approve tariffs. By engaging in such conduct ex ante, private firms can avoid the uncertainty of an ex post judicial proceeding in which courts enforce antitrust, tort, or contract law. The doctrine thus encourages a type of forum shopping, triggered primarily by private decisions to provide information in the regulatory process. If a private firm desires the protection of the filed tariff shield – immunity from antitrust and state common law suits for its market behavior – it has a strong incentive to divulge information (especially ambiguous information) to regulators ex ante, in anticipation that this information will be included in published tariffs and will minimize unpredictable, ex post judicial meddling.

Regulatory theory almost always regards additional information as a positive good for the regulatory process. Additional information for regulators has proved helpful to regulators as they determine and monitor cost-of-service rates and related terms and conditions. The filed tariff doctrine is consistent with a view of regulation based on active monitoring of an industry by regulators. Information is seen as a necessary good for regulators to perform their assigned tasks. More information improves the regulatory climate to the extent that it allows regulators to sort through issues and problems, while also acting as a check, of sorts, on capture of the agency (Kalt & Zupan, 1984; Rossi, 1997).

At the same time, however, the filed tariff shield encourages regulated firms to strategically divulge ambiguous information that is unrelated to the anticipated regulatory actions of the regulator. Where there is no check on the accuracy, clarity, and relevance of the information to the regulatory process, opportunities for manipulation of regulation – and in particular institutional choice – are present.[59] To the extent regulated firms engage in strategic conduct ex ante, an institutional bias in favor of regulatory agencies, and away from courts and markets, is likely to result. The prospect of strategic overdivulgence of information – as well as more affirmative rent seeking as firms lobby regulators to include in tariffs ambiguous terms and conditions unrelated to expected regulatory action – presents a potential cost to be balanced against the information provision incentives created by the filed tariff doctrine.

In the context of asymmetric information disclosure of nonverifiable information in contractual bargaining, Eric Talley (2001) has observed a need for judicial monitoring or verification. Other legal contexts put safeguards in place to protect the public interest from the adverse institutional

[59] Using more formal modeling, commentators warn of similar behavior in other information disclosure contexts, such as intellectual property licensing (Lichtman et al., 2000) or drug approval and merger applications (Lewis & Poitevin, 1997).

implications of overdisclosure of information ex ante to manipulate ex post enforcement. Typically, the balance between disclosure, on the one hand, and institutional decisions to regulate, on the other, is monitored by the oversight of a third party who has the ability to protect the public interest. For example, in the context of tort litigation, securities regulation, and witness immunity from criminal prosecution, each of which use information disclosure to influence regulatory choices, third-party oversight plays an important role in monitoring the divulgence of information to ensure the choice is welfare enhancing.

In medical malpractice and other tort cases, disclosure of information can give rise to defenses, including assumption of the risk (Berg, 2003; Simons, 2002). However, if disclosure of risks alone were a defense to litigation, this would encourage manufacturers and other potential defendants to provide more information with their products or services than consumers could ever process or understand. Perhaps manufacturers and other potential defendants already do so. Before allowing this information to have a legal effect on enforcement, however, courts carefully evaluate the nature of information disclosed, to determine whether an injured plaintiff had knowledge of and understood a communicated risk.

Securities regulation provides another example. In its regulations, the Securities and Exchange Commission (SEC) requires companies to disclose the risks associated with their investments, but does not allow disclosure of these risks to preclude agency enforcement proceedings against companies.[60] In fact, disclosure of information may spur the SEC to take enforcement action against companies. In the SEC context, the agency's regulations envision the agency itself, as well as courts, monitoring such information disclosure to ensure it is not materially misleading (or reckless), and thereby does not have a negative effect on the operation of securities markets (Horwich, 2000). Thus, the agency evaluates the appropriateness of disclosure to ensure the effects on the market are not adverse.

Monitored disclosure also plays an important role in influencing institutional choice in the criminal procedure context. Prosecutors routinely provide incentives for disclosure by witnesses by offering immunity in

[60] Under SEC Rule 10b-5, 17 C.F.R. § 240.10b-5 (2003), private causes of action are available against companies where "in connection with the purchase or sale of securities, the misstatement or omission of a material fact, made with scienter, upon which the plaintiff justifiably relied and which proximately caused the plaintiff's injury." See In re: *Comshare, Inc.*, 183 F.3d 542, 548 (6th Cir. 1999).

exchange for disclosure. However, when federal prosecutors offer immunity in exchange for disclosure, the prosecutor must determine that immunity is "in the public interest," and a judge must approve the grant of immunity (Sosnov, 2000: 183–84). The specific determination that the public interest is served by the prosecutor, along with independent approval by the judge, serves a third-party monitoring role, helping to ensure the institutional choice influenced by disclosure does not thwart social welfare.

In the context of many price-regulated industries, however, third-party monitoring of strategic disclosure is ineffective. Third-party monitoring of information disclosure in the utility regulation would depend on the actions of either regulators, as in the context of the SEC, or courts, as in the context of criminal immunity. To the extent that the filed tariff shield applies, however, both regulators and courts have been ineffective at policing this balance ex ante to ensure the application of the shield is not harmful to social welfare ex post in the utility regulation context.

A regulatory agency will hardly be opposed to gaining new information from the firms it regulates, particularly because the submission of tariff terms and conditions invites the prospect of future expansion of agency jurisdiction. Agencies generally acquiesce in, rather than refuse, tariff filings. In fact, often filed tariffs become effective by operation of law after the passage of time, with little or no scrutiny by agencies. So the filed tariff bar curiously aligns the incentives of both private firms and regulators to include as many terms and conditions as possible in tariffs – even when these terms and conditions are sham, in the sense that agencies often lack the power to seriously enforce them. This is not a problem with cost-of-service regulation, in which tariffs are subject to potential adjudication in a hearing, but if tariffs are not subject to these procedural safeguards the potential for manipulation is present.[61]

Courts are likewise ineffective at monitoring the costs associated with the filed tariff bar. Because the interests of regulators and firms are generally aligned in the direction of expansive tariffs, judicial appeals rarely, if ever, focus on the appropriateness of inclusion of information in a tariff. When tariffs are appealed on other grounds, courts are highly inclined to uphold tariffs under general principles of deference to agency regulators (Goldsmith, 1989; Kearney & Merrill, 1998; Pierce, 1989). Indeed, given

[61] As noted as follows, in many instances statutory limits on a regulatory agency's jurisdiction further limit the ability of agency evaluation of tariffs to serve as a safeguard on the forum effects of disclosure in private tariffing.

principles of deference to agency regulators in the late twentieth century, the judiciary has played little role in policing private behavior in the tariffing process and its relationship to the filed tariff shield. Because the interests of regulators and firms converge, and courts have little institutional capacity to police the bargains and information reflected in tariffs, there are no effective safeguards against strategic use of the regulatory process to forum shop.

B. Enforcement Gaps in the New Tariffing Environment

Private forum-shopping bias in the direction of the agency regulator does not present an enforcement problem if federal regulators fully evaluate tariffs prior to approval and have the jurisdiction and resources to adequately deter market abuses. In the cost-of-service context, for instance, regulators routinely held hearings on tariff matters. However, the shifts in the regulatory approach to tariffing accompanying deregulation, along with statutory limits on agency jurisdiction and lack of resources, may substantially undermine the agency regulator's ability to deter market abuses. Thus, the forum-shopping bias of the filed tariff doctrine can result in more radical deregulation – markets absent even antitrust or common law enforcement – than either Congress or agencies would prefer. This presents a partiular risk if courts presumptively allow the filed rate doctrine to bar judicial consideration of private conduct. Given changes in tariffing, however, a presumption against judicial consideration must be reassessed for competitive markets.

With deregulation of electric power and other traditionally regulated industries, tariffing is no longer a process in which the approval of a rate imposes firm-specific terms, such as prices. Instead, tariffing has increasingly become a regulatory tool for holding firms to market expectations regarding industry structure, particularly network access, and providing information to competitors and consumers. Tariffs, along with agency regulations, increasingly set general standards for the operation of a competitive market. In contrast to cost-of-service regulation,

> Under the new paradigm, the regulator plays a far more limited role. Instead of comprehensively overseeing an industry in order to protect the end-user, its principal function is to maximize competition among rival providers, in the expectation that competition will provide all the protection necessary for end-users.[62]

[62] Kearney & Merrill, 1998: 1361.

In light of more recent problems with deregulated markets, particularly problems with deregulation of electric power, this account seems to glorify the promise of competition. Nevertheless, it aptly describes the approach federal regulators have taken in restructuring public utility industries, such as electric power and telecommunications. As one former FERC Commissioner has stated:

> The new prevailing theory for disclosure is that where an industry is competitive, consumers are better served by the results of working market processes. Consequently, the focus of regulatory reporting and disclosure obligations should shift from what is needed for setting cost-based rates to what is needed for maintaining a competitive market and preventing an individual competitor from exercising market power.[63]

Regulators increasingly announce their approach through generally applicable rules, not in firm-specific tariff filings. To the extent that regulators continue to address firm-specific information in tariffs, they are predominantly concerned with industry structure and market information disclosure, rather than protecting consumers from price discrimination in the setting of firm-specific rates.

Mindful of such concerns, in 2004 the U.S. Court of Appeals for the Ninth Circuit rejected the presumption that the filed rate doctrine will preclude judicial consideration pf private conduct under market-based rates. *Lockyer v. FERC* held that the filed rate doctrine can apply to FERC's market-based rates, but only if FERC does something more than make a cursory finding of no market power in accepting a rate filing.[64] FERC also needs to exercise remedial authority to more actively monitor market-based rates for market abuses. If FERC does not do this, the Ninth Circuit panel suggested, "the purpose of the filed rate doctrine is undermined" and "the tariff runs afoul of . . . the FPA."[65]

In the context of electric power deregulation, in addition to adopting market-based rates regulators have significantly modified the scope of their tariff filing requirements. The FERC's Order No. 888 deregulates wholesale electric power markets and promotes competition in electric power supply by requiring each utility to file a pro forma open access transmission tariff, subject to the FERC's approval.[66] The FERC's jurisdiction is limited to wholesale transactions, so these tariffs primarily

[63] Santa, 2000: 2.

[64] 383 F.3d 1006 (9th Cir. 2004).

[65] Id. at 1016.

[66] See *Promoting Wholesale Competition Through Open Access Non-Discriminatory Transmission Services by Public Utilities*, 61 Federal Register 21,540 (1996).

govern the relationships between utilities and other utilities and wholesale suppliers, not utilities and retail customers.[67] Each utility is required to file its own standard transmission service tariff.[68] For some utilities, who voluntarily turned management of their transmission networks over to independent operators, the FERC attempted to dispense with its tariff filing requirement, instead allowing an Independent Service Operator to file transmission tariffs on behalf of its members, but the D.C. Circuit reversed, holding that Section 205 of the Federal Power Act requires the FERC to allow each individual, jurisdictional utility to file a tariff.[69] Thus, for now the FERC continues to require the filing of transmission tariffs by individual utilities, subject to its industrywide open access policies.[70]

At the same time, the FERC's regulatory authority over utilities in the electric power industry is far from plenary.[71] Although perhaps the FERC wishes to implement a uniform national policy for transmission access and pricing, the scope of the FERC's legal authority over transmission is limited: The FERC regulates wholesale sales but has no statutory jurisdiction to reach retail transmission sales.[72] Nor does the FERC have

67 The scope of the FERC's authority to regulate electricity markets was more recently addressed by the U.S. Supreme Court in *New York v. FERC*, 535 U.S. 1, 6–7 (2002) (noting the FERC's jurisdiction over wholesale sales under section 201 of the Federal Power Act).

68 61 Federal Register 21,540 (rule requiring all jurisdictional utilities to file open access transmission tariffs).

69 See *Atl. City Elec. Co. v. FERC*, 295 F.3d 1 (D.C. Cir. 2002). *Atlantic City* does not address the filed tariff doctrine, but instead focuses on a regulated utility's procedural right to agency review and consideration of its tariff changes. See Id. at 9–10. Even though the court held that the FERC could not dispense with these procedures, it also acknowledged that "FERC plays 'an essentially passive and reactive' role under Section 205." Id. at 10 [citing *City of Winnfield v. FERC*, 744 F.2d 871, 876 (D.C. Cir. 1984) (J. Scalia)].

70 It is unclear whether, and how, nondiscrimination will be protected in the context of open access to bottleneck facilities. In the telecommunications context, Jean-Jacques Laffont and Jean Tirole (2000) argue that the optimal access prices to bottleneck facilities are discriminatory because they are usage based.

71 In the electric power context, state regulators can set rates only for intrastate transactions, and these transactions also are largely off limits to federal regulators. See *Federal Power Comm'n v. Conway Corp.*, 426 U.S. 271, 271 (1976) (allowing the Federal Power Commission to consider evidence of retail rates in reviewing a nondiscrimination challenge to federally set wholesale rates, but also noting that "[t]he Commission has no power to prescribe the rates for retail sales of power companies"); *Northern States Power Co. v. FERC*, 176 F.3d 1090, 1096 (8th Cir. 1999) (holding that the FERC does not have the authority to regulate transmission for retail customers in its efforts to develop competitive wholesale power markets).

72 *New York v. FERC*, 535 U.S. at 22–23 (noting that states retain jurisdiction over retail sales, which are outside the FERC's jurisdiction).

any jurisdiction to require firms to expand transmission facilities. These limits create the potential for a jurisdictional gap, which regulated utilities might seek to fill by filing unenforceable and ambiguous firm-specific tariff terms with the FERC. For example, a utility may file an open access tariff with the FERC, using this tariff filing to specify how it will treat its retail customers in making transmission decisions; the treatment of retail customers could then fall within the scope of the filed tariff doctrine. Because the FERC does not have jurisdiction over retail sales, retail service escapes the scrutiny of both the FERC regulation and the antitrust laws in many instances. The FERC has significantly moved away from cost-of-service rate regulation of both transmission and bulk power supply;[73] even in this context, however, the FERC's jurisdiction does not include retail sales. In contrast to wholesale transmission and power supply sales, regulated by the FERC, the relationship between utilities and retail customers is largely regulated at the state level, and many states continue to require the filing and approval of tariffs governing power transmission and distribution, if not supply. As a result, the emergence of wholesale competition at the federal level, along with differing – and sometimes conflicting – approaches to deregulation at the state level (where state law consumer protections become most relevant) has led to some of the fiercest battles in the history of the electric power industry.

Like the FERC, many other regulatory agencies maintain their filing requirements in the current deregulatory environment, but today these serve predominantly general market structure, informational and evaluative, rather than firm-specific right-creating, functions. Nondiscrimination, central to rate regulation throughout the twentieth century, has evolved to incorporate the general norms of consumer protection laws, including notions of comparability.[74] Yet this is a far more general standard – aimed at defining network access and industry structure – than the traditional unjust discrimination standard – which was adjudicated in firm-specific cases. Put simply, in regulated industries, the regulator

[73] For instance, the FERC has evolved its power supply jurisdiction from cost-of-service rate making to so-called "market-based rates," for which the FERC waives certain filing requirements altogether.

[74] For example, under the FERC's comparability standard, "[a]n open access tariff that is not unduly discriminatory or anticompetitive should offer third parties access on the same or comparable basis, and under the same or comparable terms and conditions, as the transmission provider's uses of its [own] system." *Alliant Energy Corp. v. FERC*, 253 F.3d 748, 751 n. 3 (D.C. Cir. 2001) [quoting Transmission Pricing Policy Statement, 59 *Fed. Reg.* 55,031, at 55,034 (Nov. 3, 1994) (codified at 18 C.F.R. pt. 2)].

no longer perceives its role as monitoring firm-specific costs to guarantee each customer the same rate (Laffont & Tirole, 2000). Further, as the FERC's exercise of jurisdiction exemplifies, with deregulation many agencies have waived some or all their jurisdictional filing requirements with respect to entities that lack market power.

Against this backdrop, use of the filed tariff shield to bar consumer protection litigation in the context of deregulated telecommunications or electric power service is problematic. Competitive markets will, as they have in the telecommunications context, invite opportunities for service providers to offer discounts and rebates to customers. As a principle of economics, flexibility in pricing is key to effective operation of a competitive market. This allows regulators more discretion in implementing competition policy. More important, in the competitive environment it allows private firms flexibility in pricing and service. Without flexibility, private firms lack the ability to respond to market conditions, including changes in supply and demand. As courts traditionally apply the filed tariff doctrine, however, price flexibility is not allowed unless it is specifically envisioned by a previously approved tariff.

Where a tariff does envision flexibility in pricing – as if often intended for market-based rates in competitive industries – the filed tariff doctrine can present problems. Because, under the filed tariff doctrine, service providers are not bound (in any judicially enforceable way) to the terms of contracts they have entered into with customers, unless the specific contracts have been approved by regulators, providers face no disincentive for engaging in misrepresentation or even fraudulent contracts in attempting to secure customers. In addition, consumer suits under the antitrust laws, designed to protect and encourage competition, are not allowed to reach the conduct of providers to the extent it is consistent with an approved tariff. For example, it is widely suspect that wholesale energy suppliers in the West who possessed market power colluded to withhold supply, and increase price, during the California deregulation crisis (Martin, 2003). The filed tariff doctrine, however, could serve as a bar to such claims.

In the cost-of-service environment that dominated during the twentieth century, manipulation of the filed tariff shield by regulated firms posed little harm, to the extent that competition was not the norm and regulators actively used the rate-making process to protect consumers from injury. In the current environment, where competitive markets have displaced traditional rate regulation, invocation of a filed tariff shield poses a more serious risk of harm. The doctrine would be relatively harmless if regulators, in approving and monitoring tariffs, were willing and able to monitor breach of contract, fraud and other torts, and antitrust misconduct. In several ways, however, the willingness and ability of federal regulators to monitor and sanction such conduct is seriously limited. Because federal regulators do not have plenary authority, by filing overbroad tariffs regulated firms may be able to escape scrutiny altogether in their control of essential facilities, such as electric transmission.[75] For example, the FERC does not regulate retail transmission sales (e.g., how a utility allocates the costs of transmission to its retail customers), but a firm may still seek the FERC's acquiescence in its retail cost allocation, thus inviting a court to apply the filed tariff shield to conduct related to retail pricing.

Even assuming an agency clearly has jurisdiction over the tariff terms in initially approving tariffs, regulators are not likely to have an opportunity to fully assess every potential violation of the public interest. Often, as was the case with the FERC's Order No. 888, federal regulators approved tariffs with only a perfunctory review of their terms and conditions, often rubberstamping standard tariffs en masse. Further, once a violation of a tariff's terms is alleged, if a complaint is filed the agency has a broad degree of discretion – more so than courts – in deciding whether to investigate and prosecute alleged violations; this discretion may be influenced by underfunded enforcement budgets and competing priorities. Many alleged violations will simply never be investigated, pursued, or heard.

Finally, absent specific grants of authority, agencies such as the FERC and the FCC, unlike the now-defunct ICC (whose powers were at issue in *Keogh*), do not have significant powers to assess and enforce penalties against wrongdoers. In a deregulated market, enforceable remedies for misconduct are important to deter fraud and other types of strategic market manipulation. However, the agencies implementing deregulatory policies themselves frequently lack the authority to pursue or impose such remedies. For example, the FERC's remedial powers are limited to refund authority and nationwide license revocation. In its initial report on potential manipulation of electric and natural gas prices in the West,

[75] A good example is a filing PG&E Corp. made with the FERC, shielding millions of dollars in unregulated assets from creditors when PG&E declared bankruptcy. California ex rel. *Lockyer v. FERC*, 329 F.3d 700 (9th Cir. 2003); see also *9th Circuit Court of Appeals Upholds FERC Order Blessing Reorganization of PG&E Corp. to Create Corporate Shield for Credit-Hungry National Energy Group*, Foster Natural Gas Report, May 22, 2003, at 7.

focused on misconduct associated with California's deregulation conduct, the FERC's staff recommended refunds. In addition, the FERC's staff noted the possibility of the FERC's imposition of penalties through tariff monitoring and suspension.[76] Companies such as Enron, alleged to have engaged in strategic manipulation of California's market (which in Enron's case, the commission staff alleged, arose to the level of "deceit, including the submission of false information"), would thus be subject to refunds and, possibly, the threat of losing the ability to participate in deregulated markets.[77]

Yet neither of these powers is sufficient to deter misconduct in deregulated markets. Refund authority is not adequate to deter wrongdoing beyond normal breach of contract remedies, and even then it merely approximates the deterrence of the restitution remedy.[78] Nationwide license revocation authority is also not a sufficient mechanism to deter wrongdoing. Federal regulators often lack the authority to impose penalties directly, and thus must rely on their permitting and licensing powers, attempting to do indirectly what they are not authorized to do directly. For instance, as the FERC's staff noted in its report, the FERC does not have the authority to directly impose penalties.[79] In addition, no agency can specify every market rule ex ante. Agencies also frequently lack jurisdiction over every actor participating in a market.

The gap in jurisdiction is even more pronounced when agencies have waived regulatory requirements, as the FERC often does, to encourage the growth of competition. The FERC's staff acknowledged the significant of this problem when it recommended that "all market-based rate

[76] See FERC, *Initial Report on Company-Specific Separate Proceedings and Generic Reevaluations; Published Natural Gas Price Data; and Enron Trading Strategies* 3–6, Docket No. PA02-2-000 (August 2002) (hereinafter FERC *Enron Report*).

[77] Id. at 3–5.

[78] A restitution remedy might deter misconduct adequately if courts were concerned with inducing efficient behavior in plaintiffs, but the main deterrence concern in this context is the defendant. Cohen (1994) advocates a fault-based economic theory of contract damages in place of strict liability principles in order to provide the correct incentives to contracting parties. Automatic restitution would underdeter wrongdoing where the defendant's conduct is at issue. Choice of a remedy is best evaluated under contract law or other legal principles that the filed tariff shield completely forecloses.

[79] "Staff is aware that Congress is considering expanding the Commission's currently very limited civil penalty authority, and we strongly endorse expanded civil penalty authority that applies to jurisdictional companies that violate the Commission's orders and regulations, as a means to deter the types of conduct we have encountered in this investigation." *FERC Enron Report, supra,* at 6.

tariffs include standard provisions so that the Commission can go beyond simply refunding profits and impose penalties on violators."[80] Clearly, the FERC had not anticipated the market abuses that evolved when it initially approved market-based tariffs. Its failure to do so has left the FERC with little remedy against wrongdoers. Even if the FERC did have a remedy that it could legally exercise under its licensing powers, license revocation is a difficult threshold to meet. To the extent that grounds for revocation can be established, the remedy is draconian: nationwide in scope (thus excessively harsh in its consequence), harmful to consumers to the extent it overdeters, and costly for regulators. Conditioning license approval at the front end may prove simpler, but once a firm's activities are licensed it is difficult to impose new conditions on some, but not other firms, without facing protracted legal challenges.

Indeed, in many instances, the FERC may not have the ability to assert jurisdiction over deregulated market entities, even if they fail to act in compliance with filed rates, so sometimes the FERC may have had no remedies at all for abuses of deregulated power markets. It is not surprising that California's then-Governor Gray Davis (himself facing an election year run-off at the time that the FERC's report was issued) issued a stinging criticism of the FERC's report, calling it "whitewash, pure and simple." Governor Davis chastised the FERC because it "hasn't sanctioned anybody, it hasn't issued any refunds to us, it's done nothing to stop the manipulation which everyone agrees occurred here in California."[81]

Illustrative of the enforcement gap the filed tariff doctrine may create, a recent District Court decision in Texas precluded antitrust claims against energy suppliers in the deregulated Texas wholesale power market and left those harmed by market abuses without any legal or administrative remedy. In June 2004, the U.S. District Court for the Southern District of Texas, Corpus Christi Division applied the filed rate doctrine to preclude antitrust claims for illegal conduct in deregulated wholesale power markets against numerous power supply companies and the Electric Reliability Council of Texas (ERCOT).[82] The case provides a clear example of why federal courts need to revisit the filed rate doctrine in the deregulatory environment.

[80] Id.

[81] See Richard A. Oppel, Jr., *Energy Pricing Suspicious, Report Says*, N.Y. Times, Aug. 14, 2002, at C1.

[82] *Texas Commercial Energy v. TXU Energy, Inc.*, 2004–2 Trade Cases ¶ 74,497 (S.D. Tex., Corpus Christi 2004), 2004 WL 1777597.

The claim, brought by Texas Commercial Energy (TCE), alleged that 24 defendants, including TXU Energy, Inc., American Electric Power, Inc., and other energy marketers within ERCOT engaged in anticompetitive market abuses in violation of federal and state antitrust laws as well as fraud, negligent misrepresentation, breach of contract, defamation, business disparagement, civil conspiracy, and malicious and willful/flagrant conduct under state law. TCE alleged that these wrongful acts caused prices in the Balancing Energy Service Market (BES) – a bid-based market for short-term power – to rise drastically, forcing TCE to pay higher prices in the BES market and forcing it to withdraw credit-based collateral from its bilateral partners. As is typical in most cases involving the filed rate doctrine, the U.S. District Court in Texas dismissed TCE's lawsuit without addressing the substantive merits of the market abuse claims. Although FERC possesses no authority over the Texas electricity market, the court reasoned that the doctrine is intended to allow markets to operate under rules approved by state regulators. In declining to consider the merits of the federal antitrust claim, the court reasoned that the agency charged by the state legislature with overseeing the Texas electricity market, the Texas Public Utilities Commission (TPUC) possesses the "institutional competence to address rate-making issues in the BES market, one of the principles underlying the filed rate doctrine."[83] The court observed that TPUC is required by statute ensure "safe, reliable and reasonably priced electricity," including in BES markets.[84] The court noted, for example, that in August 2001 the Market Oversight Division of TPUC ordered market participants to return $30 million in illicit profits due to abusive and improper scheduling practices in the BES market. In addition, rates in the BES market are capped at $1,000 per MWh. After finding that the filed rate doctrine bars federal and state antitrust suits, the court also determined that it bars breach of contract and other claims. While the court's decision echoes the approach of many other federal courts, which often presumptively apply the filed rate doctrine to refuse consideration of a market abuse claim, it also exposes substantial flaws with the doctrine in the deregulatory environment.

Most obviously, the court's premise that TPUC's "institutional competence" precludes consideration of the claim fails entirely to confront the predicate issue of the agency's authority to remedy harms. A regulator could only possess institutional competence if it also has the authority

[83] Id. at 10 (slip opinion).
[84] Tex. Util. Code. § 39.101(a)(1).

to act. However, Texas has no express or implied private right of action for injured purchasers and TPUC also lacks authority to order refunds and damages. While the district court referred to a previous $30 million settlement in Texas as evidence of TPUC's power, this depended entirely on TPUC voluntarily assuming the role brokering a settlement agreement and persuading the companies to disgorge some of their wrongfully obtained profits. While TPUC may have the political power to broker a deal, TPUC affords customers no formal complaint and restitution process where they are injured in the BES market. Even to the extent there is a complaint and adjudication process for restitution, the filed rate doctrine precludes antitrust claims in which treble damages are available to serve a more meaningful deterrence function. Treble damages may not be necessary if agency regulators enforce 100% of market abuses (since one of the main policy reasons behind treble damages is that the likelihood of being sued is so low that meaningful penalities must be high), but regulators lack the authority or resources to guarantee restitution for every market abuse. The absence of restitution coupled with the lack of meaningful penalties means that a Texas-sized enforcement gap will exist in ERCOT's deregulated wholesale market.[85]

When, as in Texas, agency oversight lacks punch, whether due to limited jurisdiction or inadequate resources, judicial enforcement of remedies has much to offer. In many instances, courts will have distinct comparative institutional advantages over agencies in defining standards and deterring violations of market norms. Courts, unlike most regulatory agencies, are not constrained in Congress' delegation of authority as expressed in enabling or more specific statutes. Moreover, the judicial forum offers complex cases many benefits that the agency forum routinely lacks: broader discovery, wider remedial authority, and greater political independence.

[85] Moreover, in discussing the filed rate doctrine the district court in Texas completely confused federal and state law. The *Keogh* case, on which the court relied extensively, involved the application of the filed rate doctrine as a matter of federal law to suspend application of federal antitrust laws to activities regulated by a federal agency. Here, no federal agency had regulatory authority – only a Texas state agency had any claim to regulatory authority. To the extent the doctrine involves state regulation, the tariff should be treated as a matter of state law or under state action immunity – the appropriate federalism defense to the antitrust laws (see Chapter 7). The district court, however, did not reference a single Texas case involving the file rate doctrine, and failed completely to evaluate whether state regulation of the BES market gives rise to state action immunity (Rossi, 2004).

Common law and antitrust remedies are not perfect at effectuating deterrence, but absent a clear indication that regulation is intended to preempt or supersede them, these remedies play a central role in deterrence regimes for competitive service markets. Put simply, to the extent that common law or antitrust remedies are sought against service providers, absent a comprehensive regulatory scheme, courts are an essential enforcement vehicle for consumer protection norms, particularly in the context of deregulation.[86] Unless Congress expands the powers of federal agencies to directly enforce penalties against wrongdoers in deregulated markets, if given presumptive application by courts the filed tariff doctrine will invite even further strategic abuse of the regulatory process and thwart effective deterrence of market wrongdoing. If left unchecked, it can lead to more radical deregulation than either Congress or agencies envision.

IV. ALTERNATIVES FOR DEFINING THE INSTITUTIONAL ENFORCEMENT FORUM

Given the extent to which the filed tariff doctrine leaves enforcement decisions in the hands of private firms – not regulators or courts – the public interest needs to be safeguarded in enforcement decisions. Courts should not pretend that ambiguous statutory schemes necessarily reflect a congressional intent to preempt state common law claims absent some serious effort at oversight by regulators, nor should they imply antitrust immunity based solely on the filing of a tariff. Instead, courts must assess whether federal preemption is warranted and whether it is appropriate for antitrust litigation to continue against the backdrop of regulation. Existing doctrines, such as federal preemption analysis and the doctrine or primary jurisdiction, are adequate to serve this purpose and are more likely than the filed tariff doctrine to safeguard the public interest in enforcement of market norms. If the filed tariff doctrine is not abandoned altogether, it should be applied in a manner that is consistent with these doctrines.

[86] Although deregulation may make the problem more salient, the enforcement gap arguably existed under cost-of-service regulation as well. Hale and Hale (1962), for example, argued that antitrust exemptions are an appropriate exception to antitrust exemptions "when the regulatory burden is so great that effective control cannot be achieved" (58–59).

A. Substituting Federal Preemption Analysis for the Filed Tariff Shield in Vertical Jurisdiction Contexts

Federal preemption doctrine, if explicitly and carefully analyzed in the context of the specific federal approval and monitoring actions at issue, holds great promise to deter violations of market norms, providing a safeguard for consumers and competition. Article VI, cl. 2, of the U.S. Constitution states that the "Constitution, and the Laws of the United States which shall be made in Pursuance thereof . . . shall be the supreme Law of the Land. . . ." As a matter of black letter law, federal preemption jurisprudence is well established. Of course, Congress can expressly preempt state or local law by using explicit statutory language. Courts also frequently infer preemption in one of two ways: first, where federal regulation occupies the field leaving no room for supplemental regulations by the states; second, where state or local law poses an actual conflict with federal law.[87] Although established as a matter of black letter law, federal preemption analysis remains highly controversial, often resulting in split judicial decisions. Perhaps not surprisingly, despite the Supreme Court's general acknowledgment of a "presumption against the preemption of state police power regulations,"[88] many characterize the cases law as exhibiting a strong bias in favor of finding federal preemption (Davis, 2002; Spence & Murray, 1999).

If approached with caution, federal preemption analysis provides a useful framework for evaluating the implications of using the existence of a filed rate as a shorthand for reaching a preemption conclusion. In regulatory contexts such as telecommunications and electric power, Congress has envisioned a dual regulatory structure, allowing federal and state regulation to coexist. Given this, rarely, if ever, will a federally approved tariff so occupy the field as to allow no room for state regulation. Thus, it is not appropriate to treat tariff cases as "occupation of the field"-type implied preemption cases. Instead, if anything, tariff cases are best characterized as obstacle cases, in which the claim is that state regulation poses a barrier to effective federal regulation of the same activity.

The conflict between federal tariffs and state contract, tort, or fraud claims, however, is frequently hypothetical, not actual. For example, as

[87] *Capital Cities Cable, Inc. v. Crisp*, 467 U.S. 691, 699 (1984); *English v. Gen. Elec. Co.*, 496 U.S. 72, 78–79 (1990). For criticism of the development of federal preemption jurisprudence, see Nelson, 2000: 290–91; Garbaum, 1994: 809–10.

[88] *Medtronic, Inc. v. Lohr*, 518 U.S. 470, 485 (1996) [quoting *Cipollone v. Liggett Group*, 505 U.S. 504, 518, 523 (1992)].

Judge Friendly observed, the relationship between an award of contract damages and an approved rate is contingent on the disallowance of litigation awards by federal regulators. Regulators retain the power to adjust rates, even retroactively, to allow firms to recover prudently incurred costs. For courts to imply preemption in such contexts invites a serious overreaching preemption analysis. For instance, as Justice Stevens noted in his dissent to the Supreme Court's holding that the filed tariff doctrine barred state common law claims against long distance carriers in *AT&T*, an assessment of the connection between the allegedly illegal conduct and the relationship governed by the tariff is central to a full assessment of the preemptive effect of a tariff.[89] Such an analysis must evaluate the extent to which a regulatory structure is designed to allow specific conduct – in the case of AT&T, allegations of slamming – and whether the tariff approval and monitoring process conflict with the potential remedies provided under state law.

Applying a similar analysis, the rationales for the Ninth Circuit's inference of preemption in *Duke Energy* are shaky, if not completely wrong. In approving the California Power Exchange tariff, the FERC also approved the operation of the market subject to California law; California still had specific responsibilities to protect retail customers from abuses by suppliers, such as those who strategically manipulated California's newly deregulated market, and these responsibilities included the potential exercise of the governor's emergency order authority, as well as state contract and consumer protection laws. In addition, the sole basis for the Ninth Circuit's inference of preemption was that state regulation would cause an effect – a hypothetical reduction in Duke Energy's credit rating – conflicting with a term of an approved tariff. However, the relationship between the state regulation that was preempted by the federal tariff (Governor Davis' commandeering), and the conduct approved by the federal tariff (retention of Duke Energy's credit rating), is tenuous, at best.

Sometimes the Supreme Court has found implied obstacle preemption even in the absence of any federal regulation. Yet, when it does so, it has expressed a strong concern for uniformity in national law or policy.[90]

89 "[W]e have never before applied that harsh doctrine [the filed rate doctrine] to bar relief for tortuous conduct with little connection to, or effect upon, the relationship governed by the tariff." *AT & T, Co. v. Cent. Office Tel., Inc.*, 524 U.S., 214 233 (J. Stevens, dissenting).

90 See, e.g., *San Diego Bldg. Trades Council v. Garmon*, 359 U.S. 236, 246 (1959) (holding that even in the absence of a finding that the NLRB's determination that bargaining-related conduct was protected, state law affecting that conduct was prohibited). Expressing fear of nonuniformity, the Court states "[o]ur concern is with delimiting

With competition in formerly regulated industries, concerns with nondiscrimination in pricing are fading, so uniformity in pricing, terms, and conditions is not likely to be a useful standard for evaluating the legality of state regulation. To the extent that uniformity remains important, as Judge Friendly recognized in *Square D.*, the opportunity for plaintiffs to join as class provides a sufficient safeguard for uniformity interests in rates and tariff terms and conditions.

Assessment of the preemption issues reveals that courts often invoke filed tariffs as giving rise to implied preemption without careful analysis of the issue of dual regulatory enforcement in the regulatory environment. Many of the instances in which courts historically inferred preemption based solely on the existence of a firm-specific filed tariff simply would not survive the appropriate preemption analysis, for which establishment of an actual obstacle to state regulation is necessary.[91] When applying such analysis, courts must focus on the extent to which the agency itself considered the matter (McGreal, 1995) – an issue that courts applying the filed tariff doctrine frequently ignore. Careful federal preemption analysis provides a more complete picture of the regulatory problem and thus should be used by courts in considering the appropriateness of judicial enforcement against the backdrop of dual vertical jurisdiction problems, such as the claim by Southern California Edison that the state of California cannot cap retail prices in its state retail deregulation scheme, given a deregulated wholesale market. Federal preemption analysis also provides a more solid rationale for evaluating the rate structure in *Lynch,* which invoked a sweepingly broad filed tariff argument to invalidate application of the same retail price cap to PG&E.

B. Substituting an Assessment of Primary Jurisdiction as for Filed Tariff Determinations in Horizontal Jurisdictional Contexts

In the horizontal jurisdiction scenario (where the legal claim and regulation are both federal), since *Keogh* was decided courts have invoked the filed tariff shield to bar most antitrust claims, although they also recognize certain exceptions, particularly in the contexts of price squeeze, requests for injunctive relief, and suits by competitors seeking lost profits.

areas of conduct which must be free from state regulation if national policy is to be left [unchanged]." Id. at 246.

91 Where an agency has not evaluated conduct, a court should fail to find a preemptive effect. See *Ting v. AT&T*, 182 F. Supp. 2d 902, 937–38 (N.D. Cal. 2002) (refusing preemption defense based on filed tariff and finding contract provisions substantively unconscionable and void for public policy, in context of consumer class action).

Although more recent Ninth Circuit cases refuse to allow deregulation to threaten the application of the filed tariff doctrine, these cases are solidly preemption cases rather than cases applying the basic principles of *Keogh*. Federal courts have yet to fully assess *Keogh*'s fate against the backdrop of electric power and telecommunications deregulation.

Where federal regulators have approved all tariffs related to allegedly anticompetitive conduct, the continued rationale for allowing the filed rate doctrine to bar antitrust liability is questionable. The strongest rationale for invoking the filed rate doctrine in this context is an appreciation of deference to agency regulators. In *Norwood*, the First Circuit characterized the legal foundations of the filed rate doctrine as "extremely creaky,"[92] but when invoked as a bar to antitrust enforcement it is also incoherent. To begin, as with state contract and tort law claims, if misconduct requires modification of tariff terms this is something regulators could easily accommodate in future rate cases if necessary (Humphrey, 1985). However, as the court noted itself in *Norwood*, in the context of the tariff approval action the FERC had waived requirements that filed rates or tariffs be accompanied and justified by cost-of-service data, which would be necessary for the agency itself to evaluate the price squeeze claim.

Despite the fact that the agency lacked sufficient data to evaluate a claim of price squeeze, the court in *Norwood* concluded that "[i]t is the *filing* of the tariffs, and not any affirmative approval or scrutiny by the agency, that triggers the filed rate doctrine."[93] This is dangerously broad language. By focusing on the filing of tariffs by regulated firms – rather than established jurisdiction and actions on the part of the regulator – it privileges private behavior over public welfare. It is difficult to reconcile invocation of the filed rate doctrine in the context of price squeeze claims – as the court struggled with in *Norwood* – with other antitrust claims, in which the filed rate doctrine has not been successfully invoked as a bar to litigation. For example, mergers and sales of assets by utilities have been subject to antitrust challenge, even though the resulting rates were subject to federal regulation and the merger or sale had been approved by regulators.[94] Since *Otter Tail*, which allowed antitrust claims where an agency had some jurisdiction, the simple filing of tariffs has not precluded antitrust claims, even when regulators have partial jurisdiction over conduct. In a deregulated market, courts have a particular

[92] *Town of Norwood v. New England Power Co.*, 202 F.3d 408, 420.

[93] 202 F.3d at 419.

[94] Id. at 422 [citing *Northeast Utilities Service Co. v. FERC*, 993 F.2d 937 (1st Cir. 1993) and *California v. Federal Power Commission*, 369 U.S. 482 (1962)].

responsibility to carefully assess tariffs, to help ensure anticompetitive and otherwise illegal private conduct does not "escape scrutiny" of applicable legal standards.[95] Otherwise, as Judge Boudin (who penned *Norwood*) warned in an earlier-published article, through the repeated use of the filed tariff doctrine, the "metaphor is likely to exhaust itself" (Boudin, 1986: 404), undermining the very competitive process it is designed to protect.

It is questionable whether the filed tariff doctrine adds to the less intrusive tools available to courts in the horizontal context – a grounds for declining to consider a case. In the context of cases such as *Norwood*, in which the allegedly anticompetitive conduct is subject to federal regulation, apart from the filed tariff doctrine two extant legal doctrines assess the appropriateness of judicial intervention: (1) a doctrine of regulatory compliance, which has emerged in more recent years as a type of antitrust defense; and (2) the doctrine of primary jurisdiction, a general doctrine used by courts to refuse jurisdiction over agency claims. Although these are not antitrust immunities, in the sense of functioning as airtight and absolute defenses, they provide adequate safeguards for preserving agency discretion to evaluate claims of anticompetitive conduct (as the deference strand of the filed tariff doctrine also purports to safeguard), making the filed tariff shield in such circumstances completely unnecessary.[96]

Even if conduct is not expressly immune from the antitrust laws, good faith regulatory compliance can form a defense to a jury. In the context where a defendant is attempting to comply with regulatory policy, "something more than general intent should be required to establish a Sherman Act violation."[97] In addressing AT&T's rules for interconnecting other

[95] *Columbia Steel Casing Co. v. Portland Gen. Elec. Co.*, 111 F.3d 1427, 1446 (9th Cir. 1997).

[96] Where a plaintiff alleges violation of statutory provisions enforced by a federal agency, an emerging doctrine of telecommunications law would seem to preclude a federal court from considering the antitrust claim. See *Goldwasser v. Ameritech Corp.*, 222 F.3d 390 (7th Cir. 2000) (refusing antitrust jurisdiction where the FCC has enforcement authority under the 1996 Telecom Act). However, where a plaintiff has adequately pled an independent antitrust claim, the Supreme Court has held that the 1996 Telecommunication Act's antitrust savings clause preserves the claim, notwithstanding separate FCC interconnection regulation. See *Verizon v. Law Offices of Curtis V. Trinko, L.L.P.*, 124 S.Ct. 872 (2004) (exercising jurisdiction over essential facilities claim but rejecting the claim on its merits). For discussion of this emerging doctrine for refusing antitrust enforcement, see Picker (2002) and Weiser (2003).

[97] *City of Groton v. Conn. Light & Power Co.*, 662 F.2d 921, 931–32 (2d Cir. 1981) [quoting *City of Mishawaka v. American Electric Co.*, 616 F.2d 976, 985 (7th Cir. 1980), and arguing that because overall effect of utility's rates and practices suggested good faith behavior, utility was not acting unlawfully].

long distance carriers with its local service network, the Seventh Circuit stated,

> In the particular context of an industry subject to extensive and rapidly changing regulatory demands, we believe that an antitrust defendant is entitled both to raise and to have a jury consider its good faith adherence to regulatory obligations. . . .[98]

The Fifth Circuit concurred with this general standard for evaluating interconnection standards, elaborating:

> An ideal instruction would very briefly explain . . . that a carrier has an obligation under the Communications Act to interconnect, but may deny interconnections if it determines that the public interest is to the contrary; and that if the carrier at the time had a reasonable basis in regulatory policy to conclude, and in good faith concluded, that denial of interconnections is required by concrete, articulable concerns for the public interest, then there is no liability under the antitrust laws.[99]

The Supreme Court has yet to endorse this specific way of accommodating antitrust and regulatory law, but language in the Court's opinions is not inconsistent with it.[100] In the context of complex regulatory scenarios, in which careful evaluation of subjective intent and the objective standard for complying with the public interest is necessary, this defense holds greater promise for ensuring competitive safeguards are in place than short-hand invocation of a field tariff shield.[101]

Beyond the regulatory compliance jury defense, the doctrine of primary jurisdiction already provides a sufficient safeguard for those situations in which regulators actively monitor rates, terms, and conditions of service. Under the doctrine of primary jurisdiction, in "cases raising

[98] *MCI Communications Corp. v. AT&T Co.*, 708 F.2d 1081, 1109–1110 (7th Cir. 1983).

[99] Id. at 1138.

[100] See, e.g., *National Gerimedical Hosp. v. Blue Cross*, 452 U.S. 378, 393 n. 19 (1981) (noting, in the context of potential regulation of hospital's conduct by cooperative agencies, that on remand "the court should give attention to the particular economic context in which the alleged conspiracy and 'refusal to deal' took place"). See also *Phonetele, Inc. v. AT&T Co.*, 664 F.2d 716, 737–38 (9th Cir. 1981) (J. Kennedy) (stating that if a defendant can establish "it had a reasonable basis so that its actions were necessitated by concrete factual imperatives recognized as legitimate by the regulatory authority, then its actions did not violate the antitrust laws"); *Phonetele, Inc. v. AT&T Co.*, 889 F.2d 224 (9th Cir. 1989) (concluding that defendant's good faith was established).

[101] The defense echoes the Noerr/Pennington doctrine in antitrust law, which is not absolute but is qualified a "sham petitioning" exception. See *Professional Real Estate Investors, Inc. v. Columbia Pictures, Inc.*, 508 U.S. 49 (1993). Similarly, the proposal in this chapter urges courts to use established doctrine to recognize sham tariffing in deregulated markets.

issues of fact not within the conventional experience of judges or cases requiring the exercise of administrative discretion,"[102] a court defers to the agency on regulatory matters in order to allow the agency to consider them first. The Supreme Court has observed

> Uniformity and consistency in the regulation of business entrusted to a particular agency are secured, and the limited functions of review by the judiciary are more rationally exercised, by preliminary resort for ascertaining and interpreting the circumstances underlying legal issues to agencies that are better equipped than courts by specialization, by insight gained by experience, and by more flexible procedure.[103]

As Judge Friendly recognized, a court has the power to stay a judicial proceeding pending agency decisions in such a case, although it may also decide to dismiss a case altogether for present purposes.[104] In comparison to the filed tariff doctrine, the assessment of primary jurisdiction allows courts more discretion in its application.

Unlike the filed tariff doctrine, which bars present and future claims, primary jurisdiction does not confer complete immunity to the allegedly anticompetitive conduct; rather, in applying the doctrine, courts traditionally stay any judicial enforcement pending agency regulation. As Louis Jaffe (1964) recognized, the application of doctrine of primary jurisdiction emphasizes that referral of a matter from a court to an agency is not based solely on agency expertness but on the entire statutory scheme. Thus, its inquiry is more suited to the problem courts routinely address in asserting or declining jurisdiction in the horizontal context – whether the exercise of judicial power unduly trespasses onto agency expertise and decision-making authority.[105] In contrast to the filed tariff doctrine,

[102] *Far East Conference v. U.S.*, 342 U.S. 570, 574 (1952).

[103] Id. at 574–75. There are, of course, a host of practical issues in applying this doctrine (von Mehren, 1954).

[104] In *Nader v. Allegheny Airlines, Inc.*, 426 U.S. 290 (1976), the Supreme Court recognized that stays may be important for two distinct reasons. See Id. at 303–04. The agency may not have the statutory power to confer immunity but may still pass judgment on the matter (Id. at 303–04). Or, as *Far East* envisioned, a court may believe the agency is in a superior position to make findings of fact or judgments about reasonableness (Id. at 305–06) (noting common law misrepresentation not within special competence of the agency). See also *Gen. Elec. Co. v. M.V. Nedlloyd*, 817 F.2d 1022, 1027 (2d Cir. 1987) (finding it unnecessary for a court to yield jurisdiction when the issue to be resolved rests on general common law principles).

[105] The doctrine of primary jurisdiction can also play this role in lieu of the filed tariff shield in bankruptcy claims (Rouse, 1990). In the cases that preceded the U.S. Supreme Court's decision *Maislin*, the U.S. Court of Appeals for the Eighth Circuit invoked the doctrine of primary jurisdiction in evaluating jurisdiction over undercharge claims, but concluded

primary jurisdiction provides a sharper judicial instrument for respecting agency deference in a dual jurisdiction enforcement context. The sweep of per se immunity can be left entirely with implied antitrust immunity, which is not firm specific and, to the extent it is based on congressional intent, minimizes the opportunities for manipulation by private firms and judicial overreaching.

* * *

In relative quiet, the filed tariff doctrine reinforced the shape of twentieth-century regulatory law by keeping courts out of many regulatory disputes. The government relations bargaining approach illustrates the danger of treating its application as presumptive, especially in deregulated markets. When courts apply the doctrine, they have always been careful to avoid extension of the doctrine to cases involving competitors or cases seeking injunctions against firms when the regulator itself lacks such remedy. Courts have also created an exception for claims of price squeeze when regulators lack jurisdiction to remedy allegedly illegal conduct.

Even outside these narrow exceptions, the filed tariff doctrine presents serious problems, particularly where industries face deregulation or other regulatory transitions. With the decline of cost-of-service rate making, in which tariffs were adjudicated in hearings, unmonitored filings have become the norm and opportunities for strategic forum shopping have proliferated. In this environment, the filed tariff shield is unnecessary, given other legal doctrines that protect the original goals of the filed tariff doctrine. More important, it may prove harmful. Other legal doctrines safeguard the public interest and do not create the same risk of harm. At a minimum, courts should only invoke the filed tariff doctrine when it is consistent with the application of these other legal doctrines. Rather than exercising a presumption against judicial consideration of matters involving tariffs, as courts did under cost-of-service regulation, in a deregulatory environment courts should exercise caution before declining to consider the merits of claims of market wrongdoing.

that the ICC could best address the claims. See *Maislin Industries v. Primary Steel, Inc.*, 879 F.2d 400, 403 (8th Cir. 1989) (stating that "the doctrine of primary jurisdiction should be exercised if the issues in a proceeding 'turn on a determination of the reasonableness of a challenged practice'"); *INF, Ltd. v. Spectro Alloys Corp.*, 881 F.2d 546, 548–50 (8th Cir. 1989) (relying on Eighth Circuit's *Maislin* decision and addressing concerns in ICC policy).

7

Bargaining in Decentralized Lawmaking

When a federalist system allocates decision-making power between national and state governmental bodies, while also disfavoring federal regulation of an activity, bargaining is often relegated to the spheres of state and local politics. In the United States, the preference for state or local regulation in many industries, including electric power and telecommunications, is largely historical and may not survive the next century if true national markets emerge – and especially if Congress and federal regulators take serious actions to establish these markets. As long as state and local regulation continues to play a major role in these industries, however, firms in deregulated markets will often find themselves in situations in which there is a jurisdictional gap (i.e., no regulation of private conduct) or in which there is concurrent jurisdiction between the federal and state agencies (i.e., two or more potential regulators). Such gaps and overlaps not only present challenges (and some opportunities) for regulators, but also allow private firms many opportunities for strategic manipulation of forum in bargaining for regulation. As the filed tariff doctrine illustrates, the regulatory void presented by gaps and concurrent jurisdiction can encourage private firms to make tariff filings or to add tariff terms to the regulatory contract that suit their private interests, leading to particularly worrisome forum selection implications under the filed tariff doctrine where regulators lack jurisdiction or do not actively evaluate the content of tariffs. Ideally, Congress will establish a truly national market by detariffing electric power, as it has telecommunications. In the meantime, given the erosion of actively monitored cost-of-service tariff proceedings in deregulated markets, courts must evaluate the public interest in selection of an enforcement forum, rather than leave this decision entirely within the realm of private choice (see Chapter 6).

However, potential bargaining problems presented by gaps and concurrent jurisdiction are much broader than the enforcement issue problem presented by tariffs and other regulatory filings at the federal level. They also extend to the state and local law-making process that has dominated regulation of industries such as electric power throughout the twentieth century. For example, if a state within a federalist system has the authority to protect its local incumbents by erecting barriers to trade that refuse imports from other jurisdictions, the state also has the power to influence an industry more generally, shaping firm-specific structure, contracting, and other governance issues far beyond the state's own jurisdictional borders. As has been recognized since James Madison penned Federalist No. 10, state and local politics may lead to abuses – even protectionism – particularly given the lower costs to firms of manipulating state and local regulators. For this reason, public law doctrines delineating the appropriate allocation of powers between the national and state spheres of law making are fundamentally important for regulated industries in the United States.

Among historically regulated industries, federalism concerns play their most significant role in public law in the context of two legal doctrines: the dormant commerce clause of the U.S. Constitution, and state action immunity from antitrust enforcement. The "dormant" commerce clause, derived from the Commerce Clause of the U.S. Constitution, limits the power of a state to enact barriers to interstate commerce that are blatantly discriminatory against out-of-state businesses, or that have the effect of bringing about such discrimination. At the core of dormant commerce clause jurisprudence is a norm of barrier-free markets between the states, except in very limited circumstances, such as where a state itself is a market participant. Conceptually, the doctrine can be understood as responding to a type of incompleteness in bargaining; due to transaction costs, states might find it difficult to bargain with each other to ensure trade barriers are not harmful to overall social welfare, inviting individual state or local governmental bodies to defect from a market exchange norm by erecting barriers. An individual state's approach to monopoly regulation may impose spillover costs for other jurisdictions; by holding unconstitutional state legislation that does so, courts use the dormant commerce clause to internalize these costs and facilitate greater coordination between states. In this sense, the dormant commerce clause is frequently seen as procompetitive (and hence, antiprotectionist) in spirit – indeed, it is antiregulation to the extent it protects free market competition in the external (i.e., interstate) market.

In contrast, state action immunity from antitrust enforcement is seemingly proregulation, presenting an apparent contrast (some might even say contradiction) in goal and approach. Not traditionally regarded a "public law" doctrine, state action immunity suspends federal antitrust enforcement under the Sherman and Clayton Acts – statutes designed to enhance competition and free trade norms – where a state actively supervises the private activity. For example, price-regulated public utilities, including electric and telecommunications monopolies, have long escaped the scrutiny of antitrust enforcement for their regulated activities. For most of the twentieth century, cost-of-service rate proceedings served to police concerns with the exercise of market power. With deregulation, however, there is widespread recognition that antitrust enforcement will play an increasingly important role in reinforcing markets in deregulated industries, such as telecommunications, electric power, and natural gas (Baer, 1997; Bolze, Pierce, & Walsh, 2000; Dibadj, 2004; Eaton, 1994; Glazer & Little, 1999; Kolasky, 1999; McArthur, 1997; Piraino, 1997; Pitofsky, 1997). To the extent a deregulatory environment leads to increasingly incomplete state regulation, however, state action immunity from antitrust enforcement must be approached with extreme caution. Once widely taken for granted by firms in the electric power and telecommunications industries, state action immunity should no longer automatically bar antitrust suits in utility industries, any more than the filed tariff doctrine should serve as a shield to judicial claims. The erosion of state action immunity will greatly enhance the uncertainty that historically regulated monopolies face in deregulated markets, but courts have yet to adopt a principled approach to deciding when to suspend state action immunity for formerly regulated industries.

A principled approach to state action immunity would not accept state regulation at face value as providing for immunity from antitrust regulation. As a starting place, it must be recognized that other legal doctrines, such as the dormant commerce clause, play an important role in limiting state-assisted monopoly and the scope of state regulation. However, on the conventional understanding, the dormant commerce clause and state action immunity from antitrust enforcement seem inconsistent, even contradictory in their overall objectives. As Jim Chen observes, "on the crucial question of the proper balance between local sovereignty and global competition, American competition policy delivers two strikingly different, even antagonistic, answers" (Chen, 2003a: 1030). One doctrine (the dormant commerce clause) is designed to protect against state regulation that rises to protectionist levels and impedes external markets, whereas another legal doctrine (state action immunity) allows state regulation to trump federal competition policies. Put another way, one doctrine is explicitly oriented toward free trade, whereas another favors – and may even encourage – state-sanctioned monopoly. At their core, however, both legal doctrines deal with the permissible boundaries of monopoly, a fundamental form of organization for many regulated and deregulated firms. Unless carefully approached, these doctrines can present antagonistic policy approached for competition in deregulated industries.

A bargaining account of regulation illustrates how these two doctrines are not necessarily antagonistic in nature and, in fact, share public law roots. Both doctrines facilitate cooperation in the public governance process in order to sustain background norms of competition – the dormant commerce clause concerns itself with the external market, whereas state action immunity concerns itself primarily with the internal market. However, the doctrinal convergence is not limited to mere procompetitive policies that promote commercial exchange. A government relations bargaining approach to these two doctrines highlights their unified purpose of limiting the negative impact of interest group capture of the local regulatory process, without completely prohibiting rent-seeking behavior. At core, the fundamental goal of both doctrines is to protect a political process that facilitates regulatory bargaining by tempering the kind of self-interested interference that can degrade cooperative norms between the states, including a norm of free exchange of commerce between states. A bargaining approach advances the case for viewing the two doctrines as siblings, if not close cousins, in a family of public law doctrines that provides background norms not only for the operation of American capitalism but also for its governance. This has particularly important implications for the role of courts as they are asked to consider antitrust challenges against private firms in a deregulated environment. Particularly, it suggests that the standard of review applied by federal courts must go beyond mere deference to state and local politics in both constitutional and antitrust federalism contexts.

I. THE DORMANT COMMERCE CLAUSE, INTERSTATE BARGAINING, AND COMPETITION IN THE EXTERNAL MARKET

Although it is not an express mandate of the text of the U.S. Constitution's Commerce Clause, the dormant commerce clause doctrine limits the power of state governments to impair free trade. As Oliver Wendell Holmes once remarked,

> I do not think the United States would come to an end if we lost our power to declare an Act of Congress Void. I do think the Union would be imperiled if we could not make that declaration as to the laws of the several states. For one in my place sees how often a local policy prevails with those who are not trained to national views and how often action is taken that embodies what the Commerce Clause was meant to end.[1]

Among more recent judicial skeptics, such as Justices Scalia and Thomas, the doctrine is referred to as the "negative" commerce clause, indicating its lack of textual basis in the Constitution (Chen, 2003c).[2] Notwithstanding the lack of textual support for the doctrine in the Constitution, the dormant commerce clause has a long-standing basis in American constitutional jurisprudence. As Justice Cardozo famously remarked in striking down a New York law that set minimum prices all milk dealers were required to pay New York milk producers, the Commerce Clause prohibits a state law that burdens interstate commerce "when the avowed purpose of the [law], as well as its necessary tendency, is to suppress or mitigate the consequences of competition between the states."[3] This general principle was invoked to strike a New York regulatory scheme that had been used to deny a license to an out-of-state milk processing facility. Because the licensing provision had been enacted "solely [for] protection of local economic interests, such as supply for local consumption and limitation of competition," it was found to be unconstitutional.[4]

City of Philadephia v. New Jersey,[5] a well-known case addressing the dormant commerce clause limits on state regulation of waste disposal, illustrates the modern doctrine courts apply to further the purpose of protecting the external market. New Jersey prohibited the importation of most "solid or liquid waste" originating out of state.[6] The statute was first challenged in state court, but the New Jersey Supreme Court upheld

[1] Holmes, 1920: 295–96.

[2] Skeptics believe the purposes of the dormant commerce clause can readily be served by other more textually explicit constitutional doctrines, such as the Import-Export Clause of Article I, Section 10, or the Privileges and Immunities Clause of Article IV, Section 2. These alternatives are not without their own critics (Denning, 1999, 2003), but suffice it to say that the alternatives would make protections against interstate barriers much narrower.

[3] *Baldwin v. G.A.F. Selif, Inc.*, 294 U.S. 511, 522 (1935).

[4] *H.P. Hood & Sons, Inc. v. Du Mond,* 336 U.S. 525, 531 (1949).

[5] 437 U.S. 617 (1978).

[6] Id. at 618.

the law against a dormant commerce clause challenge, concluding that it "advanced vital health and environmental objectives."[7] New Jersey, however, failed to present any evidence that out-of-state garbage was more noxious than in-state garbage. Writing for a majority, Justice Stewart asserted that "where simple economic protectionism is effected by state legislation, a virtual per se rule of invalidity has been erected."[8] As the Court noted in *City of Philadelphia*, even if the New Jersey statute had not risen to the level of per se invalidity, it was not necessarily constitutional under the Commerce Clause. Instead, it would be evaluated under an alternative line of analysis: "Where the statute regulated evenhandedly to effectuate a legitimate public interest and its effects are only incidental, it will be upheld unless the burden imposed on such commerce is clearly excessive in relation to the putative local benefits...."[9] The Supreme Court struck down the New Jersey statute as a violation of the dormant commerce clause,[10] but did not clearly state which of these two rules – per se invalidity or balancing – it was applying.

In comparison to nonregulated industries, where norms of interstate competition have always prevailed, dormant commerce jurisprudence played little historical role in heavily regulated industries such as electric power and telecommunications. Without interstate competition and with largely jurisdiction-specific markets and barriers to entry, there is little need to protect interstate commerce. For instance, in an electric power industry dominated by cost-of-service regulated utilities, any notion of competition between suppliers is largely meaningless. Because a cost-of-service regulated firm does not compete in an open market, protecting interstate competition is of little constitutional concern. To the extent there is any competition between firms, it is largely limited to the political process of determining the applicability and scope of monopoly franchises.

However, as formerly regulated markets are deregulated, the introduction of competition changes market norms, inviting the dormant commerce clause to take on new importance. For instance, as the FERC has deregulated national wholesale interstate electric power markets, competition in the power supply market has emerged. Against this backdrop, certain regulatory actions by a state or local government are more likely to be constitutionally suspect. For instance, an individual state's moratorium

[7] Id. at 620.
[8] Id. at 624.
[9] Id. at 624, citing *Pike v. Bruce Church, Inc.*, 397 U.S. 137, 142 (1970).
[10] Id. at 627.

on the siting of interstate transmission lines or of merchant power plants that are intended to compete in wholesale electric supply markets can raise serious constitutional concerns under the dormant commerce clause. Such state initiatives, largely innocuous under a national policy that favors cost-of-service regulation, now serve as a barrier to interstate competition. In addition, as other authors have noted, state-imposed subsidies and rebates designed to encourage renewable power or environmental conservation may also pose a problem under the dormant commerce clause in a deregulated environment (Engel, 1999; Ferrey, 1997).

Since the 1980s, when deregulation began to take hold in a variety of industries, the Supreme Court has had several occasions to address dormant commerce jurisprudence. One of its cases on the topic, *General Motors v. Tracy*,[11] evaluated Ohio's differential tax burdens for in-state and out-of-state natural gas suppliers. Ohio had levied a 5 percent tax on all natural gas transactions, except those involving local distribution companies (LDCs), which serve as an intermediary between end users and natural gas suppliers. Under Ohio's natural gas tax, only in-state utilities qualify as tax-exempt LDCs, so Ohio's tax scheme effectively subjected in-state and out-of-state natural gas suppliers to different tax burdens.[12] The Court acknowledged that such a discriminatory scheme could violate the dormant commerce clause but refused to find a violation of the dormant commerce clause on the particular facts that had been raised. General Motors, which mounted a legal challenge to Ohio's differential tax, was a large enough customer to purchase its gas from the open market (rendered competitive by national regulators) rather than bundled gas from a state-regulated LDC. However, absent competition between the LDC and the open market serving General Motors, the Court reasoned, "there can be no local preference, whether by express discrimination against interstate commerce or undue burden upon it, to which the dormant Commerce Clause may apply."[13] The case illustrates how intrastate regulation, which may reject competition, poses a potential tension under the dormant commerce clause, which protects interstate competition where national regulators have made a policy decision favoring competitive markets.

Yet, other cases extend the dormant commerce clause beyond merely protecting the external (interstate) market. In *C&A Carbone, Inc. v. Town*

[11] 519 U.S. 278 (1997).
[12] Id. at 282–83.
[13] Id. at 301.

of Clarkstown, the Supreme Court invalidated a municipally imposed monopoly over nonrecyclable solid waste collected for processing and transfer.[14] To guarantee a minimum stream of revenues for the project, the Town of Clarkstown, New York, adopted a flow control ordinance, allowing the private operator of a transfer station to collect a fee of $81 per ton – in excess of the disposal cost of solid waste in the private market. C&A Carbone, Inc., processed solid waste and operated a recycling center, as it was permitted to do under the Clarkstown flow control ordinance. The flow control ordinance required companies like Carbone to bring nonrecylable waste to the locally franchised transfer station and pay a fee, while prohibiting them from shipping the waste themselves. "[A] financing measure," the flow control ordinance ensured that "the town-sponsored facility will be profitable so that the local contractor can build it and Clarkstown can buy it back at nominal cost in five years."[15] The Court reasoned that the local law violates the dormant commerce clause because "in practical effect and design" it bars out-of-state sanitary landfill operators from the participating in the local market for solid waste disposal.[16] In so reasoning, the majority drew from a 1925 case, written by Justice Brandeis, in which it was held that a statute prohibiting common carriers from using state highways over certain routes without a certificate of convenience and necessity is unconstitutional.[17]

If a municipal government itself were to create and own the facility, this would bring the monopoly within an exemption to the dormant commerce clause – known as the market-participant exemption.[18] In creating

[14] 511 U.S. 383 (1994).
[15] Id. at 393.
[16] Id. at 389, 394.
[17] *Buck v. Kuykendall*, 267 U.S. 307 (1925). Justice Brandeis wrote for the Court:

> [The statute's] primary purpose is not regulation with a view to safety or to conservation of the highways, but the prohibition of competition. It determines not the manner of use, but the persons by whom the highways may be used. It prohibits such use to some persons while permitting it to others for the very same purpose and in the same manner.

Id. at 315–16.

[18] *Reeves, Inc. v. Stake*, 447 U.S. 429 (1980); *Hughes v. Alexandria Scrap Corp.*, 426 U.S. 794 (1976). Although many have criticized this exemption to dormant commerce clause jurisprudence, it is defended as a pragmatic balance between competing federalism concerns (Coenen, 1989). The exemption is limited and is not automatically available where the state could expand into the market; to avail itself of the exemption, the state must establish that it is a market participant and may not use mere contractual privity to immunize downstream regulatory conduct in a market in which it is not a direct participant. *South-Central Timber Dev. v. Wunnicke*, 467 U.S. 82 (1984).

monopolies, however, local governments frequently work with private firms, using the advantages of the state – subsidies, below-market interest rates from nontaxable bonds, bypassing state or local restrictions on use of municipal tax powers, and so on – to assist firms and provide incentives for them to provide service. Because municipal governments often help to pay for privately operated infrastructure such as waste disposal facilities through the issuance of bonds, it is understandable that a local government may want to create a monopoly to ensure the facility maintains sufficient revenues to cover its costs and to avoid jeopardizing the government's bond rating. Such facilities are allowed to collect charges, which serve the same basic function as a tax. If the government itself were to build, own, and operate a facility, the political process would impose a general tax, but with private operations subsidized by a state or locally enforced monopoly, the tax implications of such projects are obscured. The Town of Clarkstown, New York, for example, guaranteed revenue for its solid waste transfer station – it promised a minimum of 120,000 tons of waste per year, allowing the firm to make more than $9.7 million in annual revenue – and, after a period of 5 years, the town agreed to buy it for $1.[19] One way of understanding the Court's rejection of the Clarkstown flow control ordinance is based on its concerns with impermissible government-assisted monopolies against the backdrop of interstate competition.

The basic animating principle of the more recent commerce clause cases has frequently been described as the protection against discrimination between in-state and out-of-state competitors (McGreal, 1998). If these decisions are taken at face value, the Supreme Court's dormant commerce clause jurisprudence might be said to embrace a procompetition stance, consistent with the ideology and goals of a neoclassical economics framework of federalism. In *Tracy*, for example, Justice Souter, writing for the Court, stated, "The dormant commerce clause protects markets and participants in markets, not tax payers as such."[20] He bolstered this vision of the dormant commerce clause by referencing the famous words of Justice Jackson:

> Our system, fostered by the Commerce Clause, is that every farmer and every craftsman shall be encouraged to produce by the certainty that he will have free access to every market in the Nation, that no home embargoes will withhold his exports, and no foreign state will by customs duties or regulations exclude them. Likewise, every consumer may look to the free

[19] 511 U.S. at 387.
[20] 519 U.S. at 825.

> competition from every producing area in the Nation to protect him from exploitation by any. Such was the vision if the Founders; such has been the doctrine of this Court which has given it reality.[21]

This – the neoclassical view of the dormant commerce clause – sees the role of federal courts as protecting states from interfering with the economic exchange of a free market economy (Eule, 1982; Gey, 1989–90; McGreal, 1998). The primary purpose of this view is to guard against balkanization by protecting free trade from state government interference in the external market.

It would be a mistake, however, to read the dormant commerce clause as a constitutional mandate for competition, let alone deregulation. As dormant commerce clause jurisprudence itself recognizes, there are exceptions to the dormant commerce clause where the state itself takes on the role of market participant. Further, the dormant commerce clause allows substantial state government intervention in the setting of prices, subsidies, and taxes, as long as a state does not engage in differential treatment in the same market in ways that burden interstate competition. Moreover, because the dormant commerce clause is not derived from the express language of the U.S. Constitution, Congress can override it by adopting a national policy that preempts, or overrides, the competitive market between individual states. *Tracy v. General Motors*, for example, seems to carve out a safe harbor for state regulation of natural gas distribution. Under the Commerce Clause, Congress has the express authority to establish an agency such as the ICC, giving it the jurisdiction to regulate railroad rates previously left to individual states. "Our Constitution," the late Julian Eule (1982) wrote, "did not attempt to solve economic parochialism by an express prohibition against interference with free trade. Instead, it shifted legislative power over economic matters that affect more than one state to a single national body" (430).

To take a more modern example than the now defunct ICC railroad regulation regime, Congress has created the FERC, which has made a major policy choice to implement regional competitive wholesale power markets. Congress has the power to override the FERC's decision to implement regional competitive wholesale markets, but no one has seriously proposed this. Alternatively, Congress might expand the FERC's jurisdiction, taking some or all regulatory authority over retail markets away from state regulators. If it were to do so, by occupying the law-making field, Congress might preclude states from enacting some laws that discriminate

[21] *H.P. Hood & Sons, Inc. v. Du Mond*, 336 U.S. 525, 539 (1949).

against out-of-state suppliers in deregulated wholesale markets, but again Congress has not done so. Congress' inaction, however, does not mean that preemption plays no role in this context. Congress' acquiescence in the FERC's competitive policies serves as the legal source for a type of federal preemption of individual states acting in ways that impair commerce between the states. Absent a change in federal policy, state efforts to curtail competition in wholesale electric power markets could be suspect under the dormant commerce clause, to the extent they undermine the interstate markets created by the FERC. Although a federal preemption argument for interstate market norms is based in a positive legal source of congressional or federal agency enactments that preclude contrary state laws, the dormant commerce clause also arguably finds some source in the cooperative behavior between two or more states that have adopted a competitive norm of exchange in which Congress acquiesces (Chen, 2003c).

Many have suggested that the neoclassical account of the dormant commerce clause – as a legal source of free trade policies between the states – is flawed (Eule, 1982; Gey, 1989–90; McGreal, 1998). An alternative view understands the dormant commerce clause not as inherently protecting competition itself, let alone free markets, but as protecting a political process that makes markets possible. For instance, in *West Lynn Creamery, Inc. v. Healy*, the Supreme Court struck down a Massachusetts tax and rebate scheme for milk, even when the tax operated neutrally without regard to the milk's place of origin, but where tax revenue went into a subsidy fund and were distributed solely to Massachusetts milk producers.[22] In writing for the majority, Justice Stevens embraced a political process account of the dormant commerce clause, in which its role is seen as representation enforcing in a manner similar to *Carolene Product*'s famous footnote 4.[23] As Justice Stevens remarked in striking down the tax and subsidy regime in *West Lynn Creamery*,

> Nondiscriminatory measures, like the evenhanded tax at issue here, are generally upheld, in spite of any adverse effects on interstate commerce, in part because 'the existence of major in-state interests adversely affected . . . is a powerful safeguard against legislative abuse.' However, when a nondiscriminatory tax is coupled with a subsidy to one of the groups hurt by the tax, a

[22] 512 U.S. 186 (1994).

[23] *United States v. Carolene Products*, 204 U.S. 344, 152 n. 4 (1938). John Hart Ely (1980) has applied the representation-reinforcing role of *Carolene Products* to equal protection jurisprudence.

> state's political process can no longer be relied upon to prevent legislative abuse, because one of the in-state interests which would otherwise lobby against the tax has been mollified by the subsidy.[24]

Rather than inherently protecting competition and free markets, the purposes of dormant commerce clause doctrine can be understood with the framework of Madisonian democracy as well as efficiency – specifically, limiting welfare-reducing interest group rent seeking in the state regulatory process.

This account of the dormant commerce clause nicely converges with the government relations bargaining approach to understanding regulation as negotiated but incomplete contract. The Compact Clause of the Constitution prevents states from entering into bilateral or multilateral agreements absent congressional approval.[25] Even absent formal agreement under the Compact Clause, states may informally undertake a coordinated procommerce regime. In this scenario, a single state – or powerful interest groups within a single state – may seek to appropriate rents by enacting legislation that is intended to defeat the coordinated regime (Stearns, 2003). The gaps and uncertainties created by jurisdictional overlaps between federal and state regulation not only create a need for gap-filling measures, but also simultaneously create incentives for firms to influence the state law-making process to advance their self-interest. Individual state defectors can cause a divergence between the ex ante and ex post expectations in maintaining the implicit contractual norm of market exchange between the states.

Drawing from this basic account of interstate coordination, Paul McGreal (1998) argued that the dormant commerce clause is best understood as a solution to a Prisoner's Dilemma defection, where individual states (as well as the interest groups that demand state regulation) stand to gain by defecting rather than cooperating with market exchange norms. Maxwell Stearns (2003) takes this argument a step further, presenting the coordinated norm of competition as a Nash equilibrium, in order to account for why only certain kinds of rent seeking are condemned under the dormant commerce clause. Nash equilibria are unique solutions or sets of available solutions that are stable, in the sense that thay maximize payoffs for each player given the expected strategies of other players in

[24] 512 U.S. at 200, citing *Minnesota v. Clover Leaf Creamery Co.*, 499 U.S. 456, 473 n. 17 (1981) and other cases.

[25] U.S. Constitution, Article 1, § 10, clause 3 ("No State shall, without the consent of Congress . . . enter into any Agreement or Compact with another State . . .").

the absence of formal cooperation. An individual state's effort to enact regulations, tariffs, or subsidies designed to appropriate the gains of the procommerce regime is non-Nash. As Stearns (2003) argues, a court striking state legislation under the dormant commerce clause "facilitates a benign multiple Nash equilibrium game, one that presumptively takes strategies inducing a mixed-strategy equilibrium outcome off the table, but that also effectively ratifies the choice of the early movants followed by other states" (12). The Court's dormant commerce clause jurisprudence values commonality in market norms between the states over any individual state's particular regulatory choice. "In effect the Court tells the state whose law is under review that while the states are free to choose any of two or more available Nash equilibrium outcomes, individual states are not free, after a common regime is in place, to supplant other states' pure Nash equilibrium with a mixed-strategy outcome, at least absent a sufficient demonstration that the motivation is other than to disrupt a pure Nash equilibrium strategy" (11).

In similar manner, a bargaining account of dormant commerce clause jurisprudence sees the doctrine as responding to an implicit bargaining failure in the market for interjurisdictional regulation. In a world of low bargaining costs, the optimal level of interstate regulation might be expected to rise, but in acuality interstate bargaining for regulation is costly and rarely occurs. For example, it may be costly for a net wine-producing state such as California to negotiate ex ante with a net wine-consuming state such as New York for lower regulations or taxes, and the low expected gains of such negotiation may not justify the costs of bargaining. A Coasian bargain for the optimal level of regulation can fail where there is imperfect information about preferences or the number of affected jurisdictions is large. At the same time, left to their own internal devices states may face incentives from interest groups to pass regulations or taxes that impose spillover costs on producers or consumers in other jurisdictions. By maintaining a norm that internalizes spillover costs, the dormant commerce clause might be understood as restoring the conditions that make tacit cooperation, or implicit bargains, between states more likely.

This is an important insight for regulatory law. Unlike the traditional public choice critique, which condemns all state and local rent seeking, the political process account of the dormant commerce clause targets only those rent-seeking laws that restrain commerce pursuant to implicit or explicit contracts between other states. Like the U.S. Congress, the state political process allows states to adopt rent-seeking legislation, in the form of regulation, subsidies, and taxes. However, an individual state cannot enact a law that undermines a desirable procommerce regime that has been put into place through the implicit or explicit cooperation of states, any more than it can undermine a procommerce regime adopted formally by Congress or a federal agency (under federal preemption principles under the Supremacy Clause).

As an illustration, in the context of deregulated wholesale power markets, individual states frequently face strong incentives to defect in order to protect firms in their own internal market, such as local utilities. Several states have adopted moratoria on exempt wholesale generators or have limited the siting of such plants to in-state utilities only. Florida's Supreme Court, for example, has interpreted a state power plant siting statute to limit plant siting to those suppliers who are Florida utilities or who have contracts with Florida utilities.[26] Effectively, merchant power plants are precluded from siting in Florida for purposes of entering the interstate market. Perhaps taking a cue from Florida's success in blocking the development of new wholesale power plants that do not directly serve in-state customers, other state and local governments, particularly in the southeastern United States, have imposed moratoria on merchant plants.[27]

States have also attempted to prohibit the siting of merchant interstate transmission lines necessary for reliable wholesale power supply markets. For example, Connecticut more recently extended to 2 years its moratorium on the siting of a new, expanded transmission line across Long Island Sound.[28] The state of Connecticut has strongly opposed the Cross-Sound Cable, a 23-mile merchant transmission line that would allow Long Island Power Authority to import power from New Haven, Connecticut to Brookhaven, Long Island. Connecticut officials raised environmental concerns in opposition to the project, such as impact on shellfish beds and dredging operations into the New Haven Harbor, but the project complies with all state siting and environmental statutes. Northeast Utilities, a major investor-owned utility whose customers reside primarily in

[26] *Tampa Electric Co. v. Garcia*, 767 So.2d 428, 435 (Fla. 2000) (holding that state's power plant siting statute "was not intended to authorize the determination of need for a proposed power plant output that is not fully committed to use by Florida customers who purchase electrical power at retail rates").

[27] Deisinger, 2000; *Nervous of NOx, Southern Govs. Put Plants on Hold*, Electricity Daily, Aug. 28, 2001; *State Limits on Merchant Plants a Growing Worry*, Generation Weekly, Aug. 22, 2001.

[28] *Conn. Governor Signs Moratorium on Grid Projects, Keeping Cross Sound in Limbo*, Power Markets Week, June 30, 2003, at 31.

Connecticut (and that also services customers in Massachusetts and New Hampshire), owns an older, competing transmission line that runs parallel to the Cross-Sound Cable and supports expanding that facility over the new transmission line. The Cross-Sound Cable, already built, was authorized to operate under an emergency order issued by the U.S. Secretary of Energy following the August 2003 blackout, but that order was lifted in early 2004. The issue is arguably within the jurisdiction of the FERC. However, Connecticut's Attorney General, backed by environmental interest groups and Northeast Utilities, threatened litigation if the Cross-Sound line is allowed to go live again, instead favoring expansion of the existing transmission line.[29] Expansion of transmission access to locations such as New York City would provide important capacity and may have helped in absorbing some of the transmission shortages that exacerbated the summer of 2003 blackout.[30] However, to the extent transmission remains entirely within the control of local, rather than national, regulators, states have strong incentives to protect their own incumbent firms or citizens, rather than supporting interstate cooperative market norms. Only when the FERC threatened to preempt the states and mandate operation of the Cross-Sound transmission line did Connecticut concede its position and allow the line to become operational.[31]

Indeed, some rent transfers are permissible, if not desirable, in state and local political processes. For example, rent seeking in the form of a neutral corporate tax exemption for utilities, or rent seeking in the setting of utility rates to favor industrial growth, is likely permissible and subject only to the safeguards of the local political process. However, rent seeking in the form of exclusionary regulation that limits access to the interstate market is more suspect as an approach to regulating economic matters, especially where market exchange is the background norm as a matter of national policy. Florida's Supreme Court rejected a dormant commerce clause challenge to use of the state's restrictive power plant siting statute to restrict the building of new plants by out-of-state suppliers,[32] but the inadequacy of a record establishing discrimination against

[29] Bruce W. Radford, *Cross-Sound Cable Puts Feds on the Spot*, Fortnightly's Spark, June 2004, at 1.

[30] The technical advantage to operating two transmission lines between Connecticut and Long Island, as opposed to one, is that this would allow electric power to travel in a semicircular loop – in and out of Long Island, depending on load.

[31] *New York and Connecticut Agree to End Cable Dispute*, New York Times, June 25, 2004, at B6.

[32] *Tampa Elec. Co. v. Garcia*, 767 So.2d 428, 436 (Fla. 2000).

out-of-state merchant suppliers may have impeded the development of this legal argument. At a minimum, dormant commerce clause jurisprudence would require states and localities to explain how regulatory actions and legislation restricting power supply in the wholesale market or transmission expansion might serve legitimate purposes, such as environmental or consumer protection.

More challenging is the constitutional status of state or local franchised monopolies against the backdrop of dormant commerce jurisprudence. On the political process account, the Town of Clarkstown, New York, violated the dormant commerce clause by granting a monopoly that imposed a veiled tax on users of waste disposal outside the locally sponsored facility, including out of state. Its monopoly franchise was invalidated. In *Carbone*, Justice Souter wrote a dissent, joined by Chief Justice Rehnquist and Justice Blackmun, arguing that the majority had ignored the distinction between private and public enterprise and that the flow control ordinance monopoly is easily distinguished from the "entrepreneurial favoritism" the Court has previous condemned as protectionist.[33] What distinguishes this monopoly from a constitutionally permissible monopoly, or do local and state electric, natural gas, and telecommunications monopolies risk the same fate if they do not open their service territories and network facilities to competitors? The historical lack of a background norm of competition excuses many historical monopolies from the constitutional reach of the dormant commerce clause: If there is no interstate market, a state or locally imposed monopoly cannot discriminate against out-of-state commerce. With the development of interstate markets in telecommunications and electric power, however, more difficult questions emerge. Will any state or local monopoly raise commerce clause problems? For example, is it unconstitutional for a utility to impose a surcharge on all users of distribution service, regardless of whether they purchase their power from local or out-of-state suppliers?

If a municipality, such as the Town of Clarkstown, operates a government-owned monopoly over telecommunications of electric distribution service, the market participant exception to the dormant commerce clause shields its conduct from the reach of the commerce clause. Franchised private utilities – such as investor-owned utilities – pose a

[33] 511 U.S. at 416 (J. Souter, dissenting). According to the dissent, "The Commerce Clause was not passed to save the citizens of Clarkstown from themselves" (Id. at 432). Thus, the dissent rejects extending the political process account beyond scenarios that discriminate between local and out-of-town participants.

potential problem but are not necessarily unconstitutional, even under the political process account of the dormant commerce clause. The political process account, however, warns state and local governments to approach the financing of such operations with care. In the *Carbone* case, the Town of Clarkstown promised to make up losses from operating the transfer facility at competitive rates, presumably by taking these losses out of its general revenues. What the dormant commerce clause seems to prohibit is a local government explicitly indemnifying a private monopoly out of the public fisc, even where these impose the same monopoly and fees on both in- and out-of-state providers of service. The Takings Clause does not require governments to take on such obligations, but the dormant commerce clause may prohibit them if they are the result of rent seeking that imposes burdens on the interstate market. Further, as in *Carbone*, authorizing above-market fees solely for purposes of maintaining the monopoly may be constitutionally suspect. As we move from local to state monopoly franchises, concerns with a single firm capturing the political process are weaker – a single firm that dominates municipal politics may have little power in statewide regulatory and political processes – so state franchised monopolies may be more likely to pass constitutional muster, but even neutral financing arrangements may be suspect if they favor local enterprise and have the "practical effect and design" of impeding out-of-state competitors.

II. JUDICIAL GATE KEEPING AND STATE ACTION IMMUNITY FROM ANTITRUST ENFORCEMENT

In contrast to the dormant commerce clause – an affirmative restriction on state power to act derived from the Constitution – state action immunity is a defense to enforcement of the antitrust statutes. Although antitrust law is not typically considered public law, state action immunity has deep public law roots. To the extent the state action defense provides private firms immunity from antitrust liability, it encourages the formation of state monopolies, or monopolistic conduct, where states intend to take private conduct outside the pale of antitrust enforcement. This judicially created antitrust defense originated when the Supreme Court rejected a Sherman Act challenge to a California marketing program brought by a grower because the program derived "its authority and its efficacy from the legislative command of the state."[34] Such immunity

[34] *Parker v. Brown*, 317 U.S. 341, 350 (1943).

serves the federalism purpose of facilitating participation in the state regulatory process, which lends legitimacy to the development of regulation (Inman & Rubinfeld, 1997).[35]

In applying state action immunity, the Supreme Court has adopted a two-part test to determine which state regulation is exempt from antitrust enforcement: "First, the challenged restraint must be 'one clearly articulated and affirmatively expressed as the state policy'; second, the policy must be 'actively supervised' by the state itself."[36] This test seems simple enough. Only if a state law expressly envisions monopolistic conduct and if the state actively supervises such conduct will the conduct escape antitrust enforcement. In application, though, courts have struggled in applying state action immunity, often because within a state different bodies take on the regulatory role and because the nature of regulation varies so much from industry to industry.

State action immunity's application to local governments, such as municipal bodies, as opposed to states, is one of the questions that has presented the most difficult challenges for courts. Local government law making presents an opportunity for extension of the political process insights of dormant commerce clause jurisprudence to the state action context. The Supreme Court has read state action immunity narrowly in the context of municipal (as opposed to state) regulation. *Community Communications Co. v. City of Boulder*,[37] for example, subjected municipal governments to antitrust enforcement for monopolistic conduct. Speaking for the majority, Justice Brennan distinguished between states regulating as states – entitled to the state action defense under a federalism rationale – and political subdivisions – exempt from antitrust enforcement only insofar as they are implementing state policy but not when they are acting as municipal governments only. The City of Boulder's moratorium on cable television expansion was thus subject to antitrust challenge because Colorado, at the state level, had not clearly expressed a policy

[35] State action immunity may also serve a judicial avoidance purpose, providing federal courts a way of disposing of complex and technical issues, especially in ways that have a binding impact on state law. Other legal doctrines, such as abstention (which advises federal courts to abstain from exercising jurisdiction out of comity), adequately protect the precedent-creating risk of federal court review of state regulation. Abstention can be invoked where a federal court is making a decision that has a binding effect on state law. In contrast, with antitrust litigation, courts are not normally passing judgments on the merits of state regulation but are focused on the merits of private conduct under federal law.

[36] *California Retail Liquor Dealers Ass'n v. Midcal Aluminum, Inc.*, 455 U.S. 97, 105 (1980) (citation omitted).

[37] 455 U.S. 40 (1982).

to regulate cable television; in fact, Justice Brennan believed it apparent that Colorado had no statewide policy – that there was a gap in state regulation.

This rationale for narrowing the availability of the state action defense for municipal governments is striking in its similarity to the political process account of dormant commerce jurisprudence. Like the municipally franchised monopoly in *Carbone*, which the Court believed to impair external market competition, the City of Boulder's moratorium on cable effectuates a tax on its citizens that goes too far. This impairs internal market competition, as well as possibly external competition. As such, a certain coherence, if not convergence, exists between these two independent doctrines. To the extent both doctrines respond to incompleteness in regulatory law and emphasize the incentives private firms face in bargaining in the law-making process with state and local governments, a narrow reading of state action immunity to antitrust enforcement against private firms is justified in the municipal context for the same reasons that the political process account of the dormant commerce clause makes sense.[38]

More recent cases, however, depart from the municipal–state distinction in antitrust immunity that Justice Brennan laid down in the context of cable television regulation. In *Town of Hallie v. City of Eau Claire*, the Court abandoned the clear articulation requirement in assessing municipal state action immunity.[39] Instead, Justice Powell reasoned in his majority opinion, as a long as a state confers permissive authority in general terms for a municipality to deal with a matter in the municipal government discretion, this is sufficient to exclude the conduct from antitrust enforcement. Thus, when the state of Wisconsin granted municipalities the authority to establish sewage treatment plants, this impliedly granted municipal government the power to make decisions about who would be served. Justice Powell recognized that municipalities may exercise "purely parochial public interests," which, at some level, could be subject to antitrust enforcement[40]; however, in his view, a state delegation to a

[38] Reacting to the prospect of liability created by the *Boulder* case, Congress abolished money damage liability under the antitrust laws for municipalities, their officials, and private persons acting under the direction of local governments and their officials in the Local Government Antitrust Act of 1984. See H.R. Rep. No. 965, 98th Cong., 2d Sess. 2, 18–19 (1984), reprinted in 5 U.S.C.C.A.N. 4602, 4619–20 (1984). Congress continued, however, to authorize antitrust liability for private conduct that is sanctioned or authorized by municipal governments.

[39] 471 U.S. 34 (1985).

[40] Id. at 42–43.

municipal government alone is sufficient to meet the "clearly expressed and fully articulated" criterion of the state action immunity test, thus exempting from antitrust enforcement a large range of municipal regulation.

In addition, state action immunity requires courts to determine how active and involved a regulatory scheme must be for purposes of deeming it "active supervision." In the *Hallie* case, however, the Supreme Court effectively abandoned the requirement of state supervision, at least insofar as it applies to municipalities.[41] In so holding, the Court explained purpose of the state supervision is to ensure regulatory policies are pursued for public purposes and not to enrich private actors. According to the Court, "Where a private party is engaging in the anticompetitive activity, there is a real danger that he is acting to further his own interests rather than the government interests of the state."[42] However, if a state has clearly authorized a municipality to act, the Court reasoned that there is no such problem. Instead, the "only real danger is that it will seek to further purely parochial public interests at the expense of more overriding state goals."[43] Thus, if it is clear that some clear state authorization exists, the Court held that there is no need for the state to actively supervise the municipality's regulation of the private activity.

Courts following this approach need only identify a clear legislative purpose but beyond this they engage in judicial restraint, deferring to state monopoly regulation under the antitrust laws. Although deference has its appeal in a complex regulatory environment, the Court's relaxation of a state supervision requirement for municipalities is counterintuitive. The premise that municipal regulation is not likely to be captured by private interests at the expense of the public good ignores the high risk of interest group capture at the local level, where the incentives for ex ante lobbying of the regulator are perhaps strongest. At the local level, the costs to firms of organizing and lobbying regulators are much lower than at the state level. Although the Court seems to embrace a federalism-based formalism as a rationale for deference to municipal regulation, this account of federalism proves too much. It can result in state delegation to municipal governments with no strings attached, insulating private behavior at the local level from almost all antitrust enforcement. Further, it places focus on the mere formalistic existence of state goals, without addressing their purpose. States, as well as municipal governments, sometimes

[41] 471 U.S. at 46–47.
[42] Id.
[43] Id.

regulate in ways that allow private interests to place their own economic well-being ahead of the public good. Allowing the law to insulate such private conduct from antitrust scrutiny may have serious consequences in deregulated markets.

The Court's state action immunity cases in the context of municipal regulation seem to view the clear articulation and active supervision requirements as one in the same. In a more recent case on the topic, however, the Court has made it clear that the active supervision requirement is alive and well as an independent criterion where what is at issue is the conduct of state, as opposed to municipal, regulators. In *FTC v. Ticor Title Insurance Co.*, the Court addressed the application of state action immunity to the rate-setting activities of title insurance companies in several states.[44] Most of the states regulating the title insurance defendants permitted private insurers to jointly file rates, which state officials could review or allow to remain in effect. The record of the case suggested that no significant review of the rates actually took place by these states.[45] The FTC had conceded that the state statutes authorizing the acceptance of jointly filed rates met the clear articulation requirement,[46] but the Court also found the agency's review did not constitute active supervision and thus failed the second step of *Midcal*.[47] Hence, the allegedly anticompetitive acts of the insurers could be challenged.

Because it plays a gate-keeping function for judicial antitrust enforcement, state action immunity will increasingly play an important role as formerly regulated firms are deregulated (Schwartz, 1999). Yet, frequently the gates of judicial scrutiny of the conduct of formerly regulated firms largely remain closed, allowing private conduct to escape antitrust evaluation. Despite *Ticor's* signal that active supervision is alive and well, lower courts generally continue to take a deferential approach to state action immunity. Even when what is at issue is state, not local, regulation and even when competitive markets for service are emerging, lower courts are not inclined to allow the Sherman Act to apply to private conduct in formerly regulated industries where there is some state regulatory scheme, however incomplete it is.

[44] 504 U.S. 621 (1992).

[45] Id. at 629–31. In Wisconsin, for example, no rate hearings had occurred (Id.).

[46] Id. at 631. The Third Circuit, following a previous decision of the First Circuit, held that the existence of a funded and authorized state program met the active supervision requirement. *Ticor Title Insurance Co. v. FTC*, 922 F.2d 1122, 1140 (3rd Cir. 1991), following *New England Motor Rate Bureau, Inc. v. FTC*, 908 F.2d 1064, 1071 (1st Cir. 1990).

[47] 504 U.S. at 640.

Illustrative of this deferential and narrowing approach to judicial review, courts have consistently provided for broad antitrust immunity for electric utilities, despite the introduction of competition to certain segments of the industry. For example, the Tenth Circuit extended antitrust immunity to Oklahoma Gas and Electric Company's (OG&E) conduct based on evidence that the state regulatory agency had "general supervision" authority over the utility, "including the power to fix all of OG&E's rates for electricity and to promulgate all the rules and regulations that affect OG&E's services, operation, and management."[48] The power to engage in review alone was deemed sufficient for meeting the active supervision requirement. Although the court Tenth Circuit cited a previous case that "found that the use of similar authority over an electric utility satisfied the active supervision requirement"[49] as a basis for this conclusion, it made no effort whatsoever to discern evidence of the affirmative use of such authority by the regulator with respect to the utility whose conduct was at issue.

The Eighth Circuit has taken a similarly deferential approach to state action. North Star Steel, a customer located within the exclusive service territory of MidAmerican, an electric utility in Iowa, sought to purchase competitively priced electricity and requested that MidAmerican wheel power to it. MidAmerican refused, and North Star sued, alleging that the utility violated the antitrust laws by refusing to allow access to its transmission lines. The court found that active supervision of the utility's conduct existed due to the fact that, by statute in Iowa, new customers were assigned to exclusive service providers and, in the event there was a conflict over which provider was in control of a given area, the regulator determined which provider should "occupy" the area.[50] According to the court, Iowa's legislation "affirmatively expressed" a policy of displacing competition in the market for retail electric service.[51] The court refused, however, to explore the substantive basis for the agency's regulatory determinations in defining exclusive service territories. For instance, even though the state had experimented with limited "pilot" retail wheeling

48 *Trigen-Oklahoma City Energy Corp. v. Okla. Gas & Elec. Co.*, 244 F.3d 1220, 1226 (10th Cir. 2001).

49 Id. [citing *Lease Light, Inc. v. Public Service Co. of Okla.*, 849 F.2d 1330, 1333 (10th Cir. 1988)].

50 *North Star Steel C. v. MidAmerican Energy Holdings Co.,* 184 F.3d 732 (8th Cir. 1999).

51 Given a previous ruling by the Iowa Supreme Court, the Eighth Circuit assumed for collateral estoppel purposes that "under Iowa law the exclusive service territory provisions include the generation of electricity for retail sales" (Id. at 732).

programs, the court did not evaluate whether the state agency's efforts to promote competition in power supply might coexist with maintaining exclusive service territories over transmission and distribution, effectively deferring to state regulators on these issues. In fact, the only regulatory action that was discussed by the court relates to the definition of distribution service territories, not the allocation of power supply or generation. As the Eighth Circuit observed, "less pervasive regulatory regimes have been held to satisfy the active supervision prong."[52]

One of these "less pervasive" regulatory regimes is state prohibitions on certain types of procompetitive conduct. For example, according to Florida's regulators and courts, Florida has adopted a statutory prohibition on retail electric competition, outside self-wheeling arrangements. Although Florida does not have a clear legislative statement regarding the issue, Florida's Public Service Commission (PSC) had adopted a regulation that prohibits retail wheeling to provide access to competitive power supply outside "self-wheeling" arrangements (e.g., a supplier transmitting power over the utility's lines for the supplier's own use). A Florida Supreme Court case had interpreted this regulation to preclude cogenerators from selling their power in the retail market.[53] Accepting both the regulation and the Florida Supreme Court's characterization of the regulation, the Eleventh Circuit applied state action immunity to preclude an antitrust action by a cogeneration facility against a utility that refused to wheel power at a competitive rate.[54] The court reasoned that "the doors to the PSC were open to all with standing to complain,"[55] but nowhere did the court identify how a cogenerator could directly raise such issues before the Florida PSC. Apart from challenging the agency rule authorizing the anticompetitive conduct, it is not clear that avenues for explicit consideration of the issue were available before the PSC. In fact, one way of understanding the claim raised before the Eleventh Circuit was as a collateral attack on the agency rule based on a substantive violation of federal antitrust law. The Eleventh Circuit opinion seems to suggest that the existence of an agency rule authorizing anticompetitive conduct is enough to trigger active supervision. If this holds, however, not only the actions of a state legislature can insulate private conduct from antitrust liability but a unilaterally adopted agency rule can also excuse

[52] Id. at 739.
[53] *PW Ventures, Inc. v. Nichols*, 533 So.2d 281 (Fla. 1988).
[54] *TEC Congeneration, Inc. v. Florida Power & Light Co.*, 76 F.3d 1560 (11th Cir. 1996).
[55] Id. at 1570.

private conduct from antitrust enforcement, even if this rule prohibits procompetitive conduct with little or no agency oversight.

Such a deferential approach to gate keeping in antitrust enforcement can have some serious implications for the enforcement of the antitrust laws in deregulated markets. As has been recognized, in California's deregulated electric power market, wholesale power suppliers possessing market power have been alleged to have engaged in tacit collusion to withhold supply and to thus artificially inflate their prices (Martin, 2003). The FERC may have made its own determinations that individual firms lack market power and had approved market-based tariffs. State agencies also had approved the sale of power by these suppliers through the state-sanctioned market exchange. To the extent that the behavior of these firms raises a plausible Section 1 (or even a Section 2) claim under the Sherman Act, mere existence of a state-sanctioned and -supervised market should not give rise to state action immunity. Courts need to devise a more principled way of assessing their gate-keeping function in such contexts.

III. RETHINKING JUDICIAL DEFERENCE IN THE STATE ACTION IMMUNITY CONTEXT

Since *Hallie*, the Supreme Court and lower courts have abandoned the political process informed municipal–state distinction in assessing state action immunity from antitrust enforcement. In place of this, courts serving as gate keepers for antitrust challenges to private conduct have adopted a highly deferential stance to applying state action immunity. If a state regulates an activity, courts reviewing private conduct under complex regulatory schemes are increasingly likely to imply a regulatory policy, even absent clear articulation of regulatory purpose by the state. As to the active supervision prong of the doctrine, this too is often judicially implied. Courts generally do not evaluate the degree of scrutiny provider by state or local regulators, let alone whether the purpose of this supervision overlaps with the procompetitive goals of the Sherman Act. The result is a serious lapse of judicial gate keeping in the consideration of antitrust challenges to private conduct in formerly regulated industries.

Judge Merrick Garland has been one of the strongest defenders of this deferential approach to considering the relevance of state regulation (Garland, 1987). He has argued that there is no principled basis for distinguishing between municipalities and states for federal antitrust law purposes. Put simply, his view is that state and local legislation should not be assessed by the federal courts for their efficiency effects in antitrust cases. Like advocates of deregulatory takings try to reinvigorate *Lochner* in determining government liability for regulatory transitions (see Chapter 5), this view sees relaxed state action immunity as invoking a *Lochner*-type review of regulation.

Not every scholar agrees with the deference approach to state action immunity defended by Judge Garland. Responding to *Eau Claire*, John Shepard Wiley proposes that courts directly address the efficiency, and in particular the public choice, implications of state and local legislation in deciding whether to invoke state action immunity. According to him, if anticompetitive legislation is inefficient and the result of producer interest lobbying, state action immunity should not protect it from invalidation under the Sherman Act (Wiley, 1986). In similar spirit, Matthew Spitzer (1988) argues that federal courts should invalidate state or local legislation if it is inefficient or if it transfers wealth from consumers to producers. John Cirace (1982) also argues that courts should employ an efficiency test to assess the validity of state and local legislation under the Sherman Act.

Defenders of judicial deference to state regulators argue that, in effect, reviewing state and local laws for efficiency and public choice implications is tantamount to federal courts returning to *Lochner*-like review, encroaching on the states' ability to engage in economic regulation. Judge Garland (1987), for example, favors exempting from judicial review under the Sherman Act all regulatory actions by state and local governments except for delegations of the power to restrain the market to private parties. However, if judicial review of private conduct is approached with care, a deferential stance to antitrust immunity would certainly not be necessary to limit the scope of judicial review. As Daniel Gifford (1995) argued, federal courts have the capacity to review state and local legislation without directly addressing their substantive efficiency effects. Gifford would have courts apply the same "free market" approach in the state action immunity context that they apply under the dormant commerce clause. State action immunity would protect the internal market from trade restraints, whereas the dormant commerce clause extends to the external market.

State action immunity from antitrust enforcement serves purposes similar to those the political process account of the dormant commerce clause embraces but only on rare occasions is this recognized. Some scholars explicitly make the connection between the two doctrines, recognizing state action immunity as a public law doctrine that is closely related to the dormant commerce clause (Chen, 2003a; Gifford, 1995).[56] Although they do not draw out the similarities between the two public law doctrines, Inman and Rubinfeld (1997) argue that state action immunity should only be invoked where regulation impose substantial spillover costs on out-of-state interests. State action immunity should not free all private monopolies from antitrust enforcement; instead, the defense should only be recognized for those monopolies that are actively supervised by the state for purposes of limiting the harms that flow from unregulated monopoly. State supervision is not inherently anticommerce but recognizes the necessity for regulation to correct for market failures. On this understanding, for state action immunity to make sense in its application, enforcement of procommerce norms is necessary where the federalism-based value of participation comes into conflict with efficiency, as may occur if state regulation creates spillover costs for non-participants in the relevant political process.

Here, state action immunity can explicitly acknowledge its roots by taking a lesson from its public law cousin, dormant commerce clause jurisprudence, which is also attentive to spillover costs in bargaining. Specifically, in markets with competitive background norms courts must have a relatively high doctrinal threshold for invoking a gate-keeping function, as they do in determining when state action immunity precludes antitrust enforcement. More recent cases involving utility restructuring illustrate the problem of the low threshold many lower courts currently embrace. Especially in a process of restructuring or deregulation – which gives birth to the norms of competition – private firms face strong incentives to use the regulatory process to enact partial regulatory schemes for purposes of establishing immunity from the antitrust laws. As states have begun to deregulate industries such as telecommunications and electric power, the nature of state regulation has changed. As one Department of Justice lawyer has recognized, "If a state opens its retail market to competition, then the state action doctrine would not apply to conduct that related directly to retail competion."[57] The reality is not always so simple because states frequently endorse competition in some, but not all, aspects of formerly regulated industries such as electric power and

[56] One of those rare occasions is *Parker v. Brown*, which raised both dormant commerce clause and antitrust challenges to the California raisin marketing program [317 U.S. 341 (1943)].

[57] Jospeh F. Schuler, *State Action Doctrine Losing Relevance, Department of Justice Attorney Says*, Public Utilities Fortnightly, May 15, 1999, at 70 (quoting Milton A. Marquis, attorney with U.S. Department of Justice, Antitrust Division).

telecommunications. Rather than regulating utilities through firm-specific rate and traditional certificate-of-necessity proceedings, regulators are increasingly laying down general structural rules or approving structural tariffs.

A government relations bargaining framework is not only consistent with the overall goal of protecting markets, in both the internal and external contexts, but also advises a different emphasis for state action immunity than previous efforts, such as Gifford's, to read dormant commerce jurisprudence and state action immunity in ways that are consistent with free market principles. Understanding state and local legislation as based in bargains focuses on the negotiation process of decentralized law making, rather than on unregulated markets themselves. Between states, bargaining frequently fails and may be costly to achieve, given the Compact Clause. Within a state, as in other law-making processes, private interest groups frequently face incentives to lobby law makers to secure benefits and may prefer open-ended regulatory schemes that leave details to be worked out by an agency firm by firm. The more local the law-making process, the less costly it is for such interest groups to organize and influence the process. At the local level, such capture may be not only more visible, but also more stable, given the ability to capture the political and the regulatory process. Thus, if courts focused on the quality of the political process leading to enactment of a market restraint, the municipal–state distinction in state action immunity law makes sense; it requires courts to apply more scrutiny to local, as opposed to state, regulations in restraint of trade. Instead of protecting markets per se, state action immunity, like the dormant commerce clause, can be understood as a representation-reinforcing doctrine. One main difference is that, in the Sherman Act context, Congress has already declared an overriding purpose of competition, so the primary source of the competitive norm is legislative, not necessarily based on implicit cooperation between the states.

This understanding also has implications for the approach courts should take in applying state action immunity to law making at the state level. As Frank Easterbook (1984) suggested, legal presumptions can play an important role in antitrust law, particularly when they serve as gatekeeping filters for judicial consideration of antitrust claims. If approached as a type of default rule for guiding judicial intervention, such presumptions can set incentives in the bargaining process of state law making.

First, as to the clear purpose requirement, some have argued that courts should interpret this as a type of clear statement rule designed to promote more democratic decision making at the state level. State action immunity, implied from the Sherman Act, affords immunity for purposes of promoting federalism – valued for the democratic legitimacy it affords, not because state decisions in and of themselves are sacrosanct. Clear statement rules skew decision making toward the political process (Eskridge & Frickey, 1992). If the state legislature adopts a clear statement, or expressly articulates policy to regulate in restraint of trade, courts will decline to interfere under the first prong of the *Midcal* test, but otherwise the legislature will play an important role in deciding whether courts review the action. As William Page (1981, 1987) argued in some of the leading articles on state action immunity, such a clear statement heightens the visibility of legislation, encouraging participants in the political process to acquire information about and debate policies. Absent such a statement, private conduct that is consistent with or authorized by broad delegations to municipal governments or regulatory agencies would be subject to review under the Sherman Act.

Dillon's rule, a canon that only broadly applied in states to invalidate broad state delegations to municipalities (most states have moved away from this with the growth of "home rule"), may serve the same overall goal of providing a higher level of supervision for municipal law making (Gillette, 1991). The effect of the clear articulation requirement, however, is not to create a federally enforced version of Dillon's rule. Dillon's rule invalidates delegations to municipalities absent express consideration by the state legislature; in contrast to Dillon's rule, which automatically invalidates the delegation, the clear articulation requirement would subject the delegation to scrutiny under the Sherman Act but may still allow it to stand if it does not unlawfully restrain trade or is not otherwise anticompetitive.

Yet, traditional clear statement rules have their limits as they assume a legislature itself speaks with a single purpose and voice. As Kenneth Shepsle (1992) and many others before and after him have put it, a legislature is a they, not an it. A clear statement rule is a hermeneutic effort to get at legislative intent – to pay fidelity to past preferences, which are judicially constructed as a fiction – but a legislature will rarely have a clear intent on an issue of complex economic regulation. Courts may abuse clear statement rules by using them as a backdoor way to impose a constitutional design, allowing "judicial modesty to cloak judicial activism" (Eskridge & Frickey, 1992: 646). Moreover, a clear statement rule assumes the major problem is the legislature, not the interest groups that interact with it. By contrast, a different type of interpretive canon could be a better way of conceptualizing the clear articulation requirement. Einer Elhauge (2002) argued for a "penalty default rule" in judicial interpretation of statutes: Where a court interpreting a statute is unsure of Congress' intent, the court adopts the interpretation of the statute that is most unfavorable to the interest group that is most capable of persuading Congress to reverse the interpretation. Much as penalty default rules in contract law (Ayres & Gertner, 1992), such an approach encourages a different type of private behavior in future transactions. Specifically, Elhauge envisions such an approach as influencing private behavior to procure more explicit legislative action in the future, which can increase the accountability of the political process. The clear articulation requirement might serve a similar purpose. Understood as a penalty-enhancing default rule, a clear articulation requirement would not give rise to automatic state action immunity. Instead, it would relegate legislative ambiguity to a purpose that the interest groups most likely to reverse the interpretation (i.e., those with monopoly power in an industry) would disfavor – antitrust enforcement.

A preference-eliciting default rule is only a partial solution to the problems created by regulatory incompleteness in state law making. A clear articulation of purpose is necessary and does much of the heavy lifting in state action immunity analysis, but it is not a sufficient basis for suspending judicial review of market conduct under the Sherman Act. For example, Oregon has clearly expressed a legislative policy to remove market competition by authorizing regulators to approve allocations of service territories. What matters in judicial gate keeping in the consideration of antitrust claims is not just the legislature's clarity in delegating to the regulator but also what the regulator does in exercising its discretion. Recognizing this, the Ninth Circuit properly refused to extend state action immunity to a utility's purported anticompetitive conduct in dividing Portland into exclusive service territories, given that regulators had not made firm-specific decisions to displace competition with regulation.[58] Although the utility claimed that its conduct was consistent with previous contracts and orders, agreed to under generally delegated rate-making authority, the only way the regulator could have mandated service territories was pursuant to a statute under which the regulator had not acted. According to the Ninth Circuit, mere "state authorization, approval, encouragement, or participation in restrictive private conduct confers no antitrust immunity."[59]

[58] *Columbia Steel Casing, Inc. v. Portland General Electric Co.*, 111 F.3d 1427 (9th Cir. 1997).
[59] Id. at 1440–41 [quoting *Phonetele, Inc. v. American Tel. & Tel. Co.*, 664 F.2d 716, 736 (9th Cir. 1981) (other citations omitted)].

If clear articulation alone were sufficient to provide a shield from the Sherman Act, private interests could lobby for a delegation under a clear statutory language (however broad) and then engage in conduct that would otherwise be impermissible under the Sherman Act, even where the conduct completely escapes the scrutiny of agency regulators. By encouraging firms to lobby for antitrust exclusion in state legislation, this could have forum selection effects. For example, a state restructuring plan that states that a scheme of competitive restructuring is intended to displace antitrust enforcement could alone eviscerate the competitive norms of the antitrust laws, regardless of how such a scheme organizes the industry and monitors firm behavior. Although the Sherman Act allows positive state regulation, it does not authorize state repeal of federal antitrust law through ambiguous delegations or even through plain language overrides (Page & Lopatka, 1993). Thus, to the extent the preference-eliciting default rule interpretation of state action immunity eviscerates the active scrutiny requirement, it concedes too much. This result is not required by deference or notions of federalism and may prove harmful to social welfare.

Under existing doctrine, active supervision of the conduct, as well as a clear statement of purpose, is required in order to trigger state action immunity from antitrust enforcement. Although the U.S. Supreme Court has not had the recent occasion to address this issue in the context of deregulated telecommunications and electric power markets, lower courts are alarmingly deferential to regulators in applying this prong of the *Midcal* test. Consistent with the Supreme Court's pronouncements in the context of municipal regulation, lower courts deemphasize state supervision, focusing instead on whether the legislature has delegated authority to supervise an agency. In most cases, potential supervision of conduct alone has been sufficient to trigger state action immunity from enforcement of the antitrust laws.

However, without any specific evidence of state regulation, judicial deference to regulatory power – or the mere potential of agency regulation – invites interest group manipulation of the regulatory forum for enforcement of competitive norms. For example, in the context of electric power restructuring debates at the state level, firms seeking immunity from the antitrust laws might lobby for delegation of decisions regarding competitive access to essential facilities, as well as pricing, to the regulator. Legislative delegation of this authority does not mean that the regulator has exercised it in ways that are consistent with the procompetitive goals of the Sherman Act. Allowing state action immunity to preclude antitrust enforcement in such circumstances creates strong incentives for delegation to state regulators with little or no guarantee that such authority is exercised in ways that promote federalism or social welfare, not to mention competition.

Courts thus need to depart from their current and past practice of diluting the active supervision requirement. Again, a preference-eliciting approach (Elhauge, 2002) would be useful. Rather than implying active supervision from the historical fact of delegation, a general presumption against active supervision would force litigants to present evidence of a pattern or regulatory activity and would elicit more explicit future lobbying of regulators by monopolies. Put simply, an opportunity for regulation is not the same as active supervision – although courts seem to consistently reach this conclusion. The opportunity for regulation is a first step of the active supervision analysis, but it hardly concludes it. A preference-eliciting default rule approach would also have courts assess how frequently, and under what circumstances, supervisory authority is exercised.

The Ninth Circuit has recognized as much in allowing an electric cooperative to sue a utility for refusing access to essential transmission facilities. Although the utility claimed that the state regulatory scheme clearly envisioned the utility refusing to wheel – to the extent the state had adopted a clear policy to displace competition among electric suppliers – the Ninth Circuit did not allow this to trigger immunity from antitrust liability. Under Idaho state law, the utility could decline the customer's wheeling request without the substantive review of a state agency or state courts, but the court reasoned that "[t]his is the type of private regulatory power that the active supervision prong of *Midcal* is designed to prevent."[60] Thus, the Ninth Circuit reasoned, a self-policing regulatory scheme may not require active supervision to qualify for state action immunity,[61] but where the regulator has discretion to exercise active supervision it is an appropriate inquiry for a court. Similarly, departing from its previously deferential approach, the Tenth Circuit refused to extend state action immunity to lock-up contracts between Southwestern Bell that were "neither mandated, nor authorized, nor reviewed, nor even known" about by state regulators.[62]

[60] *Snake River Valley Elec. Ass'n v. Pacificorp*, 238 F.3d 1189 (9th Cir. 2001).

[61] Id. at 1194 [citing *Liquor Corp. v. Duffy*, 479 U.S. 335, 344, n. 6 (1987) and *FTC v. Ticor Title Ins. Co.*, 504 U.S. 621, 640 (1992)].

[62] *Telecor Communications, Inc. v. Southwestern Bell Telephone Co.*, 305 F.3d 1124, 1140 (10th Cir. 2002).

Cognizant of the potential gap that a low active supervision threshold can create, some lower courts recognize that active supervision "would be satisfied if the state or state agencies held rate-making hearings on a consistent basis."[63] Such an inference is a good starting point for analysis of the application of antitrust laws in a deregulated environment and might be a sound basis for a limited presumption of state action immunity. In *Ticor*, for instance, the Supreme Court found it relevant that the Wisconsin state regulatory body had not held rate hearings prior to approving on jointly filed insurance rates.[64] Mere private contracts, however, do not meet this standard. For example, a contract provision prohibiting a customer from entering into the electricity market as a competitor in the future, offered by a utility in exchange for a discounted rate, is not protected by state action immunity.[65] Without meaningful agency review of the specific private conduct at issue, state action immunity can be abused in a deregulatory environment.

In interpreting the active supervision requirement, courts must be true to the overall federalism purposes of state action immunity. Fidelity to federalism would not only limit assessment of supervision to states, but would also include other local regulatory bodies, such as municipalities. In addition, fidelity to federalism would require some attention to the process that gives rise to regulatory supervision. If the purposes of regulatory action overlap with the overall consumer welfare goals of the Sherman Act, deference to supervision by the state or local actor is appropriate. However, if the purpose is blatantly protectionist, in ways that do not even arguably improve consumer welfare and that impose spillover costs on those in other jurisdictions who have not participated in the process leading to the adoption of regulation, intervention of the antitrust laws may be appropriate. A penalty-enhancing default rule would align private incentives to ensure more explicit procurement of state action immunity via legislation and regulatory activity.

Although the Ninth Circuit should be applauded for recognizing the importance of active supervision, a later case addressing the state antitrust immunity in the very same antitrust claim undermines the active supervision prong by allowing it to hinge on the nature of the regulatory

[63] See *Green v. People's Energy Corp.*, 2003–1 Trade Cases (CCH) ¶ 73,999 (N.D. Ill. 2003) (finding active supervision where lengthy hearings were held on gas supplier's rates on a consistent basis).

[64] 504 U.S. at 629–31.

[65] *United States v. Rochester Gas & Elec. Corp.*, 4 F. Supp. 2d 172, 176 (W.D. N.Y. 1998).

program put in place by a state legislature. Following the Ninth Circuit's recognition that there was no state action immunity, the Idaho legislature amended its Electric Supplier Stablization Act, under which the utility had previously declined a wheeling request absent agency review. The amendments allowed an electric supplier to refuse to wheel power if the requested wheeling "results in retail wheeling and/or a sham wholesale transaction," subject to review of the state regulatory agency.[66] In addition, the Idaho legislature prohibited competing suppliers from serving customers or former customers of other electric suppliers unless the competing supplier petitions the Idaho regulator and the regulator issues an order allowing the service.[67] The Ninth Circuit held that, unlike the previous statutory arrangement, which left the decision not to wheel entirely to private choice, the amended statute "has not left unregulated a private preserve without competition" and thus meets the active supervision requirement for state action immunity.[68] The Ninth Circuit emphasized that the Idaho statute precluded a private utility from wheeling without a contrary decision by the state regulator. The result of this is that statutes and regulations that prohibit competitive conduct can eviscerate any active supervision requirement. If a private firm is successful in lobbying for a statute that prohibits them from engaging in competitive conduct, they will be immune from antitrust challenge. However, a court should not take a prohibition on allowing access to a network facility at face value; instead, it should carefully evaluate the scope of the regulator's discretion to override the private choice, including the criteria the regulator is to apply in making such a decision.

Revival of the active supervision portion of judicial review in state action immunity analysis does not imply that courts should subject state and local regulation to strict scrutiny review, as advocates of deference seem to imply. Rather, to make the connection explicit, the type of judicial review called for in evaluating state action immunity is more akin to what courts provide under the political process account of the dormant commerce clause. State action immunity is less consequential than other judicial review of legislation or regulation because it does not result in condemning public conduct or necessarily striking legislation, but instead it merely subjects private conduct to review under the antitrust laws. If the type of regulation does not present veiled wealth transfers – benign rent

[66] Idaho Code § 61-322D9A.

[67] Idaho Code § 61-334B.

[68] *Snake River Valley Electric Association v. PacifiCorp.*, 357 F.3d 1042, 1049 (9th Cir. 2004).

seeking would not impair the political process – private conduct that is supervised by the regulator generally would be shielded from the scope of the Sherman Act. Rent seeking that thwarts the representative political process, however, would not be used by private firms as a strategy to escape judicial review under the antitrust standards of the Sherman Act. Such an approach preserves federalism values by protecting the type of democratic participation that forms the core of federalism. It also reduces the incentive for private interest groups to lobby state and local regulators in ways that allow state action immunity to become a strategy (much like the filed tariff doctrine) for opting out of antitrust enforcement in ways that impose spillover costs outside a state.

* * *

A government relations bargaining approach to economic regulation recognizes how public law is important for state and local regulation, especially in deregulated markets. Judicial deference to state regulation in the contexts of the dormant commerce clause and in the judicial gate-keeping function of applying state action immunity to antitrust claims can come at a high cost to competitive markets. If approached with the goal of avoiding spillover costs in bargaining, these two independent judicial doctrines hold promise to improve the lawmaking process, both between and within states.

8

Overcoming Federal–State Bargaining Failures

Although state and local regulation may hold some promise as a vertical forum for regulating industries, decentralized regulation is commonly understood to present a serious tension for competitive markets. National regulation is more likely to facilitate the development of competitive interstate markets because localities face stronger incentives than the federal government to erect barriers to trade. Especially in the context of network facilitities, which rely on interstate markets, state and local regulation may create patchwork approaches to regulatory problems. For these reasons, commentators commonly embrace national regulation as necessary to address many of the problems confronting economic regulation of network industries, such as electric power and telecommunications (Chen, 2003b; Cudahy, 2002b; Pierce, 1994).

Electric power transmission for deregulated wholesale power markets illustrates the need for a national-led approach to network regulation, such as the issue of high-voltage transmission line expansion and siting. If left to its own devices, a state or local political process is not likely to yield stable regulatory solutions for an interstate market in competitive power sales. To the extent states have the power to site transmission lines, for example, interstate markets will not always develop around congested transmission areas. Bottlenecks in power transmission will impair the development of interstate power markets and competition. Protectionist state regulatory action, discussed in Chapter 7, is one problem. State or local inaction and recalcitrant state legislatures pose an equally, if not more substantial, impediment to competitive markets in a dual jurisdiction framework. If a state refuses to develop its own regulatory solution to such a network capacity problem or if individual state regulatory approaches create a patchwork of transmission-congested areas that thwart deregulated wholesale power markets, a national solution to the problem of transmission congestion will be inevitable.[1] For this reason, leading scholars of the industry, such as Richard Pierce, see a need for amendments to the Federal Power Act (FPA) expanding the FERC's authority over electric power transmission, much as the Natural Gas Act gives the FERC authority to mandate pipeline expansion (Pierce, 1994).

Congress could readily solve the jurisdictional problem in electric power transmission by expanding the authority of federal agencies, such as the FERC,[2] to site and regulate transmission lines; however, Congress has consistently (and somewhat unbelievably) failed to act to expand and clarify the FERC's jurisdiction. Congress is not the only public institution with a capacity and willingness to approach the jurisdictional problem. Courts too play a primary role in solving the regulatory coordination problems facing deregulated industries in a dual jurisdiction framework. Conventionally, courts respond to the problem by expansively interpreting federal regulatory authority under statutes and regulations to preempt state and local regulators, even when Congress or federal regulators are ambiguous regarding their regulatory intent. For example, under the *Chevron* doctrine, which federal courts frequently invoke to defer to reasonable agency interpretations of law,[3] a federal agency's construction of its jurisdictional statutes is generally upheld. Because deference to a federal agency leads to a national uniformity, judicial

[1] Where it is each state's interest to expand a network facility, such as electric power transmission, and bargaining costs are low, coordinated solutions between states may emerge. Doctrines such as the dormant commerce clause, discussed in Chapter 7, deter unilateral state erection of trade barriers and can assist in allowing such coordination to emerge voluntarily where states themselves take the regulatory initiative. It is overly optimistic, however, to think that such solutions will always arise or that states will always be sufficient political fora to take the lead in bringing them about. In some instances, a state legislature will not take any regulatory action. For instance, by holding out – avoiding decisions about transmission expansion or limiting who can petition to raise such concerns – a state can protect its transmission infrastructure from becoming an open access superhighway for electric power supply producers or consumers in other states. Although the dormant commerce clause might help solve coordination problems where states take affirmative regulatory actions and bargaining costs are low, other public law doctrines may be needed to overcome inertia where bargaining costs are high and states do not affirmatively take regulatory action, as well as to overcome the potential problem with regulatory inaction at the federal level.

[2] As Edward Rubin and Malcolm Feeley (1994) suggested, the benefits of decentralization – touted as a goal by many federalism advocates – can readily be achieved by delegating power to a federal agency.

[3] *Chevron U.S.A., Inc. v. Natural Resources Defense Council, Inc.*, 467 U.S. 837 (1984). As the Supreme Court stated in *Chevron*, "an agency to which Congress has delegated policymaking responsibilities may, within the limits of that delegation, properly rely upon the incumbent administration's views of wise policy to inform its judgments" (Id. at 865).

deference in reviewing regulations involving federalism issues implicitly adopts a national supremacy understanding of federalism. Courts have a general preference for a federal supremacy approach to the resolution of jurisdictional battles and for uniformity in their legal resolution (Silverstein, 1991; Spence & Murray, 1999). To the extent that courts embrace a default rule in favor of federal preemption they might provide free and clear space for federal authorities to fill with regulatory content. In theory, this could allow federal law to presumptively close any regulatory gaps and resolve jurisdictional conflicts between institutions of public governance. In addition, a nationally uniform, agency-developed solution would be less likely to respond to the most powerful and extreme interest groups that are more likely to hold sway in state or local as opposed to national political processes (Chen, 2003b; Rossi, 2002).[4]

In operation, however, congressional statutes (even when interpreted by federal courts) rarely extend plenary authority to federal agencies. Federal preemption doctrine – including the broad, implied flavor of preemption routinely embraced by courts – may not be powerful enough to close all jurisdictional gaps between the federal government and states or to eliminate jurisdictional overlaps. Without some help from Congress, courts do not have the authority to use federal preemption to completely rewrite federal statutes; they are bound by the clear language of statutes, which might leave certain issues within the clear jurisdiction of states, as well as by past precedents that limit the scope of federal authority. It has been noted by scholars that decentralized governmental bodies are imperfect institutions for bringing about policy innovation (Rose-Ackerman, 1980). However, it is less acknowledged that national authorities – agencies, Congress, and courts – often face pragmatic limits as innovators, too. Given such limits in the national political process, this chapter lays out a contrarian case for state-led deregulation initiatives as a second-best solution to problems of vertical regulatory coordination in a bargaining context. Public law, I argue, can be reformulated to play a more central role in facilitiating coordination between federal regulators and the states in the realm of economic regulation.

[4] Federalism as market mechanism is perhaps most suspect in developing economies (Rodden & Rose-Ackerman, 1997). If a national government cannot guard against corruption, it is even more likely that local governmental bodies will also be corrupt. Absent mechanisms to correct for local corruption and to internalize spillover costs of local politics in regulation (e.g., dormant commerce clause jurisprudence), localism is probably not a useful means of implementing markets in network industries.

Although the federal supremacy approach promotes uniformity and predictability in competition policies – and thus is commonly seen as favoring markets[5] – where Congress or federal regulators fail to act the imperfections of a national regulatory scheme can also pose barriers to the development of competitive markets. Federal courts' efforts to define jurisdiction can work to exaggerate any gaps between state and federal regulators. Further, to the extent both federal and state regulators expect courts to interpret federal jurisdiction broadly, in bargaining situations where there is potential concurrent jurisdiction, the commons presented in jurisdictional bargaining space may cause an impasse to occur in which neither federal nor state regulators act to fill the substantive void. When courts attempt to imply federal jurisdiction expansively without requiring federal regulatory action, this unnecessarily interferes with state experimentation and may contribute to the disincentives for coordinated solutions between the states. In contrast to a judicial deference approach – which, under *Chevron* envisions expansive (but not plenary) federal regulatory authority – some basic default rules to guide judicial interpretation of statutes and regulations can facilitate a more coordinated approach between the federal government and the states. Although not perfect, in the context of economic regulation, coordinated federalism approaches to regulatory problems provide an opportunity to overcome the political inertia that arises from jurisdictional limits and ambiguity. Even absent congressional action, courts can play an important role in formulating default rules against preemption – and in favor of state and local jurisdiction to address national goals even when a state legislature is tacitly recalcitrant – as way of facilitating greater vertical coordination in regulatory policy.

I. JURISDICTIONAL FEDERALISM AND ITS LIMITS

Regulatory issues are frequently left to uncoordinated federal and state action in separate spheres of authority. These aspects of federalism are sometimes referred to as "preemptive" federalism or "dual" federalism (Weiser, 2001a: 1697). Under the predominant federalism model in public law – jurisdictional federalism – the judiciary determines the allocation of power between the federal government and the states where federal and state sources of law do not speak to the issue or are incomplete.

[5] Jim Chen (2003b), for instance, argues that there is an "irreconcilable conflict between decentralization and deregulation" (317).

However, when federal regulators speak to jurisdictional issues, they sometimes do so in vague or ambiguous terms; regularly jurisdictional issues are ignored altogether by Congress or federal agencies. Under the conventional approach, courts reviewing regulatory disputes must define the extent to which state regulation is preempted by Congress or a regulatory agency against the backdrop of ambiguity or silence. Even where federal preemption does not come into play, courts may need to define whether Congress has the power to act. Hence, under preemptive federalism, public law and courts perform a jurisdiction defining function, with a goal of reducing jurisdictional conflict by maximizing the jurisdictional independence of regulatory bodies.

Preemptive or dual federalism gives federal courts the primary role of defining jurisdiction for federal and state regulators.[6] Indeed, the power of federal courts to draw jurisdictional lines, even where Congress or federal agencies have not been clear about the scope of their jurisdiction, is a long-accepted premise of the law of economic regulation. Early on in the context of railroad regulation, for instance, in *Wabash Railway*, it was recognized that states had limited authority to regulate the intrastate aspects of interstate shipping.[7] After Congress passed the ICA, courts were forced to define the jurisdictional scope of federal regulatory power, as in the *Shreveport Rate Case*,[8] and Congress eventually expanded the ICC's power to extend to intrastate rates in the Transportation Act of 1920, creating a single national railroad system (Hovenkamp, 1991). This approach has also been applied under the Communications Act of 1934 (Weiser, 2001a), which courts interpreted to extend the jurisdictional reach of federal regulation of the telephone industry. To the extent that states are autonomous actors, separated from the federal government (Yoo, 1998), the federal judiciary is regularly called on to declare winners in jurisdictional battles, allowing the emergence of a "specialized federal common law" under such regulatory statutes (Friendly, 1964; Mishkin, 1957).

Jurisdictional federalism best describes the historical and current judicial approach to defining federal jurisdiction in electric power regulation. For instance, when the state of Rhode Island attempted to

[6] The jurisdictional source for courts exercising such authority is the Commerce Clause of the U.S. Constitution, along with the Supremacy Clause and the statutory review powers of Article III courts.

[7] See, e.g., *Wabash, St. Louis & Pac. Ry. Co. v. Illinois*, 118 U.S. 557 (1886) (holding that states do not have authority over the intrastate portion of an interstate shipment).

[8] See, e.g., *Houston, East & West Texas Ry. Co. v. United States*, 234 U.S. 342 (1914) (holding that the ICC has authority over intrastate rates that burden interstate traffic).

regulate the rates charged by a Rhode Island plant selling electricity to a Massachusetts company, which then resold electricity to the city of Attleboro, Massachusetts, the U.S. Supreme Court invalidated the regulation because it imposed a "direct burden upon interstate commerce."[9] This limitation on state regulation created the "Attleboro gap" (a gap in which neither federal nor state regulators had jurisdiction), leading Congress to adopt part II of the FPA in 1935. This statute gives federal regulators wide jurisdiction over interstate electricity transactions that are beyond the scope of state authority, but courts are still called on occasionally to define the jurisdictional space for federal and state regulators.

Jurisdictional line drawing continues to predominant discussions of federalism in electric power transmission regulation. The language of the FPA gives the FERC jurisdiction over the "transmission of electric energy in interstate commerce and . . . the sale of such energy at wholesale in interstate commerce."[10] In upholding the FERC's Order No. 888, which implemented open access for transmission in deregulated wholesale power markets, the Supreme Court held that the FPA "unquestionably supports" the FERC's assertion of jurisdiction "to regulate the unbundled transmissions of electricity retailers."[11] According to the Court, the language of the FPA limits the FERC's jurisdiction over the sale of power to the wholesale market, but authorizes the FERC's jurisdiction over most transmission pricing, without regard to whether transmission is sold to a reseller or directly to a retail customer. Effectively, the Court held that the FPA is not only limited in its scope to closing the "Attleboro gap," but also potentially extends federal jurisdiction to the regulation of aspects of transmission that had previously been subject to state jurisdiction. The Court further elaborated on the scope of the FERC's jurisdiction under the FPA by suggesting that the FERC had the authority to remedy undue discrimination in bundled retail transmissions, notwithstanding statutory language that was ambiguous and arguably precluded the assertion of such authority.[12]

When state and federal regulatory authorities compete for jurisdiction – that is, where both jurisdictional bodies attempt to assert power, as

[9] *Public Utility Commission of Rhode Island v. Attleboro Steam & Electric Co.*, 273 U.S. 83, 89 (1927).

[10] 16 U.S.C. § 824(b).

[11] *New York v. FERC*, 535 U.S. 1, 23–24 (2002).

[12] Id. at 27–28. 16 U.S.C. § 824(d) precludes the FERC from asserting jurisdiction "over facilities used for the generation of electric energy or over facilities used in local distribution. . . ."

is frequently the case under the traditional model – federal regulators will almost always win legal battles on issues of economic regulation. Federal agency regulators have the power to preempt state law (McGreal, 1995), although their victory may take time to establish when they have not settled on an approach. In this sense, the conventional jurisdiction-defining approach to regulatory federalism can produce temporary periods of instability. Eventually, however, courts will draw the jurisdictional lines and a period of stability will ensue in the jurisdictional bargaining space. For instance, in the electric power industry, once courts determined in the first two decades of the FPA's existence that the jurisdiction of federal regulators is limited to wholesale power sales,[13] a period of jurisdictional stability over the regulation of power transmission ensued for nearly 50 years. This jurisdictional balance was aided by a relatively consistent framework of price regulation at both federal and state levels, as well as a fairly tight jurisdictional match between firms and state regulators because few utilities maintained business in multiple states without organizing the firm's structure to reflect jurisdictional ordering. As firms begin to operate in multiple states in newly deregulated markets, a new period of instability will ensue, even if courts adhere to the traditional dual federalism model in which the judiciary consistently embraces an expansive interpretation of federal law.

When federal agency regulators win these jurisdictional battles – as they routinely do – to the extent federal and state jurisdiction potentially overlap traditional regulatory federalism presents a difficult problem. Sometimes vertical coordination evolves voluntarily through the political process to allow both federal and state regulators to simultaneously pursue their goals. However, overlapping jurisdiction sometimes presents difficult coordination problems. One issue that regulatory federalism generally ignores is how vertical jurisdictional overlaps, or ambiguity in jurisdictional spheres, can create a regulatory impasse. Overlapping jurisdiction may invite inaction on the part of one or both regulators, particularly where the costs of taking regulatory action – political and otherwise – are high. William Buzbee (2003) identifies one potential problem in this context as a "regulatory commons." As he describes it, "the regulator cannot take control of the social ill, cannot exclude others from similarly deciding

[13] *United States v. Public Utilities Commission of California*, 345 U.S. 295 (1953) (holding Federal Power Commission has jurisdiction over "sales for resale" in power, but federal power does not begin where local power ends, notwithstanding a more general clause of the FPA, which purports to extend federal regulation to matters not regulated by states).

to try their hand at regulating, and cannot stop others from free riding on the regulator's investment in investigating the social ill and designing a regulatory response" (28). It is well recognized that concurrent jurisdiction might lead to "overregulation" (Becker, 1983; Peltzman, 1976; Stigler, 1971) or "regulatory accretion" (Ruhl & Salzman, 2003) problems. Yet, regulatory *inaction* due to perceived jurisdictional commons poses an equally serious challenge for regulatory law in a federalist system such as the United States.

A good example is the early impasse over California's failed deregulation policies. Federal regulators blamed the state's self-imposed price cap on retail sales for placing utilities and other suppliers between a rock and a hard place, given skyrocketing wholesale power procurement costs. They were not the only ones passing blame for inaction in the regulatory commons. California regulators blamed the FERC for failing to adequately regulate prices in the wholesale power market under the FPA's "just and reasonable" mandate. Eventually, federal and state regulators settled on approaches that solved problems with California's electricity market, but the ambiguity of jurisdiction encouraged finger pointing in the media and inaction on the part of both federal and state authorities in the midst of a serious crisis in economic regulation (Rossi, 2002).

Traditional public law doctrines invite courts to play the central role of defining the authority of state and federal regulators. One approach is to use judicial power to interpret statutes and regulation to avoid jurisdictional overlaps, to the extent these can lead to conflicts or regulatory impasse. Courts are forced to make a choice between expanded federal authority or in favor of the states, but the major judicial strategy to avoid conflict is to use judicial power to draw the jurisdictional line in the proverbial sand. A cost of such an approach is to make less likely, if not to entirely preclude, regulatory coordination between state and federal regulators.

Moreover, sometimes the traditional jurisdiction-defining approach to federalism issues can produce regulatory gaps: To the extent courts err on the side of narrowing both federal and state authority (under sloppily drafted statutory language), state or federal authorities may lack the power to resolve important disputes. Regulatory overlaps, and perhaps more obviously, regulatory gaps can also contribute to regulatory inaction by both federal and state regulators. For instance, in the electric power context, under traditional siting laws state regulators frequently lack the authority to mandate the expansion of transmission capacity for reasons that would not benefit in-state (or so-called "native load") customers. Under the FPA, federal authorities also have traditionally lacked the authority to mandate firms to expand transmission capacity, even when network access to transmission would enhance wholesale power competition. As a result, a regulatory gap between the state and federal regulators exists; neither governmental body is equipped with the jurisdictional authority to directly solve the problem with transmission congestion that plagues competitive power markets. Under such circumstances, it is hardly surprising that congestion on the interstate electric power transmission network – a major contributing factor to the summer of 2003 blackouts – still exists.

Although preemptive federalism may ultimately be necessary to resolve certain disputes, absent clear congressional exercises of jurisdiction it cannot be relied on to resolve all jurisdictional disputes. Together, regulatory overlaps, which can create impasses, and regulatory gaps, which can make welfare-enhancing regulation impossible, pose a serious problem for regulatory law – particularly where there is an active tradition of state regulation of an industry. Traditional jurisdictional federalism, which implicitly assumes jurisdictional competition between federal and state regulators (but almost always favors federal regulation), is ill equipped to overcome, and may even exacerbate, the problem.

II. COORDINATED FEDERALISM AND ITS LIMITS

Since the mid-1970s, an alternative approach to federalism issues has emerged as a solution to regulatory overlaps and gaps. In contrast to the jurisdiction-defining flavor of federalism, which relegates state and federal authorities to independent jurisdictional spheres, "cooperative" federalism envisions overlap between federal and state regulators as a positive good. Generally, cooperative federalism has been defined as follows:

> Cooperative federalism programs set forth some uniform federal standards – as embodied in the statute, federal agency regulations, or both – but leave state agencies with discretion to implement the federal law, supplement it with more stringent standards, and, in some cases, receive an exemption from federal requirements. This power allows states to experiment with different approaches and tailor federal law to local conditions.[14]

Such an approach recognizes that state and federal regulators do not operate in hermetically sealed jurisdictional spheres. Rather, the overlap in their authority is "messy and chaotic" (Weiser, 2001a: 1693). Federal

[14] Weiser, 2001a: 1696 (footnotes and citations omitted).

and state regulators often must work together – that is, cooperate or at least coordinate – in implementing regulatory goals.[15]

In contrast to the predominant model, coordinated federalism sees jurisdictional overlap as a positive good. It recognizes the ultimate need for federal goals – and the ideal of interstate uniformity in approach – but also claims to draw on some of the benefits localism has to offer the regulatory process. For example, given the reduced cost to political mobilization of interest groups at the state and local level, involving states in the regulatory process may increase participation. This can have obvious payoffs for regulatory compliance, legitimacy, and efficiency. States are also more likely to experiment in a regulatory approach, trying out regulatory mechanisms that would be unlikely to be adopted without experience by Congress or federal regulators, particularly given the costly congressional decision-making process. State enforcement and state-adopted programs encourage experimentation with different approaches and allow tailoring of federal goals to local conditions (Weiser, 2001b).

Perhaps attentive to these goals, Congress has endorsed coordinated federalism in several federal statutes. For example, it was endorsed in the major environmental law statutes passed in the 1970s. Congress set forth minimum standards for environmental issues such as water pollution, but left states considerable discretion to implement the federal law. For example, under "savings clauses" states are often allowed the flexibility to adopt more stringent standards.[16] As the Second Circuit describes the role of the states under this approach,

> By the contemplation of minimum federal standards, however, Congress did not intend to relegate the states to the status of enforcement agents for the executive branch of the federal government. To the contrary, it is indisputable that Congress specifically declined to attempt a preemption of the field in the area of water pollution legislation, and as much as invited the States to enact requirements more stringent than the federal standards.[17]

In some cases, state agencies implement their own programs that exempt them from federal requirements (Markell, 2000; Percival, 1995).

15 Jim Chen (2003b) identifies cooperative federalism as the "Colorado School" of regulation, given that some of its key proponents in the telecommunications context, such as Professor Philip Weiser of the University of Colorado law faculty and Judge Stephen Williams of the U.S. Court of Appeals for the D.C. Circuit, have strong connections with, or live in, that state.

16 See, e.g., Clean Water Act, 33 U.S.C. § 1370; Comprehensive Environmental Response, Compensation and Liability Act, 42 U.S.C. § 9614(a).

17 *Mianus River Pres. Comm. v. EPA*, 541 F.2d 899, 906 (2d Cir. 1976).

The Telecom Act of 1996 also adopts a coordinated federalism solution, replacing the dual federalism model of the Telecommunications Act of 1934 with a more coordinated regulatory regime. Under the Telecom Act of 1996, the first major overhaul of federal communications statutes in more than 60 years, Congress established a "pro-competitive, deregulatory national policy framework" for the telecommunications industry.[18] Under the Telecom Act of 1996, incumbent providers of local telephone service are required to negotiate in good faith with new entrants to agree on the terms and conditions for any interconnection service between them,[19] submitting interconnection agreements to the relevant state public utilities commission (PUC) for approval.[20] If the incumbent and new entrant cannot reach agreement, a party may petition the state PUC to arbitrate any dispute[21] and, if the state PUC declines to arbitrate the dispute, the FCC steps in to resolve it.[22] If a party believes that the arbitrated settlement does not comport with the Telecom Act of 1996, a federal district court is authorized to consider appeals, even if they are arbitrated by a state PUC.[23]

This is a significant departure from the traditional process – long accepted in telecommunications and energy regulation – of appealing state PUC orders to state courts. As the Supreme Court has observed, the Telecom Act of 1996

> broadly extended [federal] law into the field of intrastate telecommunications, but in a few specified areas (ratemaking, interconnection agreements, etc.) has left the policy implications of that extension to be determined by state commissions, which – within the broad range of lawful policymaking open to administrative agencies – are beyond federal control. Such a scheme is decidedly novel, and the attendant legal questions, such as whether federal courts must defer to state agency interpretations of federal law, are novel as well.[24]

In an important trilogy of articles on the topic, Philip Weiser (1999, 2001a, 2001b) addressed the implications of cooperative federalism principles for regulatory law. Some of his effort is aimed at proposing a way for federal courts to approach the ambiguities of the Telecom Act of 1996,

[18] Senate Conference Report No. 104–230, at 1 (1996).
[19] 47 U.S.C. §§ 251(c)(1), 252(a)(1).
[20] Id. at § 252(e)(1).
[21] Id. at § 252(b).
[22] Id. at § 252(e)(5).
[23] Id. at § 252(e)(6).
[24] *AT&T v. Iowa Utilities Board*, 525 U.S. 366, 385 n. 10 (1999).

while still promoting cooperative federalism principles.[25] First, Weiser argues that the FCC ought to have implied authority to adopt remedial rules. Under *Chevron*, courts defer to federal agency construction of their statutes and regulations. Weiser (2001a) argues that a vertical *Chevron* principle should apply, allowing an agency the implied authority to adopt remedial rules. Second, and of equal importance, where the FCC fails to adopt remedial rules to enforce interconnection agreements, Weiser argues that the states should be allowed to apply their own remedies for violations of interconnection agreements. Thus, according to Weiser, federal regulators have the implied authority to adopt remedial measures, but if they fail to do so state law remedies apply.

This results in a complex architecture for federalism,[26] but one that furthers federal goals while also respecting states for their experimentation and locally tailored solutions to regulatory problems. The issue of regulatory overlap presents a common problem for regulatory law, but the brand of cooperative federalism Weiser endorses is well suited to deal with this in the context of telecommunications deregulation. For example, if neither the FCC nor states applies remedies to interconnection agreements, each relying on the other to assume the costs – to take the political heat – for imposing penalties on industry actors, an instable regulatory balance is likely to ensue. The solution proposed by Weiser implements a series of incentives that arguably make the development of a stable regulatory solution in the context of coordinated federalism more likely. If the FCC decides to adopt remedial rules, this will preempt states, and a uniform regulatory approach to enforcing interconnection agreements will reign. However, if the FCC does not adopt remedial rules, individual state remedies will be used as a default to fill in the gaps. To the extent individual state remedies impose a costly and unpredictable approach for firms or the industry as a whole, this is not necessarily the end state of affairs. Such a patchwork would create strong incentives for these firms

[25] The Telecom Act of 1996 is silent on one key question: Beyond reviewing agreements for compliance with the Telecom Act of 1996 – an interpretive task – what role, if any, do federal courts have in enforcing state-approved interconnection agreements? Do federal courts have the authority to read their own remedies into the Telecom Act of 1996 or to impose remedies under state law?

[26] One issue, for example, is that at some point cooperative federalism becomes coerced federalism. Constitutional limits on cooperative federalism solutions are implicated where federal law requires actions by certain states as may arise under commandeering and spending clause challenges to federal programs. However, where federal law does not require action by states, these challenges are less likely to pose serious problems for cooperative federalism programs.

to lobby federal regulators for a more uniform and predictable solution. Even where states do not impose remedies for interconnection agreements, state common law can be used to fill the regulatory gap, but this may produce even more uncertainty, causing interest groups to favor a federal solution even more. In this sense, the incentives created by the cooperative federalism solution to interconnection in the telecommunications context aim at overcoming inertia to create some degree of balance and stability for the industry, even though when compared with a national regulatory solution the cooperative federalism framework within which these incentives operate is complex and may present short-term uncertainties for consumers or firms in the industry.

Although Congress has not yet moved in a coordinated federalism direction in the context of electric power regulation, a similarly formulated approach to vertical jurisdiction could break the impasse that currently exists over regulation of electric power transmission in deregulated markets. Similar to the environmental statutes William Buzbee describes, jurisdiction over electric power transmission under the FPA is plagued by gaps – in which neither states nor federal bodies can regulate – and overlaps – in which an impasse frequently exists due to concurrent jurisdiction. Ensuing regulatory problems have developed, including the failure of federal or state regulators to mandate sufficient expansion of transmission capacity to accommodate deregulated wholesale power markets. A coordinated federalism approach to transmission regulation would articulate national goals, while also giving the FERC authority, where necessary, to mandate expansion of transmission and to allocate the costs of expansion to the beneficiaries. Such an approach need not preempt state power plant or transmission line siting processes. Instead, such an approach would allow the FERC, or perhaps regional regulatory authorities, the authority to step in where state and cooperative regional siting processes have failed to provide a sufficient solution to the problem of transmission siting or pricing in deregulated wholesale power supply markets (Pierce, 1994). National energy legislation that has been introduced to Congress attempts to extend the FERC's authority in these respects, but Congress has consistently failed to overcome political obstacles to its adoption.

Cooperative federalism also holds promise for the establishment of a more reliable governance regime for existing transmission infrastructure in the electric power industry. Currently, transmission reliability standards are enforced by the NERC, a voluntary organization of transmitting utilities in the electric power industry. Recently proposed energy legislation, which Congress has also failed to adopt, would have moved beyond the voluntary compliance regime, requiring the FERC to adopt NERC reliability standards (e.g., the requirement that a transmitting utility maintain a certain reserve margin in transmission) and enforce these by assessing penalties against violators. This legislation gave the NERC the power to dictate the content of reliability standards, but left the FERC little role in defining how the public interest would be served by different reliability standards.[27] In contrast, a coodinated federalism regime that allows the FERC independent discretion in evaluating such standards, as well as enforcing them, would allow for a more reliable transmission system that considers the public interest in deregulated markets than the current model, which relies almost entirely on voluntarily adopted standards and voluntary compliance to ensure transmission reliability.

A recent issue arising in deregulated electric power markets poses an even more difficult challenge for coordinated federalism solutions for economic regulation of electric power transmission. In many regions of the United States, decisions about transmission pricing and reliability are increasingly being made by regional transmission organizations (RTOs). RTOs are voluntary organizations comprised of transmitting utilities in certain regions of the country, and designed to make decisions about the expansion and operation of electric power transmission. The FERC has taken several steps to encourage the formation of RTOs, although there are considerable statutory limits on the FERC's authority to mandate participation in RTOs.

Some of the major battles brewing today in the electric power industry today are conflicts between RTOs, which generally take a pro-wholesale competition view, and state regulators, which may be more concerned with more statewide or local concerns. For instance, the state of Kentucky opposed ceding jurisdiction over American Electric Power, a Kentucky utility, to PJM Interconnection, an RTO in Pennsylvania. Kentucky state regulators determined that it is not in the public interest to allow AEP to join the RTO, but the FERC has taken a contrary view.[28] In 2003, the FERC made a determination that it can exempt utilities from state law where this poses an obstacle to a utility's voluntary participation in an RTO.[29] However, a federal district court judge agreed

[27] See Matthew L. Wald, *Few Indications Efforts to Cut Blackouts Are Under Way*, New York Times, Dec. 13, 2003, at C1.

[28] Bill Wolfe, *Kentucky Battles U.S. Over Regulating Utilities*, Courier-Journal (Louisville, Kentucky), Jan. 25, 2004, at 1E.

[29] New PJM Companies, American Electric Power Service Corp., 105 FERC ¶ 61,251 (2003).

with Kentucky's position that the FERC lacks jurisdiction over service adequacy for "native load," which the FPA leaves within the jurisdiction of state regulators.[30] Virginia has also enacted a statute that limits the ability of Virginia utilities to join an RTO without state approval.

A standard claim, made by the FERC in conflicts in Kentucky, Virginia, and other states, is that RTOs should override state regulators as a matter of public law under the implied preemption strand of the Supremacy Clause. Such a view, however, relies on an extremely broad assessment of implied preemption under both the FPA and the FERC's regulations. It is not clear that implied preemption jurisprudence would support RTO preemption of the states, but to the extent RTOs preempt state regulators, public law produces an astonishingly perverse set of incentives for large incumbent firms in the electric power industry. Large transmitting utilities would be able to bypass the state political process, in which they must participate as an interest group alongside other stakeholders, including consumer and environmental groups, in favor of a regional coordinated solution of relatively homogenous transmission-owning firms. If state and RTO law making are compared as bargaining processes, the RTO process may be quite capable of producing stable interstate solutions. These solutions, however, have an effect on the incentives of key stakeholders in the industry, encouraging them to bypass state law-making processes for a regional governance proves that excludes participation by important stakeholders with different concerns.[31] A more legitimate governance process would draw on state or federal regulatory processes, rather than end run these for regional solutions without state approval. To the extent the FERC's RTO approach attempts to do this without clearly preempting state law under the Supremacy Clause, it differs from other cooperative federalism solutions. It may also bump up against the Compact Clause of the Constitution, forcing states to participate (by opt-in of the largest incumbent utilities in a state) in interstate compacts without state consent or congressional approval.[32] Without

[30] Tina Davis, *Federal Judge: FERC Lack's Authority on Native Load Service*, The Energy Daily, Jan. 6, 2004.

[31] One set of commentators observes that RTOs attempt to mediate the conflict between the commons nature of the transmission system and the fragmented state and federal regulatory apparatus that governs it. By confusing incentives in the industry, in many states retail state regulation is left in tact – creating a "half market" in electric power (Van Doren & Taylor, 2004: 16).

[32] The Compact Clause (Art. I, Sec. 10, U.S. Constitution) requires congressional approval for "any agreement or compact" among the states. The Supreme Court held, in *United States Steel Corp. v. Multistate Tax Commission*, that the clause applies only to state

doubt, there is a serious need to protect against abuses of state regulatory process that are protectionist because state regulation is more inclined to capture than its federal counterpart; however, the dormant commerce clause could facilitate this without replacing the state political process with a privately governed regional organization of limited membership.

III. BREAKING THE IMPASSE FOR DEREGULATED INDUSTRIES

Greater self-consciousness about coordinated federalism by all public actors – Congress, agencies, and courts – is necessary to resolve the jurisdictional impasse in network industries such as electric power. Where Congress has already adopted a cooperative federalism approach, as it has in the Telecom Act of 1996, perhaps the greatest cost presented by such an approach is temporary instability. A coordinated federalism solution is admittedly messy and complex. Its primary strength is in the way it aligns incentives to facilitate bargaining in the adoption of regulatory solutions in ways that federal preemption of states (with its concomitant regulatory gaps and overlaps) does not. In addition, coordinated federalism facilitates state experimentation and locally tailored solutions (Dorf & Sabel, 1998), which may present legitimacy and regulatory commitment benefits for private stakeholders above overly broad federal solutions. Coordinated federalism can work to align interest groups toward stable solutions without abandoning federal goals or state political processes.

In industries such as electric power, however, Congress itself has failed to affirmatively adopt a coordinated vertical solution to federalism conflicts and jurisdictional overlaps. Congress and courts continue to adhere to the dual federalism model of the FPA.[33] This approach is more likely to result in regulatory commons, confusing incentives for political solutions, or regulatory gaps, making effective regulation by either state or federal authorities unlikely. Some recognition of this by courts in applying public

compacts that "encroach" upon federal supremacy [434 U.S. 452 (1978)]. Of course, the presence of such agreements without explicit congressional consent is hardly new (Frankfurter & Landis, 1925).

33 Congress did adopt a cooperative federalism approach in the Public Utilities Regulatory Policies Act of 1978 (PURPA), which used state regulations to adopt standards for alternative power generation facilities. PURPA directs the FERC to promulgate rules requiring utilities to purchase electricity from "qualifying cogeneration and small power production facilities" [16 U.S.C. § 824a-3(a)]. Although the FERC certifies such facilities, states were required to develop their own schemes for providing avoided cost rates to qualifying facilities [*FERC v. Mississippi*, 456 U.S. 742 (1982)].

law doctrines to jurisdictional disputes could help to overcome the obstacles to a more coordinated regulatory regime for electric power markets. Specifically, public law doctrines regarding federal preemption and allocation of powers within states could benefit from keeping a coordinated federalism framework in mind.

A. A Presumption Against Federal Preemption of State Economic Regulation

To begin, a fundamentally different judicial orientation in interpreting federal jurisdiction might work to overcome the political impasse presented by imperfect jurisdictional federalism in regulated industries such as electric power. Rather than implying federal authority to regulate under dual jurisdictional statutes such as the FPA (or pursuant to federal regulations), courts might play a role in helping move regulated industries in the direction of coordinated solutions by focusing the judicial role on default rules for statutory interpretation. The default rule that predominates in dual federalism – a rule favoring federal preemption – should be reversed to favor a presumption against preemption in the context of industries historically regulated at the state and local levels. If embraced by federal courts, such an approach would align incentives for political reform in the direction of more coordinated jurisdictional solutions. If presumptively authorized to regulate where Congress or federal regulatory agencies are ambiguous, states would play an integral role in the formulation of national solutions to regulatory problems, while also allowing state political processes the opportunity to formulate locally tailored regulatory and compliance solutions where Congress has failed to adopt a uniform national solution on its own.

Einer Elhauge (2002) made a compelling case for a "penalty default rule" in judicial interpretation of statutes: Where a court interpreting a statute is unsure of Congress' intent, the court adopts the interpretation of the statute that is most unfavorable to the coalition most capable of persuading Congress to reverse the interpretation. Echoing this suggestion in the context of federalism jurisprudence, Roderick Hills (2003) argues against implied federal preemption – clear statement rules in the federalism context might serve a role of facilitating the process of national solutions regulatory problems. For instance, as Justice Stevens suggested, a presumption against federal preemption may be appropriate.[34]

[34] See, e.g., *Medtronic v. Lohr*, 518 U.S. 470 (1996). See also *Geier v. American Honda Motor Company, Inc.*, 529 U.S. 861 (1990) (J. Stevens, dissenting).

Hills defends the presumption against preemption as superior to other approaches to federal preemption not because it protects states rights, advances civic republican participatory values, or is mandated by the text of the Constitution, as other writers on federalism have argued. Instead, Hills suggests that a presumption against federal preemption allows states and localities to effectively set national agendas before Congress, overcoming the obstacles to debate and participation that often plague the national regulatory process.

Hills' argument against federal preemption rejects the two dominant views of the judicial approach to federal preemption under dual federalism – one federalism promoting, the other federalism ignoring. Many writing in federalism with a state or local orientation embrace a judicial approach similar to Hills', but dominant views draw on traditional jurisdictional federalism and its dual federalism assumptions.

The federalism-promoting view is perhaps best known. As Cass Sunstein argued:

> In the system of American public law, the basic assumption is that states have authority to regulate their own citizens and territory. This assumption justifies an interpretive principle requiring a clear statement before judges will find federal preemption of state law. Although no substitute for an inquiry into the relationship between federal and state law in the particular context, this principle will frequently aid interpretation in such cases.[35]

Candice Hoke (1991) similarly argues that "federal preemption decisions impede the ability of those governmental bodies that are structured to be the most responsive to citizens' public values and ideas – state and local governments – and have concomitantly undermined citizens' rights to participate directly in governing themselves" (687). According to this view, a clear statement is valuable for purposes of enhancing state's rights or decentralized participation in state political processes as goods in and of themselves. Hills' approach, in contrast, does not rely on state's rights or on any idealization of states as favored bodies for governance but sees states as cogs in the national law-making machine.

Another dominant critique of preemption is that the Constitution requires courts to ignore states in interpreting federal law. Caleb Nelson (2000) develops the creative originalist argument that the *non obstatante* clause – a provision of the Supremacy Clause of the U.S. Constitution that refers to "any Thing in the Constitution or Laws of any State to the Contrary nothwithstanding" – requires courts to treat preemption of state

[35] Sunstein, 1989: 469.

law as analogous to the repeal of existing laws. As Hills suggests, however, Nelson's originalist interpretation of the Supremacy Clause relies on both a doctrine of enumerated powers and dual federalism. To the extent modern courts do not see the federal government's power to regulate as limited (as some more recent Commerce Clause cases would suggest) and dual federalism does not accurately describe the modern interactions between federal and state governments, Nelson's federalism-ignoring view of preemption is off base.

Adding another important layer to these arguments, Hills sees preemption as playing an entirely different role in helping Congress to set its law-making agenda. Its role is not to promote decentralization per se or to recognize the inherent supremacy of federal law but to facilitate a higher-quality national political process. Effectively, Hills would treat states as sophisticated legislative committees which could experiment with and focus reform efforts.

His argument for this approach is based on three main lawmaking failures in the federal government. For example, Hills observes that collective action problems allow narrowly focused interest groups to control even national regulatory processes, echoing what Richard Stewart (1990) referred to as "Madison's Nightmare" – a faction-ridden maze of the capture of national majoritarian political processes by interest groups. In the context of energy legislation before Congress, it is quite common for Congress to bundle together multiple unregulated reforms, producing log-rolling solutions that may confront obstacles due to one or two high-profile objectionable provisions. To illustrate, the main energy bill before Congress in 2003 contained provisions that would have more clearly expanded the FERC's authority over transmission in order to enhance reliability. This bill failed to pass primarily because of unrelated statutory provisions limiting state tort liability for the fuel oxygenate methyl tertiary butyl ether.[36]

In addition, as Hills suggests, individual representatives are frequently preoccupied with pleasing constituents – by approving earmarks and pork-loaded packages – leading Congress to neglect general policy making (Cain, Ferejohn & Fiorina, 1987). Again, energy legislation provides an example of the failures of the national political process. The 2003 energy bill contained multiple provisions on different topics aimed at local or

[36] Peter Berh & Dan Morgan, *Without Energy Legislation, Grid, Power Policy in Limbo*, Washington Post, Nov. 27, 2003, at E01; Carl Hulse, *Even With Bush's Support Wide-Ranging Legislation May Have Been Sunk With Excess*, New York Times, Nov. 26, 2003, at A17.

regional constituents, such as provisions aimed to provide federal aid for a Shreveport, Louisiana, shopping mall that houses the chain restaurant "Hooters."[37]

Further, what Samuel Beer (1977) called "political overload" plagues the ability of Congress to set the regulatory agenda because only a small number of issues can effectively occupy Congress' decision agenda (Kingdon, 1995). In the energy context, again Congress is unlikely to even consider national energy legislation unless a major national or international crisis brings it to the agenda – the mideast oil embargo (leading to passage of Carter's energy plan in 1978), the Gulf War (leading to passage of the Energy Policy Act of 1992), or post–September 11 concerns over the relationship between terrorism and oil (leading to Congress' failed energy bill in 2003). On occasion, individual members of Congress propose stand-alone bill designed to expand the FERC's authority, but these generally have little support in Congress and frequently disappear without hearing.[38]

Drawing on such decision-making failures, Hills argues that state politics can help correct for national deficiencies in congressional decision-making processes. In effect, if authorized to act, state governments might be more likely to serve as agenda setters for national governments. In addition, as Hill suggests, antipreemption rules can serve as debate-eliciting incentives in the political process. They do so by aligning pro-preemption interests to seek regulatory uniformity through the political process and by promoting public over special interest groups. For instance in the electric power context, a patchwork of state-led reforms, such as California's, can help force the national decision-making agenda in favor of bringing issues such as the FERC's jurisdiction directly onto Congress' agenda and mobilizing interest groups to support congressional action. By contrast, a serious of judicial decisions attempting to clarify federal preemption of the states might be more likely to lead to more impasses, as federal and state regulators increasingly occupy concurrent jurisdiction or reach their limits – each looking to the other to make difficult

[37] Hence, Senator John McCain dubbed the proposed legislation a bill for "Hooters and polluters." Dan Morgan, *The GOP Congress, High on the Hog*, Washington Post, Jan. 18, 2004, at B01.

[38] In 2004, Senator Hillary Clinton proposed a stand-alone reliability bill, presumably because she concluded that the larger energy bill was doomed. *See Senator Clinton to Push Reliability Bill, Urges Lawmakers to Pass It Apart from the Energy Bill*, Electric Utility Week, Jan. 20, 2004, at 3. However, because 2004 was an election year, it was unlikely that a more streamlined bill would have been passed by Congress unless it was very modest.

regulatory decisions, much as occurred in the California deregulation crisis (Rossi, 2002).

The case for a presumption against preemption in the economic regulation context has much to commend, but it needs to be extended to federal agencies and statutes. Under *Chevron*, many cases in which preemption becomes an issue involve federal regulation by administrative agencies, not statutes (McGreal, 1995). In many instances, there are regulatory overlaps between Congress and administrative agencies, such as the FCC and the FERC, that might play a dysfunctional role similar to the overlaps between Congress and the states. Some commentators use the existence of such overlaps to argue for a nondelegation doctrine (Baker & Krawiec, 2004), which most legal scholars find unworkable, if not welfare reducing (Seidenfeld, 2004). Like Congress, agencies are prone to agenda setting and other political failures. If an agency clearly acts pursuant to validly delegated authority, then no presumption against preemption should apply. However, where an agency's policies remain as ambiguous as Congress', courts should not find federal preemption. Hills' suggestion of a clear statement default rule in preemption cases could be extended to federal agencies and Congress. So understood, a presumption against preemption is not only aimed at using states to force congressional agendas, but also at forcing regulatory agendas more broadly at the national level, before the federal agencies charged by Congress with regulating economic activities.

B. Dissecting the State to Overcome Recalcitrant Legislatures

In addition to considering whether state-led regulation might have some benefits for national lawmaking process, it is also fundamental for public law to confront whether state and local political processes are exogenous to the legal framework of economic regulation. A bargaining approach should be mindful of the regulatory limits that are internal to state decisionmaking processes. It is tempting to dismiss states from any analysis of regulatory law due to these limits, but in some contexts public law may be able to overcome limits internal to states where they serve as a barrier to regulatory bargaining that would advance the more general goals of a legal system.

Those who would dismiss states from the scope of regulatory law have many insights from political science on their side. Jim Chen (2003b) forcefully critiques cooperative federalism programs for favoring power incumbents at the local level over a federal regulatory process. Chen's analysis focuses on state implementation of universal service funds under the Telecom Act of 1996. He draws on the economics of interest group decision making, which would suggest a greater likelihood of faction, if not interest group capture, at the state and local level, as opposed to in national politics, as Madison's Federalist No. 10 predicted long ago. As a solution to this decision-making pathology with state and local political processes, Chen suggests "deregulatory discipline from above" – expansion of federal agency authority by Congress or heightened judicial review of state regulatory decisions pursuant to federal preemption principles (373).

Chen's description of local interest group behavior may be sound, but if internal state political processes are included within jurisdictional bargaining space the solution of judicially expanding federal authority is idealistic and perhaps too blunt. As has been suggested, Congress and federal regulatory agencies frequently fail to clearly preempt state law, leaving the task of clarification to courts under implied preemption doctrine. Congress and agencies frequently fail to clearly preempt state law, and when courts enter into the picture they too may create regulatory commons independent of the specific goals of an area of law. Perhaps the dormant commerce clause, as described in Chapter 7, is a more narrowly tailored judicial doctrine than federal preemption jurisprudence for dealing with the problems presented by state regulations presenting spillover costs on interstate markets as a result of interest group behavior. The prospect of challenges to state decisions under the dormant commerce clause can provide a safeguard against state regulation that protects incumbents in ways that impose external costs without forgoing the incentive and agenda-setting benefits provided by a coordinated federalism solution to economic regulation issues. Rather than looking to courts to broaden federal authority in ways that may produce counterproductive impasses in regulatory enforcement, where there is state action the dormant commerce clause focuses on the real problem: state imposition of externalities on other governing bodies.

An equally complex problem is presented where a state legislature adheres to old regulatory statutes (such as those adopted with a nationally uniform cost-of-service structure in mind), failing to authorize state or local regulators to do anything to open up their network access facilities. To the extent the problem is state legislature recalcitrance (whether tacit or explicit), coordinated federalism may hold greater promise if courts could find a way to introduce greater competition in the state political process, reducing the power of any one branch or level of state or local government to be recalcitrant through inaction. As an illustration, consider the issue of a state legislature's authorization of regulatory action by state or local agencies. As Roderick Hills (1999) argued elsewhere, cooperative federalism can be facilitated by "dissecting the state" – if state and local agencies are presumptively authorized to implement federal goals, even where state enabling legislation is ambiguous as to state agency jurisdiction. When a federal program gives grant money directly to a state governor or local governments, it plays the executive branch or local governments off against the state legislature. Similarly, when Congress has passed a statute such as the FPA and a federal agency has clearly articulated general goals in implementing this statute, even if Congress has not delegated specific implementation authority to the agency it might be implied that it has given remedial implementation authority to state agencies, overriding state constitutional doctrines such as separation of powers. Presumptive preemption of structural constraints in state constitutions might function to allow a state political process to correct for some of the gaps that remain in regulatory law due to the failure of national institutional bodies – Congress, agencies, and courts – to solve these jurisdictional problems on their own.

For example, due to the inertia of many state and local statutes adopted with a cost-of-service framework in mind, in many states today economic regulation proceeds as if states operate independently of federal goals. Where a state legislature is recalcitrant in updating its laws and fails to authorize a local or statewide regulatory agency to take into account federal goals while siting transmission lines or power plants (e.g., concerns with reliability in deregulated wholesale power markets), courts could presumptively authorize such officials to act to pursue federal goals. In Florida, for instance, when state agency officials wanted to consider an application to site a merchant power plant to be built by Duke Energy with the purpose of generating power to sell in deregulated wholesale markets, an existing statute was interpreted by the Supreme Court to preclude out-of-state suppliers from filing such applications. Pursuant to the siting statute passed by the Florida Legislature prior to wholesale power deregulation, Duke Energy's application was rejected by the state Supreme Court, even though the state agency initially had accepted it under a belief that it had the legal jurisdiction to do so. An alternative approach to reviewing the agency's jurisdiction would have ignored the ambiguous jurisdictional limits in the state statute, presumptively authorizing state officials to consider the application – and to site – the facility if this were related to the pursuit of clear (albeit general) federal goals in reliable deregulated wholesale power markets. This presumption would be overcome only if the state legislature is explicit in its recalcitrance, adopting a statute that precludes consideration of the issue by state regulators.

By simultaneously embracing a presumption against federal preemption in interpretation of statutes and regulations and a presumption in favor of state or local regulatory action (i.e., authorizing state and local officials to act, notwithstanding a tacitly recalcitrant legislature), public law could better align incentives to favor national reform of statutes or regulations or, as a second best solution, state implementation of federal goals. In contrast to the current approach, a presumption against preemption would leave responsibility clearly in the hands of state actors. State and local officials would presumptively be authorized to act to pursue federal goals, although if a state legislature wants to override the authority of a state agency to implement a federal program, it would possess the authority to do so expressly. So understood, a judicially imposed set of default rules could promote coordinated federalism, even where Congress has not acted. In industries in transition, such as electric power, judicially led coordinated federalism could replace judicial line drawing between the federal government and the states – which often leads to regulatory impasse – with a more cooperative pursuit of national goals. Simultaneously, federal courts may stimulate some regulatory action to address interstate network problems states where none currently exits by introducing competition within the branches of state government. There are two primary objections to such a set of default rules: First, that federal courts lack the power to implement them and that they are internally inconsistent. Second, that this approach glorifies states' rights or idealizes states as innovators.

To address the second objection first, this is not a states' rights view of economic regulation. Indeed, there is no such thing, given that Congress has broad power to override states on most, if not all, issues of economic regulation. Even this, though, does not make states black boxes in discussion of the allocation of jurisdictional authority. States have an important role to play. The point is not, however, that states are inherently superior over the national government as innovator. Nor is it to promote decentralization as an end state of affairs. Instead, states would act as facilitators and agenda setters in national law making, helping national solutions to adapt to regulatory problems where the national law-making process fails to on its own. Judicially led coordinated federalism is a second best solution to congressional reforms of national regulatory statutes that fail to give federal agency regulators the necessary jurisdiction, but it also may prove necessary to overcome existing obstacles to regulatory reform in network industries.

The first objection – that federal courts lack the power to apply these default rules and they are internally inconsistent – also does not withstand scrutiny. These proposals are not premised on any constitutional power that that the conventional set of default rules in public law do not also rely on. The power to vest state and local officials with authority to implement federal goals can be derived from the Commerce Clause, as is the conventionally accepted judicial power to create implied preemption. Where Congress or federal regulators, within their constitutional authority, have stated a general goal, courts presumably would look to state or local regulators to implement it. This is not coercive because state political actors still would have to make the choice to regulate. If the state political process, such as a legislature, explicitly overrides this choice, state action is more likely to exist for purposes of mounting a dormant commerce clause challenge if the state approach imposes spillover costs on interstate commerce. This approach downplays the significance of "independent" state constitutions, but many states already recognize in their constitutional jurisprudence that state constitutions are not to be interpreted in isolation where a state is implementing a federal program.[39] As a matter of constitutional law, federal courts have as much power to implement such a set of default rules as they do to read implied preemption of state law into federal statures and regulations. In fact, to the extent the presumptive authorization of state executive or local agency regulation to implement federal goals is based on political process considerations, rather than a substantive legal mandate that altogether precludes state regulation, it should be less controversial than implied preemption of substantive law, under which a federal court forces a state to make a substantive policy choice that is consistent with federal law even where Congress has not clearly spoken. Rather than reading judicial power broadly by expansive

[39] See, e.g., *Ex Parte Elliott*, 973 SW.2d 737 (Tex. App. 1998); *McFaddin v. Jackson*, 738 S.W.2d 176 (Tenn. 1987); *Department of Legal Affairs v. Rogers*, 329 So.2d 257 (Fla. 1976). Thus, even where federal courts do not exercise such authority, state courts might authorize such action as the best interpretation of state constitutional separation of powers doctrine. As I argue elsewhere, implicit authorization for state executive and local agencies to act on behalf of federal goals is the best interpretation of state separation of powers – a matter of state constitutional law (Rossi, forthcoming 2005).

jurisdictional readings of federal statutes and regulations – as traditional jurisdictional federalism would envision – the default rules for preemption envision a more modest roles for the courts because they align political incentives to favor cooperative federalism approaches even where Congress has not explicitly done so. Although a presumption against preemption of substantive statutes and regulations may seem at odds with a presumption that preempts state constitution allocations of powers, these default rules are no less inconsistent than the conventional public law approach, which favors preemption of substantive law but disfavors preemption of state constitutions.

Such an approach gives state and local governments a more positive role to play in deregulated markets than judicial federalism currently envisions under public law. It creates a political process that is more likely to clarify jurisdictional responsibility, while also lowering the costs of using state government to implement federal goals. In the long run, it might also promote a more stable national solution on important issues than the conventional public law approach of relying on courts to draw the lines between incomplete federal regulation and the states.

For example, in the context of electricity transmission siting, if state and local regulatory commissions are granted presumptive authority to consider national goals in reliable wholesale power markets, states would more clearly share responsibility with Congress for transmission expansion. At least some regulators in each state would clearly possess the regulatory power to expand transmission to accommodate deregulated markets. States might also be implicitly authorized to build pricing for such transmission expansion into their own regulatory structures for retail rates. This will not solve every problem with regulation of electric power transmission, for which a national solution is necessary. Some states may choose to expand transmission, allowing deregulated markets to work, whereas others may not, creating chokehold regions that could force consideration of a more national solution to state-based transmission regulation. At the same time, responsibility for the lag would clearly sit with the either states or Congress. If states are presumptively authorized to take such goals into account, presumably a state's failure to act to site transmission in response to requests for transmission expansion could be brought within the realm of the dormant commerce clause, ultimately facilitating the emergence of more cooperative solutions between states where national regulators fail to take action. At a minimum, a recalcitrant state legislature would be required to explicitly reject that state's participation in national markets. Designing default rules for judicial review with these bargaining problems in mind will not bring an end to all jurisdictional problems in public law. Such design can, however, make explicit previously hidden institutional preferences within states for recalcitrance with national competition policies, better facilitating disruption of the jurisdictional impasses that plague the current approach to federal preemption in economic regulation.

9

Conclusion

Incomplete Regulatory Bargaining and the Lessons for Judicial Review

Most economic theory looks to the doctrines of regulatory law as a way for agency regulators to correct for problems presented by market failure. Theories of economic regulation frequently ignore that the political process, as well as the market, does not always function perfectly. Particularly with deregulation, which changes the number, type, and frequency of interactions between firms and the government, as well as between regulatory bodies and jurisdisctions, imperfect political processes will present new challenges for regulators. Regulatory law must pay attention to questions of public governance and the process for the adoption and implementation of regulation, as well as the extent to which regulation corrects for market failures.

Bargaining insights from incomplete contracts not only provide a robust theory of the firm. Within the framework of government relations bargaining, they also provide an insightful framework for students of law, economics, and political science who are concerned with questions of public governance in deregulated markets. The primary objective of the framework is not to explain history, nor is it to critique the substantive efficiency of differing regulatory arrangements. Instead, by highlighting incentives and bargaining conditions, a bargaining approach asks a different set of questions about public law and its roles than other theories of regulation. These questions are particularly important as we begin to seriously study the law and economics of a deregulatory era and, in particular, the role of judicial review in deregulated industries.

I. TOWARD A FACILITATIVE, NOT COERCIVE, ACCOUNT OF REGULATORY LAW

Predominant accounts of regulatory law see it as maintaining or restoring a preexisting equilibrium, treating the political process as largely exogenous to doctrines of regulatory law. By analogizing regulation to a contract – but one that is subject to constant renegotiation – the incomplete contracts approach to regulation provides a different focus for regulatory law than competing accounts. If the political and regulatory process are not considered exogenous to the theory of regulation, regulatory law and public law issues take on a different shape and scope than traditional understandings of regulation as contract would suggest.

In what remains one of the best treatments to date of regulatory law for the deregulatory era, Joseph Kearney and Thomas Merrill sum up the mind-set of most scholars and lawyers:

> Most legal scholars and lawyers are only dimly aware of the monumental changes that have been taking place in common carrier and public utility law in recent years. A small number have some grasp of the changes taking place in one industry. Only a handful have any sense of how the legal landscape has shifted overall. The fact that the changes that we have discussed are widely advertised as "deregulation" probably contributes to the complacent sense that public law has no on-going role to play with respect to common carrier and public utility services.[1]

Clearly, I have argued, public law has some role to play, especially as these industries are deregulated. Further, I have suggested, the approach courts take to reviewing public law disputes will be tantamount to the success or failure of deregulated markets.

Other efforts to analogize regulation to legalistic contracts (Sidak & Spulber, 1997) are backward looking in approaching the topic of public law, in general, and judicial review, in particular. First, the legalistic contract approach makes an effort to discern the regulatory contract as a deal between firms, the state, and other stakeholders. Then, if the state modifies the terms of the deal, the legalistic contract approach to regulation looks primarily to courts to enforce it. A deal is a deal, on this approach. The primary point of regulatory law is to enforce existing deals with the goal of creating incentives for firms and stakeholders to enter into new deals in the future. Especially in contexts where economies are developing, or political institutions are unstable, regulatory commitment is of primary

[1] Kearney & Merrill, 1998: 1408.

importance. In such contexts, the legalistic contract approach is perhaps most useful (Levy & Spiller, 1996).[2]

However, backward-looking interpretation and enforcement of deals by courts is not the only – and certainly not always the best – way that regulatory law can achieve stable equilibria and promote commitments. If not backward looking, what role might law play? Robert Ahdieh (2004) argued that law has a "cueing" function to play in legal transitions, particularly where markets are at issue. In contrast to other approaches to law, in which law serves primarily to sanction and coerce, Ahdieh's cueing theory sees law as focusing on a "variety of instructional, informational, and participatory mechanisms" (220). The goal is to facilitate, not dictate, effective private (and public) coordination. Such an approach sees stability and equilibrium states as important but recognizes these as focal points rather than unique solutions to regulatory problems (Schelling, 1980; Sugden, 1995). Shaping expectations is fundamental to such a project (Ahdieh, 2004).

In fact, I have argued, it is not revolutionary to see regulatory law as playing such a role. It always has coordinated expectations, often without playing a coercive role. During the era of natural monopoly regulation that predominated industries such as electric power and telecommunications for most of the twentieth century in the United States, a facilitative role better describes what courts did than the legalistic contract approach to regulation. For most of the twentieth century, courts deferred to a legislative and agency regulatory process that, I have argued, was largely self-enforcing (see Chapters 2 and 5). Outside the short-lived *Lochner* era, during which the U.S. Constitution was invoked to protecting economic property, courts were rarely even called on to interpret and enforce deals.[3] The legalistic contracts approach thus does not accurately describe the judicial role taken by U.S. courts, even at the height of the twentieth-century regulatory state.

A bargaining account does not always see courts as providing the solution to the problem of regulatory instability. Other political institutions – agencies, legislatures, and state and local governmental

[2] Levy and Spiller (1996) argue that the effectiveness of market reforms depends on a country's legislative, executive system. I do not disagree with this important insight; however, I seek to outline what an effective system of judicial review might entail in order for such market reforms to work in a developed federalist system such as the United States.

[3] Even at the height of the *Lochner* era, during the 1920s, the Supreme Court upheld most regulatory laws challenged under the Due Process clause of the Constitution (Bernstein, 2003: 4, n. 14).

bodies – can generate stable solutions against a backdrop of occasional legal change. Private stakeholders may also play this role. Radical deregulation envisions private enforcement regimes as the predominant solution to regulatory commitment problems. Although spontaneous ordering might be appropriate for some aspects of formerly regulated markets, unsupervised markets may present their own problems, such as lack of meaningful penalties for opportunistic conduct, and diverge from the broader public interest. This does not mean, however, that courts must search for and dictate that public interest. Frequently, political or regulatory institutions may be better equipped than the judiciary to determine appropriateness and degree of stability, while also taking into account the public interest. State or federal agencies, or Congress or state legislatures, may be better equipped than courts to produce and facilitate regulatory commitments. When courts provide the solution to regulatory commitment problems, their role is not necessarily one of looking backward to find and enforce regulatory bargains. Courts may also play a forward-looking role, setting up conditions and incentives for future regulatory bargaining with, and between, other private and public institutions of governance. Thus, in contrast to other theories of regulation, which see courts approximating the efficient substantive result, or interpreting and enforcing preexisting bargains, the government relations bargaining approach positions the judicial role within the political process.

The approach also has important implications for how this political and regulatory process is understood. In contrast to some public choice accounts, which condemn rent seeking to protect against capture, an incomplete contract approach recognizes that not all rent seeking is undesirable. Capture of regulatory agencies is an extreme story – one that probably does not characterize most regulated industries and one that is hard pressed to explain the movement toward deregulation (see Chapter 3). The incomplete contracts approach is neutral toward most rent seeking – recognizing that this is a necessary feature of any pluralist political theory – but also recognizes that some rent seeking may present some collective action barriers or impose spillover costs. The role of regulatory law thus is not necessarily to stop rent seeking completely but to channel it into more socially desirable regulation.

A bargaining account also parts ways with the progressive theory that regulation is designed to promote the public interest or civic virtue. Unlike the public interest theories of regulation, the incomplete contracts account provides some focus for reforms apart from progressive politics. The primary focus is not on the substance of regulation or its impact on social welfare but on the instititutional framework for its enactment and enforcement. An incomplete contracts account of regulation also provides more guidance for evaluation than appeals to the amorphous "public interest." It also does not make idealistic assumptions about private behavior but assumes that private firms will often act with their self-interest in mind – even in the public regulatory process.

Finally, a government relations bargaining framework extends efforts to displace traditional theories of the regulatory state with "collaborative governance." Collaborative governance approaches typically emphasize private contracting over public mandates in the regulatory state (Ayres & Braithwaite, 1992; Freeman, 1997). For instance, Jody Freeman's (1997, 2000) influential theory of collaborative governance looks to contractual mechanisms, not just as a tool for privatization, but as a way to infuse public governance ideals into private regulatory interactions. The overarching goal of collaborative governance is to simultaneously enhance flexibility and legitimacy by providing additional or new access points for private participation in the regulatory process. At the same time, on this approach private decisions would be informed by public purposes and goals.

Contractual concepts are central to the collaborative governance project. The government relations bargaining approach, which draws on incomplete contracts, is also compatible with this approach. However, government relations bargaining does not limit the contractual analogy to bargains between private and public entities (e.g., between a firm and the state). Discussion of public law must include bargains between governmental bodies, as well as bargains between government bodies and private stakeholders. The government relations bargaining approach thus extends the collaborative governance project to address the unique structural roles of institutions such as legislatures, agencies, and courts in the bargaining process. In addition, the approach has more to say about the role of courts than collaborative governance accounts, which generally favor deference to government decisions to deregulate or privatize.

II. IMPLICATIONS OF THE BARGAINING PERSPECTIVE FOR JUDICIAL REVIEW

Throughout this book, a government relations bargaining account of economic regulation, informed by incomplete contracts insights, has been presented and applied to a series of public law problems in deregulated electric power markets. A few final observations about the implications of a government relations bargaining framework can illustrate the relevance of the inquiry for regulatory law, as well as for economics and political science.

First, the renegotiation-neutral approach of the framework casts light on a different set of issues for public law than other theories of regulation typically emphasize. Any effort to articulate ex ante rules for a regulatory system must strike the balance between optimal certainty in the form of specificity and flexibility. Certainty is not the main objective of regulatory law. Similarly, the overarching goal of regulatory law is not completeness. Regulatory law serves to mediate between the two extremes of specificity and flexibility, taking into account the effects on private behavior each extreme might have in the making and implementation of law. More than many competing accounts, the government relations bargaining approach envisions flexibility and experimentation in the development of regulation as well as in deregulated markets.

Second, a bargaining account does not just recognize that incompleteness exists. Instead, like accounts of incomplete contracts in private law (Ayres & Gertner, 1992), it asks *why* incompleteness exists. To the extent incompleteness is the product of strategic private behavior, public law can play a role in limiting this kind of incompleteness where it has adverse implications for social welfare. Incompleteness may exist by no fault of the parties, due to asymmetry of information or unknowable exogenous changes. Even so, regulatory law might play a role in correcting for such asymmetry or uncertainties in the future in order to facilitate higher-quality bargaining. The government relations bargaining framework approaches public law questions with this role in mind – not to produce completeness as an inherent good, but to minimize strategic abuses of incomplete regulatory law.

Third, to the extent the bargaining conditions contributing to incompleteness come into play, a government relations bargaining approach opens regulatory law to a broadly informed institutional analysis. The focus thus is not primarily on courts. Nor is it on regulatory agencies. It also includes within its scope legislatures and state regulators, rather than national regulators. Each institution has an important role to play in deregulated markets. In contrast to natural monopoly regulation, which focused almost exclusively on state agency regulators, this greatly increases the chances of political failures in governing deregulated markets.

Fourth, as the applications in the book should suggest, the recommendations for institutions are practically focused on existing public law doctrine and, in particular, on the role of courts. The incomplete contracts approach does not see courts as passive partners to a type of regulatory "deal," merely enforcing an independent bargain between the state and powerful firms. For instance, one of the major implications of the framework presented in this book is that it recognizes the limitations of judicial review, as is apparent from analysis of judicial review of takings (see Chapter 5). In contrast to other contractual accounts of regulation, such as those embraced by advocates of deregulatory takings (Sidak & Spulber, 1997; Spulber & Yoo, 2003), an incomplete contracts approach is judicially conservative, advising judicial humility over activism. However, an incomplete contracts approach does not relegate courts a role as passive referees, blindly deferring to other public governance bodies. Courts have a positive role to play in deregulated markets. The success or failure of deregulation may depend on how courts set the tone for bargaining in the regulatory process. As in other bargaining contexts, default rules – rather than substantive review of regulation – provide the best opportunity to enhance the legitimacy of judicial review.

The government relations bargaining framework suggest a much more modest, yet forward-looking, approach to judicial review than the legalistic contracts approach to regulatory law. In many instances, judicial deference to legislators and regulators is appropriate. For instance, judicial deference to governmental decisions to deregulate where private firms seek redress in the form of compensation (see Chapter 5) avoids creating incentives for overinvestment in the current regulatory regime and may also have political process benefits. Often, such deference will be appropriate during regulatory transitions. However, the incomplete contracts perspective also illustrates how, in other instances, including many regulatory transitions, judicial deference to private and public governance decisions is not appropriate. For example, where private behavior influences the regulatory forum, as may be the case with the filed tariff doctrine (see Chapter 6) and state action immunity from antitrust enforcement (see Chapter 7), judicial safeguards are important to the success of competitive markets. Although national solutions to many economic regulation problems may ultimately prove inevitable, judicial limits on federal jurisdiction and incentives for overcoming the recalcitrance of state legislatures can also have some positive effects in promoting coordinated federalism solutions to difficult jurisdictional problems (see Chapter 8).

An approach to judicial review informed by deference and "clear statement" rules has many advantages, among them transparency and political accountability for regulatory decisions. However, in many instances judicial safeguards must go beyond mere deference to the political branches or clear statement rules. A basic presumption in favor of deference is appropriate in the context of judicial review of governmental liability for regulatory change, but in other instances courts must police private influence on, and selection of, the mechanisms for regulatory enforcement. Tariffs and federalism conflicts are two main contexts in which a more active process-based approach to public law issues is justified in judicial review.

* * *

A bargaining framework asks some new questions, but it certainly does not provide answers to every public law issue confronting economic regulation in infrastructure industries today. Although the questions raised by the bargaining framework are useful, in present form its recommendations are tentative. The flexibility of the approach allows for experimentation and thus may minimize errors in the adoption of the recommendations presented in this book, but the ultimate merits of the approach will ultimately depend on further study. The questions and recommendations suggested by a bargaining analysis of deregulation of telecommunications and electric power raises many issues for additional research in law, as well as for empirical study in political science and economics.

References*

Adams, Henry Carter. 1887 (January). "Relation of the State to Industrial Action." *Publications of the American Economics Association.* 1: 55.

Ahdieh, Robert B. 2004. "Law's Signal: A Cueing Theory of Law in Market Transition." *Southern California Law Review*. 77: 215.

Alexander, Barbara & The National Consumer Law Center. 1996. *Consumer Protection Proposals for Retail Electric Competition: Model Legislation and Regulations.* Boston: National Consumer Law Center.

Alexander, Gregory S. 1996. "Ten Years of Takings." *Journal of Legal Education.* 46: 586.

Alston, Lee J., Thráinn Eggertsson & Douglas C. North, eds. *Empirical Studies in Institutional Change*. Cambridge: Cambridge University Press.

Areeda, Phillip E. & Herbert Hovenkamp. 2000. *IA Antitrust Law*, Second edition. Boston: Little, Brown.

Arteburn, Norman F. 1927. "The Origin and First Test of Public Callings." *University of Pennsylvania Law Review.* 75: 411.

Austin, Regina. 1983. "The Insurance Classification Controversy." *University of Pennsylvania Law Review*. 131: 517.

Averch, Harvey & Johnson, Leland L. 1962. "Behavior of the Firm Under Regulatory Constraint." *American Economic Review*. 52: 1052.

Aviram, Amitai. 2003. "Regulation by Networks." *Brigham Young University Law Review*. 2003: 1179.

Ayres, Ian & John Braithwaite. 1992. *Responsive Regulation: Transcending the Deregulation Debate*. New York: Oxford University Press.

Ayres, Ian & Robert Gertner. 1992. "Strategic Contractual Inefficiency and the Optimal Choice of Legal Rules." *Yale Law Journal*. 101: 729.

* This references list includes all books, academic journal, and major trade press articles cited in short form throughout the book. For convenience of reference, judicial and agency cases, statutes and regulations, and some government reports are cited in complete form in text and footnotes throughout the book. These do not appear in this references list but in a separate Index of Primary Legal Authorities (p. 257). Also for convenience, popular newspaper articles are not included in this references list, but are cited in full in footnotes in the text of the book.

Baer, William J. 1997. "FTC Perspectives on Competition Policy and Enforcement Initiatives in Electric Power." Presented at the Conference on the New Rules of the Game for Electric Power: Antitrust and Anticompetitive Behavior, Bureau of Competition, Federal Trade Commission, Washington, D.C., December 4. Available at http://www.ftc.gov/speeches/other/elec1204.htm

Baker, Scott and Kimberly Krawiec. 2004. "The Penalty Default Canon." *George Washington Law Review*. 72: 663.

Baron, David & John Ferejohn. 1989. "Bargaining in Legislatures." *American Political Science Review*. 83: 1181.

Baumol, William J. & Merrill, Thomas W. 1996. "Deregulatory Takings, Breach of the Regulatory Contract, and the Telecommunications Act of 1996." *New York University Law Review*. 72: 1037.

Becker, Gary. 1983. "A Theory of Competition Among Pressure Groups for Political Influence." *Quarterly Journal of Economics*. 98: 371.

Beer, Samuel H. 1977. "Political Overload and Federalism." *Polity*. 10: 5.

Berg, Jessica Wilen. 2003. "Understanding Waiver." *Houston Law Review*. 40: 281.

Bernheim, B. Douglas & Michael D. Whinston. 1998. "Incomplete Contracts and Strategic Ambiguity." *American Economic Review*. 88: 902.

Bernstein, David E. 2003. "*Lochner*'s Legacy's Legacy." *Texas Law Review*. 82: 1.

Bernstein, Lisa. 1992. "Opting Out of the Legal System: Extra Legal Contractual Relations in the Diamond Industry." *Journal of Legal Studies*. 21: 115.

Bernstein, Lisa. 2001. "Private Commercial Law in the Cotton Industry: Creating Cooperation Through Rules, Norms and Institutions." *Michigan Law Review*. 99: 1724.

Bolze, Ray S., John C. Pierce & Linda L. Walsh, 2000. "Antitrust Law Regulation: A New Focus for a Competitive Energy Industry." *Energy Law Journal*. 21: 79.

Borenstein, Severin. 2002. "The Trouble with Electricity Markets: Understanding California's Restructuring Disaster." *Journal of Economic Perspectives*. 16(1): 191.

Borenstein, Severin & James D. Bushnell. 2000. "Electricity Restructuring: Deregulation or Reregulation?" *Regulation*. 23(2): 46.

Boudin, Michael. 1986. "Antitrust Doctrine and the Sway of Metaphor." *Georgetown Law Journal*. 75: 395.

Bouknight J. A. & David B. Raskin. 1987. "Planning for Wholesale Customer Loads in a Competitive Environment: The Obligation to Provide Wholesale Service under the Federal Power Act." *Energy Law Journal*. 8: 237.

Boyes, William J. 1976. "An Empirical Examination of the Averch-Johnson Effect." *Economic Inquiry*. 14: 25.

Bradley, Robert L., Jr. 2003. "The Origins and Development of Electric Power Regulation." In Grossman, Peter Z. & Daniel H. Cole, eds. *The End of a Natural Monopoly: Deregulation and Competition in the Electric Power Industry*. Amsterdam: Elsevier Science (JAI Imprint).

Brennan, Timothy J. & Boyd, James. 1997. "Stranded Costs, Takings, and the Law and Economics of Implicit Contracts." *Journal of Regulatory Economics*. 11: 41.

Breyer, Stephen. 1982. *Regulation and its Reform*. Cambridge, Mass.: Harvard University Press.

Brown, Stephen J. & David S. Sibley. 1986. *The Theory of Public Utility Pricing*. New York: Cambridge University Press.

Burdick, Charles K. 1911. "The Origin of the Peculiar Duties of Public Service Companies." *Columbia Law Review*. 11: 514.

Buzbee, William W. 2003. "Recognizing the Regulatory Commons: A Theory of Regulatory Gaps." *Iowa Law Review*. 89: 1.

Cain, Bruce, John Ferejohn & Morris Fiorina. 1987. *The Personal Vote: Constituency Service and Electoral Independence*. Cambridge, Mass.: Harvard University Press.

Calabresi, Guido & Douglas A. Melamed. 1972. "Property Rules, Liability Rules, and Inalienability: One View of the Cathedral." *Harvard Law Review*. 85: 1089.

Candeub, Adam. 2004. "Network Interconnection and Takings." *Syracuse Law Review*. 54: 369.

Carron, Andrew S. & Paul W. MacAvoy. 1981. *The Decline of Service in Regulated Industries*. Washington, D.C.: American Enterprise Institute.

Casson, Mark. 1997. *Information and Organization: A New Perspective on the Theory of the Firm*. New York: Clarendon Press.

Chen, Jim. 1999. "The Second Coming of *Smyth v. Ames*." *Texas Law Review*. 77: 1535.

Chen, Jim. 2000. "Standing in the Shadows of Giants: The Role of Intergenerational Equity in Telecommunications Reform." *University of Colorado Law Review*. 71: 921.

Chen, Jim. 2003a. "The Vertical Dimension of Cooperative Competition Policy." *Antitrust Bulletin*. 48: 1005.

Chen, Jim. 2003b. "Subsidized Rural Telephony and the Public Interest: A Case Study in Cooperative Federalism and Its Pitfalls." *Journal on Telecommunications & High Technology Law*. 2: 307.

Chen, Jim. 2003c. "A Vision Softly Creeping: Congressional Acquiesence and the Dormant Commerce Clause." *Minnesota Law Review*. 88: 1764.

Chen, Jim. 2004. "The Nature of the Public Utility: Infrastructure, the Market, and the Law." *Northwestern University Law Review*. 98: 1617.

Cirace, John. 1982. "An Economic Analysis of the 'State-Municipal Action' Antitrust Cases." *Texas Law Review*. 61: 481.

Coase, Ronald H. 1937. "The Nature of the Firm." *Economica*. 4: 386.

Coase, Ronald H. 1960. "The Problem of Social Costs." *Journal of Law and Economics*. 3: 1.

Coenen, Dan T. 1989. "Untangling the Market-Participant Exception to the Dormant Commerce Clause." *Michigan Law Review*. 88: 395.

Cohen, George M. 1994. "The Fault Lines in Contract Damages." *Virginia Law Review*. 80: 1225.

Cole, Daniel H. 2003. "The Regulatory Contract." in Grossman, Peter Z. & Daniel H. Cole, eds. *The End of a Natural Monopoly: Deregulation and Competition in the Electric Power Industry*. Amsterdam: Elsevier Science (JAI Imprint).

Colton, Roger. 1991. "A Cost-Based Response to Low-Income Energy Problems." *Public Utilities Fortnightly*. March 1: 31.

Colton, Roger. 1997. *The 'Obligation to Serve' and a Competitive Electric Industry*. Report of DOE Office of Economic, Electricity and Natural Gas Analysis, May.

Costello, Kenneth W. & Robert J. Graniere. 1997. *Deregulation-Restructuring: Evidence from Individual Industries.* Columbus, Ohio: National Regulatory Research Institute.

Costello, Kenneth W. & J. Rodney Lemon. 1996. *Unbundling the Retail Natural Gas Market: Current Activities and Guidance for Serving Residential and Small Consumers*. Columbus, Ohio: National Regulatory Research Institute.

Courville, Leon. 1974. "Regulation and Efficiency in the Electric Utility Industry." *Bell Journal of Economic and Management Science.* 5: 53.

Cramton, Roger C. 1986. "Demystifying Legal Scholarship." *Georgetown Law Journal.* 75: 1.

Cudahy, Richard D. 2002a. "Electric Deregulation after California: Down But Not Out." *Administrative Law Review*. 54: 333.

Cudahy, Richard D. 2002b. "Full Circle in the Formerly Regulated Industries?" *Loyola University of Chicago Law Journal.* 33: 767.

Davis, Mary J. 2002. "Unmasking the Presumption in Favor of Preemption." *Southern California Law Review*. 53: 967.

de Figueiredo, John M. & Rui J. P. de Figueiredo, Jr. 2002. "The Allocation of Resources by Interest Groups: Lobbying, Litigation and Administrative Regulation." *Business and Politics*. 4(2): 161

Dechert, W. Davis. 1984. "Has the Averch-Johnson Effect Been Theoretically Justified?" *Journal of Economic Dynamics and Control.* 8: 1.

Deisinger, Chris. 2000. "The Backlash Against Merchant Plants and the Need for a New Regulatory Model." *Electricity Journal.* 13: 51.

Demsetz, Harold. 1968. "Why Regulate Utilities?" *Journal of Law & Economics.* 11: 55.

Denning, Brannon P. 1999. "Justice Thomas, the Import-Export Clause, and *Camps Newfound/Owatonna v. Harrison*." *University of Colorado Law Review*. 70: 155.

Denning, Brannon P. 2003. "Why the Privileges and Immunities Clause of Article IV Cannot Replace the Dormant Commerce Clause Doctrine." *Minnesota Law Review*. 84: 284.

Derthick, Martha & Paul J. Quirk. 1985. *The Politics of Deregulation*. Washington, D.C.: Brookings.

Dibadj, Reza. 2004. "Saving Antitrust." *University of Colorado Law Review*. 75: 745.

Diver, Colin. 1983. "The Optimal Precision of Administrative Rules." *Yale Law Journal.* 93: 65.

Dorf, Michael H. & Charles F. Sabel. 1998. "A Constitution of Democratic Experimentalism." *Columbia Law Review*. 98: 267.

Easterbrook, Frank H. 1984. "The Limits of Antitrust." *Texas Law Review*. 63: 1.

Easterbrook, Frank H. 1988. "The Role of Original Intent in Statutory Construction." *Harvard Journal of Law and Public Policy.* 11: 59.

Eaton, Jade Alice. 1994. "Recent United States Department of Justice Actions in the Electric Utility Industry." *Connecticut Journal of International Law.* 9: 857.

Economides, Nicholas. 2003. "The Tragic Inefficiency of the M-ECPR." in Shampine, Allan L., ed. *Down to the Wire: Studies in the Diffusion and Regulation of Telecommunications Technologies*. Hauppauge, N.Y.: Nova Science Publishers.

Eggertsson, Thráinn. 1996. "A Note on the Economics of Institutions." in Alston, Lee J., Thráinn Eggertsson & Douglas C. North, eds. *Empirical Studies in Institutional Change*. Cambridge: Cambridge University Press.

Elhauge, Einer. 2002. "Preference-Eliciting Statutory Default Rules." *Columbia Law Review*. 102: 2163.

Ellickson, Robert. 1994. *Order Without Law: How Neighbors Settle Disputes*. Cambridge, Mass.: Harvard University Press.

Ely, John Hart. 1980. *Democracy and Distrust: A Theory of Judicial Review*. Cambridge, Mass.: Harvard University Press.

Ely, Richard T. 1887. "The Nature and Significance of the Corporation." *Harper's Magazine*. 75: 71.

Engel, Kristen H. 1999. "The Dormant Commerce Clause Threat to Market-Based Regulation: The Case of Electricity Deregulation." *Ecology Law Quarterly*. 26: 243.

Epstein, Richard A. 1984. "Toward a Revitalization of the Contract Clause." *University of Chicago Law Review*. 51: 703.

Epstein, Richard A. 1985. *Takings: Private Property and the Power of Eminent Domain*. Cambridge, Mass.: Harvard University Press.

Epstein, Richard A. 1995. "The Permit Power Meets the Constitution." *Iowa Law Review*. 81: 407.

Epstein, Richard A. 1997a. "A Clear View from *The Cathedral*: The Dominance of Property Rules." *Yale Law Journal*. 106: 2091, 2128.

Epstein, Richard A. 1997b. "Takings, Exclusivity and Speech: The Legacy of *PruneYard v. Robins*." *University of Chicago Law Review*. 64: 21.

Eskridge, William N., Jr. & Philip P. Frickey. 1992. "Quasi-Constitutional Law: Clear Statement Rules as Constitutional Lawmaking." *Vanderbilt Law Review*. 45: 593.

Eule, Julian N. 1982. "Laying the Dormant Commerce Clause to Rest." *Yale Law Journal*. 91: 425.

Farber, Daniel A. 1991. Legislative Deals and Statutory Bequests. *Minnesota Law Review*. 75: 667.

Farber, Daniel A. & Philip Frickey. 1991. *Law and Public Choice: A Critical Introduction*. Chicago: University of Chicago Press.

Ferrey, Steven. 1997. "Renewable Subsidies in the Age of Deregulation: State-Imposed Preferences May Have Come to the Wrong Place at the Wrong Time." *Fortnightly*. December: 22.

Fisch, Jill E. 1997. "Retroactivity and Legal Change: An Equilibrium Approach." *Harvard Law Review*. 110: 1055.

Fox-Penner, Peter. 1997. *Electric Utility Restructuring: A Guide to the Competitive Era*. Vienna, Virginia: Public Utility Reports.

Frankfurter, Felix & James Landis. 1925. "The Compact Clause of the Constitution – A Study in Interstate Adjustments." *Yale Law Journal*. 34: 685.

Freeman, Jody. 1997. "Collaborative Governance in the Administrative State." *UCLA Law Review*. 45: 1.

Freeman, Jody. 2000. "The Contracting State." *Florida State University Law Review.* 28: 155.

Friendly, Henry J. 1964. "In Praise of *Erie* – And of the New Federal Common Law." *New York University Law Review*. 39: 383.

Furubotn, Eirik G. & Rudolf Richter. 1998. *Institutions and Economic Theory: The Contribution of the New Institutional Economics*. Ann Arbor: University of Michigan Press.

Garbaum, Stephen A. 1994. "The Nature of Preemption." *Cornell Law Review*. 79: 767.

Garland, Merrick B. 1987. "Antitrust and State Action: Economic Efficiency and the Political Process." *Yale Law Journal.* 96: 486.

Gey, Steven G. 1989–90. "The Political Economy of the Dormant Commerce Clause." *NYU Review of Law & Social Change*. 17: 1.

Gifford, Daniel J. 1995. "Federalism, Efficiency, the Commerce Clause, and the Sherman Act: Why We Should Follow a Consistent Free Market Policy." *Emory Law Journal.* 44: 1227.

Gillette, Clayton. 1991. "In Partial Praise of Dillon's Rule, or, Can Public Choice Theory Justify Local Government Law?" *Chicago-Kent Law Review.* 67: 959.

Gilliam, Thomas J., Jr. 1997. "Contracting with the United States in its Role as Regulator: Striking a Bargain with an Equitable Sovereign or Capricious Siren." *Mississippi College Law Review*. 18: 247.

Glazer, Craig A. & M. Bryan Little. 1999. "The Roles of Antitrust Law and Regulatory Oversight in the Restructured Electricity Industry." *Electricity Journal.* 12: 21.

Goldberg, Victor. 1976. "Regulation and Administered Contracts." *Bell Journal of Economics.* 7: 444.

Goldsmith, Richard. 1989. "Utility Rates and 'Takings'." *Energy Law Journal.* 10: 241.

Gómez-Ibáñez, José A. 2003. *Regulating Infrastructure: Monopoly Contracts and Discretion*. Cambridge, Mass.: Harvard University Press.

Goodin, Robert E. 1982. *Political Theory and Public Policy*. Chicago: University of Chicago Press.

Goodman, James. 2003. *Blackout.* New York: North Point Press.

Gormley, William T., Jr. 1983. *The Politics of Public Utility Regulation*. Pittsburgh: University of Pittsburgh Press.

Grossman, Peter Z. 2003. "Is Anything Naturally a Monopoly?" in Grossman, Peter Z. & Daniel H. Cole, eds. *The End of a Natural Monopoly: Deregulation and Competition in the Electric Power Industry*. Amsterdam: Elsevier Science (JAI Imprint).

Grossman, Peter Z. & Daniel H. Cole. 2003. *The End of a Natural Monopoly: Deregulation and Competition in the Electric Power Industry*. Amsterdam: Elsevier Science (JAI Imprint).

Haar, Charles M. & Daniel W. Fessler. 1986. *The Wrong Side of the Tracks: A Revolutionary Rediscovery of the Common Law Tradition of Fairness in the Struggle Against Inequality*. New York: Simon & Schuster.

Hadfield, Gillian. 1999. "Of Sovereignty and Contract: Damages for Breach of Contract by the Government." *Southern California Interdisciplinary Law Journal.* 8: 467.

Hale, G. E. & Rosemary Hale. 1962. "Competition or Control VI: Application of Antitrust Laws to Regulated Industries." *University of Pennsylvania Law Review*. 111: 46.

Hall, Gus & Richard Pierce., 1997. "Retail Gas Reform: Learning from the Georgia Model." *Public Utilities Fortnightly.* April 15: 22.

Hart, Oliver & Moore, John. 1999. "Foundations of Incomplete Contracts." *Review of Economic Studies*. 66: 115.

Hart, Oliver D. 1988. "Incomplete Contracts and the Theory of the Firm." *Journal of Law, Economics and Organization.* 4: 119.

Hart, Oliver D. 1995. *Firms, Contracts, and Financial Structure*. Oxford: Oxford University Press.

Hills, Roderick M., Jr. 1999. "Dissecting the State: The Use of Federal Law to Free State and Local Officials from State Legislatures' Control." *Michigan Law Review*. 97: 1201.

Hills, Roderick M., Jr. 2003. "Against Preemption: How Federalism Can Improve the National Lawmaking Process." Working paper available at http://papers.ssrn.com/sol3/papers.cfm?abstract_id=412000.

Hirsh, Richard F. 1999. *Power Loss: The Origins of Deregulation and Restructuring in the American Electric Utility Industry*. Cambridge, Mass.: MIT Press.

Hirst, Eric & Lester Baxter. 1995. "How Stranded Will Electric Utilities Be?" *Public Utilities Fortnightly*. Feb. 15: 30–32.

Hoke, S. Candice. 1991. "Preemption Pathologies and Civic Republican Values." *Boston University Law Review*. 71: 685.

Holmes, Oliver Wendell. 1920. *Collected Legal Papers*. New York: Harcourt, Brace & Co.

Horwich, Allan. 2000. "The Neglected Relationship of Materiality and Recklessness in Actions under Rule 10b-5." *Business Lawyer*. 55: 1023.

Hovenkamp, Herbert. 1991. *Enterprise and American Law*, 1836–1937. Cambridge, Mass.: Harvard University Press.

Hovenkamp, Herbert. 1999a. *Federal Antitrust Policy: The Law of Competition and Its Practice*. St. Paul, Minnesota: West Group.

Hovenkamp, Herbert. 1999b. "The Takings Clause and Improvident Regulatory Bargains." *Yale Law Journal.* 108: 801.

Humphrey, Andrew G. 1985. "Antitrust Jurisdiction and Remedies in an Electric Utility Price Squeeze." University of Chicago Law Review. 52: 1090.

Inman, Robert P. & Daniel L. Rubinfeld. 1997. "Making Sense of the Antitrust State-Action Doctrine: Balancing Political Participation and Economic Efficiency in Regulatory Federalism." *Texas Law Review*. 75: 1203.

Isser, Steve & Steven A. Mitnick. 1998. "Enron's Battle with PECO." *Public Utilities Fortnightly* Mar. 1: 38.

Jaffe, Louis L. 1964. "Primary Jurisdiction." *Harvard Law Review*. 77: 1037.

Joskow, Paul. 1977. "Commercial Impossibility, the Uranium Market, and the Westinghouse Case." *Journal of Legal Studies.* 6: 119.

Joskow, Paul J. 2001. "California's Electricity Crisis." *Oxford Journal of Economic Policy.* 17: 365.

Joskow, Paul & Roger G. Noll. 1981. "Regulation in Theory and Practice: An Overview." in Fromm, Gary, ed. *Studies in Public Utility Regulation.* Cambridge, Massachusetts: MIT Press.

Joskow, Paul & Richard Schmalensee. 1983. *Markets for Power: An Analysis of Electrical Utility Deregulation*. Cambridge, Massachusetts: MIT Press.

Kalt, Joseph P. & Mark A. Zupan. 1984. "Capture and Ideology in the Economic Theory of Politics." *American Economic Review*. 74: 279.

Kaplow, Louis. 1985. "Extension of Monopoly Power Through Leverage." *Columbia Law Review*. 85: 515.

Kaplow, Louis. 1986. "An Economic Analysis of Legal Transitions." *Harvard Law Review*. 99: 509.

Kearney, Joseph D. & Thomas W. Merrill. 1998. The Great Transformation of Regulated Industries Law. *Columbia Law Review*. 98: 1323.

Kelly, Kevin. 1997. "New Rules for the New Economy." *Wired*. Sept.: 140, 142–43.

Kingdon, John W. 1995. *Agendas, Alternatives, and Public Policies*. Boston: Addison Wesley.

Kolasky, William J. 1999. "Network Effects: A Contrarian View." *George Mason Law Review*. 7: 577.

Komesar, Neil K. 2001. *Law's Limits: The Rule of Law and the Supply and Demand of Rights*. Cambridge: Cambridge University Press.

Kutler, Stanley. 1971. *Privilege and Creative Destruction: The Charles River Bridge Case*. Baltimore: John Hopkins University Press.

Kuttner, Robert. 1999. *Everything for Sale: The Virtues and Limits of Markets*. Chicago: University of Chicago Press.

Laffont, Jean-Jacques & Jean Tirole. 1990. "Adverse Selection and Renegotiation in Procurement." *Review of Economic Studies*. 57: 597–626.

Laffont, Jean-Jacques & Jean Tirole. 1993. *A Theory of Incentives in Procurement and Regulation*. Cambridge, Mass.: MIT Press.

Laffont, Jean-Jacques & Jean Tirole. 2000. *Competition in Telecommunications*. Cambridge, Mass.: MIT Press.

Laswell, Harold. 1971. *A Pre-View of the Policy Sciences*. New York: American Elsevier.

Lemley, Mark & David McGowan. 1998. "Legal Implications of Network Economic Effects." *California Law Review*. 86: 479.

Lesser, Jonathon A. & Malcolm D. Ainspan. 1994. "Retail Wheeling: Deja Vu All Over Again?" *The Electricity Journal*. Apr.: 34.

Levinson, Daryl. 2000. "Making Government Pay: Markets, Politics, and the Allocation of Constitutional Costs." *University of Chicago Law Review*. 67: 345.

Lewis, Tracy & Michael Poitevin. 1997. "Disclosure of Information in Regulatory Proceedings." *Journal of Law, Economics & Organization*. 13: 50.

Levy, Brian & Pablo T. Spiller. 1996. *Regulations, Institutions and Commitment: Comparative Studies of Telecommunications*. Cambridge: Cambridge University Press.

Lichtman, Douglas, Scott Baker & Kate Krause. 2000. "Strategic Disclosure in the Patent System." *Vanderbilt Law Review*. 53: 2175.

Lopatka, John E. 1984. "The Electric Utility Price Squeeze as an Antitrust Cause of Action." *UCLA Law Review*. 31: 563.

MacAvoy, Paul W., Daniel F. Spulber & Bruce Stangle. 1989. "Is Competitive Entry Free? Bypass and Partial Deregulation in Natural Gas Markets." *Yale Journal on Regulation*. 6: 209.

Macey, Jonathan R. 1986. "Promoting Public-Regarding Legislation Through Statutory Interpretation: An Interest Group Model." *Columbia Law Review*. 86: 223.

Macey, Jonathan R. 1998. "Public Choice and the Law." in Newman, Peter, ed. *The New Palgrave Dictionary of Economics and the Law*. London: United Kingdom: Macmillan Reference Limited.

Macleod, W. Bentley. 1996. "Decision, Contract, and Emotion: Some Economics for a Complex and Confusing World." *Canadian Journal of Economics*. 29: 788.

Macneil, Ian R. 1978. "Contracts: Adjustment of Long-term Economic Relations Under Classical, Neo-Classical, and Relational Contract Law." *Northwestern University Law Review*. 72: 854.

Mahoney, Paul G. & Chris William Sanchirico. 2003. "Norms, Repeated Games and the Role of Law." *California Law Review*. 91: 1281.

Malloy, Michael. 1998. "When You Wish Upon a *Winstar*: Contract Analysis and the Future of Regulatory Action." *Saint Louis University Law Journal*. 42: 409.

Markell, David L. 2000. "The Role of Deterrence-Based Enforcement in a 'Reinvented' State/Federal Relationship: The Divide Between Theory and Reality." Harvard Environmental Law Review. 24: 1.

Martimort, David, Phillip De Donder & Etienne Billette de Villemeur. 2003. "An Incomplete Contract Perspective on Public Good Provision." Toulouse Institut d'Economie Industrielle Working Paper, available at http://www.idei.fr/doc/wp/2003/public_good_provision.pdf

Martin, Robert B., III. 2003. "Sherman Shorts Outs: The Dimming of Antitrust Enforcement in the California Electricity Crisis." *Hastings Law Journal*. 55: 271.

Mashaw, Jerry. 1997. *Greed, Chaos & Governance: Using Public Choice to Improve Public Law*. New Haven, Conn.: Yale University Press.

Maskin, Eric & Jean Tirole. 1999. "Unforeseen Contingencies and Incomplete Contracts." *Review of Economic Studies*. 66: 83.

McArthur, John Burritt. 1997. "Anti-Trust in the New [De]Regulated Natural Gas Industry." *Energy Law Journal*. 18: 1.

McGreal, Paul E. 1995. "Some *Rice* with Your *Chevron*?: Presumption and Deference in Regulatory Preemption." *Case Western Reserve Law Review*. 45: 823.

McGreal, Paul E. 1998. "The Flawed Economics of the Dormant Commerce Clause." *William & Mary Law Review*. 39: 1191.

McNollgast. 1992. "Positive Canons: The Role of Legislative Bargains in Statutory Interpretation." *Georgetown Law Journal*. 80: 705.

McUsic, Molly S. 1996. "The Ghost of *Lochner*: Modern Takings Doctrine and Its Impact on Economic Legislation." *Boston University Law Review*. 76: 605.

Merrill, Thomas W. 1999. "Supplier of Last Resort: Who, What, Why?" *Public Utilities Fortnightly*. July 15: 18.

Merrill, Thomas W. & Henry E. Smith. 2002. "The Property/Contract Interface." *Columbia Law Review*. 101: 773.

Michaels, Robert J. 1996. "Stranded Investments, Stranded Intellectuals." *Regulation*. 47: 51.

Michelman, Frank. 1968. "Property, Utility, and Fairness: Comments on the Ethical Foundations of 'Just Compensation' Law." *Harvard Law Review*. 80: 1165.

Michelman, Frank. 1988. "Takings 1987." *Columbia Law Review.* 88: 1600.
Mishkin, Paul J. 1957. "The Variousness of 'Federal Law': Competence and Discretion in the Choice of National and State Rules for Decision." *University of Pennsylvania Law Review*. 105: 797.
Mitnick, Barry M. 1980. *The Political Economy of Regulation: Creating, Designing, and Removing Regulatory Forms*. New York: Columbia University Press.
Movsesian, Mark. 1998. "Are Statutes Really 'Legislative Bargains?' The Failure of the Contract Analogy in Statutory Interpretation." *North Carolina Law Review*. 76: 1145.
Mueller, Milton J., Jr. 1997. *Universal Service: Competition, Interconnection, and Monopoly in the Making of the American Telephone System.* Washington, D.C.: American Enterprise Institute.
Nagle, John Copeland. 1995. "Waiving Sovereign Immunity in an Age of Clear Statement Rules." *Wisconsin Law Review*. 1995: 771.
Nelson, Caleb. 2000. "Preemption." *Virginia Law Review*. 86: 225.
Noam, Eli. 1997. "Will Universal Service and Common Carriage Survive the Telecommunications Act of 1996?" *Columbia Law Review.* 97: 955.
Noll, Roger. 1971. *Reforming Regulation: Studies in the Regulation of Economic Activity*. Washington, D.C.: Brookings.
Norlander, Gerald A. 1998. "Retail Choice: A Race to the Bottom." *Public Utilities Fortnightly.* Jan. 1: 8 (letter to the editor).
North, Douglass C. 1996. "Epilogue: Economic Performance Through Time." in Alston, Lee J., Thráinn Eggertsson & Douglas C. North, eds. *Empirical Studies in Institutional Change*. Cambridge: Cambridge University Press.
Norton, Floyd & Mark Spivak. 1985. "The Wholesale Service Obligation of Electric Utilities." *Energy Law Journal.* 6: 179.
Note. 1923. "The Sherman Act as Applied to Railroads Regulated Under the Interstate Commerce Act." *Harvard Law Review.* 36: 456.
Note. 1953. "Recent Cases: Antitrust – Primary Jurisdiction Applied in Action Against Members of Regulated Industries." *University of Pennsylvania Law Review*. 101: 678.
Pace, Joe D. 1987. "Wheeling and the Obligation to Serve." *Energy Law Journal.* 8: 265.
Page, William H. 1981. "Antitrust, Federalism and the Regulatory Process." *Boston University Law Review*. 61: 1099.
Page, William H. 1987. "Interest Groups, Antitrust, and State Regulation: *Parker v. Brown* in the Economic Theory of Legislation." *Duke Law Journal.* 1987: 618.
Page, William H. & John E. Lopatka. 1993. "State Regulation in the Shadow of Antitrust: *FTC v. Ticor Title Insurance Co*." *Supreme Court Economic Review*. 3: 189.
Pechman, Carl. 1993. *Regulating Power: The Economics of Electricity in the Information Age*. Dordrecht: Kluwer Academic Press.
Peltzman, Sam. 1976. "Toward a More General Theory of Regulation." *Journal of Law and Economics.* 19: 211.

Peltzman, Sam. 1989. "The Economic Theory of Regulation after a Decade of Deregulation." *Brookings Papers on Economic Activity: Microeconomics.* 1989: 1.

Percival, Robert V. 1995. "Environmental Federalism: Historical Roots and Contemporary Models." *Maryland Law Review*. 54: 1141.

Persson, Torsten, Gerard Roland & Guido Tabellini. 1997. "Separation of Powers and Political Accountability." *Quarterly Journal of Economics.* 112: 1163.

Peterson, Andrea. 1989. "The Takings Clause: In Search of Underlying Principles. Part I – A Critique of Current Takings Clause Doctrine." *California Law Review*. 77: 1299.

Peterson, H. Craig. 1975. "An Empirical Test of Regulatory Effects." *Bell Journal of Economics and Management Science.* 6: 111.

Phillips, Charles F. 1993. *The Regulation of Public Utilities*. Fairfax, Virginia: Public Utility Reports.

Picker, Randal C. 2002. "Understanding Statutory Bundles: Does the Sherman Act Come with the 1996 Telecommunications Act?" University of Chicago John M. Olin Program in Law & Economics, Working Paper No. 177, 2002. Available at http://www.law.uchicago.edu/Picker/Papers/Manhattan200.pdf

Pierce, Richard J., Jr. 1984. "Regulatory Treatment of Mistakes in Retrospect: Cancelled Plants and Excess Capacity." *University of Pennsylvania Law Review*. 132: 497.

Pierce, Richard J., Jr. 1988. "Reconstituting the Natural Gas Industry from Wellhead to Burnertip." *Energy Law Journal.* 9: 1.

Pierce, Richard J., Jr. 1989. "Public Utility Regulatory Takings: Should the Judiciary Attempt to Police the Political Institutions?" *Georgetown Law Journal.* 77: 2031.

Pierce, Richard J., Jr. 1991. "The Unintended Effects of Judicial Review of Agency Rules: How Federal Courts Have Contributed to the Electricity Crisis of the 1990s." *Administrative Law Review.* 43: 7.

Pierce, Richard J., Jr. 1994. "The State of the Transition to Competitive Markets in Natural Gas and Electricity." *Energy Law Journal.* 15: 323.

Piraino, Thomas A., Jr. 1997. "A Proposed Antitrust Analysis of Telecommunications Joint Ventures." *Wisconsin Law Review.* 1997: 639.

Pitofsky, Robert. 1997. "Competition Policy in Communications Industries: New Antitrust Approaches." Remarks presented at Glasser Legal Works Seminar on Competitive Policy in Communications Industries: New Antitrust Approaches, Federal Trade Commission, Washington, D.C., March 10. Available at http://www.ftc.gov/speeches/pitofsky/newcomm.htm

Platt, Harold. 1991. *The Electric City: Energy and the Growth of the Chicago Area 880–1930.* Chicago: University of Chicago Press.

Pleatt, George R. 1998. "Should Metering Stay at the Stand-Alone Disco?" *Public Utilities Fortnightly.* Feb. 1.

Poirier, Marc R. 2002. "The Virtue of Vagueness in Takings Doctrine." *Cardozo Law Review*. 24: 93.

Posner, Eric. 1995. "Contract Law in the Welfare State: A Defense of the Unconscionability Doctrine, Usury Laws, and Related Limits on the Freedom to Contract." *Journal of Legal Studies.* 24: 283.

Posner, Eric. 2003. "Economic Analysis of Contract Law after Three Decades: Success or Failure?" *Yale Law Journal.* 112: 829.

Posner, Richard A. 1974. "Theories of Economic Regulation." *Bell Journal of Economics and Management Science.* 5: 335.

Posner, Richard A. 1979. "The Chicago School of Antitrust Analysis." *University of Pennsylvania Law Review*. 127: 925.

Posner, Richard & Andrew Rosenfield. 1977. "Impossibility and Related Doctrines in Contract Law: An Economic Analysis." *Journal of Legal Studies.* 6: 83.

Priest, George. 1992. "The Origins of Utility Regulation and the 'Theories of Regulation' Debate." *Journal of Law & Economics.* 36: 289.

Quirk, Paul J. 1981. *Industry Influence in Federal Regulatory Agencies*. Princeton, N.J.: Princeton University Press.

Robinson, Gustavus H. 1928. "The Public Utility Concept in American Law." *Harvard Law Review.* 41: 277.

Rockefeller John D., IV. 1991. "A Call for Action: The Pepper Commission's Blueprint for Health Care Reform." *Journal of the American Medical Association.* 265: 2507.

Rodden, Jonathan & Susan Rose-Ackerman. 1997. "Does Federalism Preserve Markets?" *Virginia Law Review*. 83: 1521.

Rose-Ackerman, Susan. 1980. "Risk Taking and Reelection: Does Federalism Promote Innovation?" *Journal of Legal Studies.* 9: 593.

Rose-Ackerman, Susan. 1988. "Against Ad Hocery: A Comment on Michelman." *Columbia Law Review*. 88: 1697.

Rose-Ackerman, Susan. 1992. "Regulatory Takings: Policy Analysis and Democratic Principles." in Merucro, Nicholas, ed. *Taking Property and Just Compensation: Law and Economic Perspectives of the Takings Issue.* Dordrecht: Kluwer Academic Press.

Rose-Ackerman, Susan & Jim Rossi. 2000. "Disentangling Deregulatory Takings." *Virginia Law Review*. 86: 1435.

Rossi, Jim. 1994. "Redeeming Judicial Review: The Hard Look Doctrine and Federal Regulatory Efforts to Restructure the Electric Utility Industry." *Wisconsin Law Review*. 1994: 763.

Rossi, Jim. 1997. "Participation Run Amok: The Costs of Mass Participation for Deliberative Agency Decisionmaking." *Northwestern University Law Review.* 92: 173.

Rossi, Jim. 1998a. "The Common Law 'Duty to Serve' and Protection of Consumers in an Age of Competitive Retail Public Utility Restructuring." *Vanderbilt Law Review* 51: 1233.

Rossi, Jim. 1998b. "The Irony of Deregulatory Takings." *Texas Law Review*. 77: 297.

Rossi, Jim. 2002. "The Electric Power Deregulation Fiasco: Looking to Regulatory Federalism to Promote a Balance Between Markets and the Provision of Public Goods." *Michigan Law Review*. 100: 1768.

Rossi, Jim. 2003. "Lowering the Filed Tariff Shield: Judicial Enforcement for a Deregulatory Era." *Vanderbilt Law Review*. 56: 1591.

Rossi, Jim. 2004. "Debilitating Doctrine: How the Filed Rate Policy Wreaks Havoc – And What Courts Can Do About It." *Public Utilities Fortnightly*, November: 16.

Rossi, Jim. Forthcoming 2005. "Dual Constitutions and Constitutional Duels." *William & Mary Law Review.*

Rouse, Michael A. 1990. "A Re-Evaluation of the "Filed Rate" Doctrine in Light of Revised Regulatory Policy and Carriers' Practices: *INF, Ltd. v. Spectro Alloys Corp.*" *Creighton Law Review*. 23: 669.

Rubin, Edward L. & Malcolm Feeley. 1994. "Federalism: Some Notes on a National Neurosis." *UCLA Law Review*. 41: 903.

Rubin, Paul H., Christopher Curran & John Curran. 2001. "Litigation versus Legislation: Forum Shopping by Rent-Seekers." *Public Choice*. 107: 295.

Ruhl, J. B. & James Salzman. 2003. "Regulatory Accretion in the Administrative State. *Georgetown Law Journal.* 91: 75.

Santa, Donald F., Jr. 2000. "Who Needs What, and Why? Reporting and Disclosure Obligations in Emerging Competitive Electricity Markets." *Energy Law Journal.* 21: 1.

Savage, Leonard J. 1972. *The Foundations of Statistics.* New York: Dover Publications.

Schelling, Thomas. 1980. *Strategy of Conflict*, Second edition. Cambridge, Mass.: Harvard University Press.

Schwartz, Jeffrey D. 1999. "The Use of Antitrust State Action Doctrine in the Deregulated Electric Utility Industry." *American University Law Review*. 48: 1449.

Schwartz, Joshua I. 1997. "Assembling *Winstar*: Triumpth of the Ideal of Congruence in Government Contracts Law?" *Public Contract Law Journal.* 26: 481.

Seidenfeld, Mark. 2004. "Pyrrhic Political Penalties: Why the Public Would Lose Under the 'Penalty Default Canon.'" *George Washington Law Review*. 72: 724.

Shepsle, Kenneth A. 1992. "Congress is a 'They,' Not an 'It': Legislative Intent as an Oxymoron." *International Review of Law & Economics.* 12: 239.

Sidak, J. Gregory & Daniel Spulber. 1997. *Deregulatory Takings and the Regulatory Contract: The Transformation of Network Industries in the United States.* New York: Cambridge University Press.

Sillin, John O. 2003. "Why We Fell into the Heart of Darkness." *Public Utilities Fortnightly*. September 15: 30.

Silverstein, Eileen. 1991. "Against Preemption in Labor Law." *Connecticut Law Review*. 24: 1.

Simon, Herbert. 1961. *Administrative Behavior*, Second edition. New York: Macmillan.

Simons, Kenneth W. 2002. "Reflections on Assumption of the Risk." *UCLA Law Review*. 50: 481.

Simpson, James B. & Sarah D. Strum. 1991. "How a Good Samaritan? Federal Income Tax Exemption for Charitable Hospitals Reconsidered." *University of Puget Sound Law Review.* 14: 633.

Singer, Joseph. 1996. "No Right to Exclude: Public Accommodations and Private Property." *Northwestern University Law Review.* 90: 1283.

Smith, Vernon. 1993. "Can Electric Power – A 'Natural Monopoly' – Be Deregulated?" in Landsberg, Hans H., ed. *Making National Energy Policy*. Washington, D.C.: Resources for the Future.

Sosnov, Leonard N. 2000. "Separation of Powers Shell Game: The Federal Witness Immunity Act." *Temple Law Review*. 73: 171.

Spann, Robert M. 1974. "Rate of Return Regulation and Efficiency in Production: An Empirical Test of the Averch-Johnson Thesis." *Bell Journal of Economic and Management Science*. 5: 38.

Speidel, Richard. 1981. "Court-Imposed Price Adjustments Under Long-Term Supply Contracts." *Northwestern University Law Review*. 76: 369, 381–94.

Spence, David B. & Paula Murray. 1999. "The Law, Economics, and Politics of Federal Preemption Analysis: A Quantitative Analysis." *California Law Review*. 87: 1125.

Spitzer, Matthew. 1988. "Antitrust, Federalism, and the Rational Choice Political Economy: A Critique of Capture Theory." *Southern California Law Review*. 61: 1293.

Spulber, Daniel F. & Christopher S. Yoo. 2003. Access to Networks: Constitutional and Economic Connections. *Cornell Law Review*. 88: 885.

Stearns, Maxell L. 2003. "A Beautiful Mend: A Game Theoretical Analysis of the Dormant Commerce Clause Doctrine." *William & Mary Law Review*. 45: 1.

Stewart, Richard B. 1990. "Madison's Nightmare." *University of Chicago Law Review*. 57: 335.

Stigler, George. 1971. "The Theory of Economic Regulation." *Bell Journal of Economic and Management Science*. 2: 3.

Stigler, George & Claire Friedland. 1962. "What Can Regulators Regulate? The Case of Electricity." *Journal of Law & Economics*. 5: 1.

Sugden, Robert. 1995. "A Theory of Focal Points." *Economic Journal*. 105: 533.

Sullivan, Lawrence A. 1992. "Section 2 of the Sherman Act and Vertical Strategies by Dominant Firms." *Southwestern University Law Review*. 21: 1227.

Sunstein, Cass. 1989. "Interpreting Statutes in the Regulatory State." *Harvard Law Review*. 103: 405.

Sunstein, Cass. 1995. "Incompletely Theorized Agreements." *Harvard Law Review*. 108: 1733.

Symposium. 2003. "Is There an Ideal Way to Deal with the Non-Ideal World of Legal Change?" *Journal of Contemporary Legal Issues*. 13: 1.

Talley, Eric. 2001. "Disclosure Norms." *University of Pennsylvania Law Review*. 149: 1955.

Tirole, Jean. 2002. *The Theory of Industrial Organization*. Cambridge, Mass.: MIT Press.

Tomain, Joseph P. & Sidney Shapiro. 1997. "Analyzing Government Regulation." *Administrative Law Review*. 39: 377.

U.S. Energy Information Administration. 1997. *Electricity Prices in a Competitive Environment: Marginal Cost Pricing of Generation Services and Financial Status of Electric Utilities – A Preliminary Analysis Through 2015*. Washington, D.C.: U.S. Department of Energy.

Van Alstine, Michael P. 2002. "The Costs of Legal Change." *UCLA Law Review*. 49: 789

Van Doren, Peter & Jerry Taylor. 2004. "Rethinking Restructuring." *Public Utilities Fortnightly*. February: 12.

von Mehren, Robert B. 1954. "The Antitrust Laws and Regulated Industries: The Doctrine of Primary Jurisdiction." *Harvard Law Review.* 67: 929.

Watts, Duncan J. 2003. *Six Degrees of Separation: The Science of a Connected Age.* New York: W.W. Norton & Co.

Weaver, Jacqueline. 2004. "Can Energy Markets Be Trusted?" *Houston Business and Tax Law Journal.* 4: 1.

Weiser, Philip J. 1999. "*Chevron*, Cooperative Federalism, and Telecommunications Reform." *Vanderbilt Law Review*. 52: 1.

Weiser, Philip J. 2001a. "Federal Common Law, Cooperative Federalism, and the Enforcement of the Telcom Act." *New York University Law Review*. 76: 1692.

Weiser, Philip J. 2001b. "Towards a Constitutional Architecture for Cooperative Federalism." *North Carolina Law Review*. 79: 663.

Weiser, Philip J. 2003. "*Goldwasser*, The Telecom Act, and Reflections on Antitrust Remedies." *Administrative Law Review.* 55: 1.

White, Matthew W. 1996. "Power Struggles: Explaining Deregulatory Reforms in Electricity Markets." *Brookings Papers: Microeconomics*. 1996: 201.

Wiley, John Shepard, Jr. 1986. "A Capture Theory of Antitrust Federalism." *Harvard Law Review.* 99: 713.

Williamson, Oliver. 1975. *Markets and Hierarchies: Analysis and Antitrust Implications.* New York: Free Press.

Williamson, Oliver. 1976. "Franchise Bidding for Natural Monopolies – In General and with Respect to CATV." *Bell Journal of Economics.* 7: 73.

Williamson, Oliver. 1979. "Transaction Cost Economics: The Governance of Contractual Relations." *Journal of Law & Economics.* 22: 233.

Williamson, Oliver. 1996a. *The Mechanisms of Governance.* New York: Oxford University Press.

Williamson, Oliver. 1996b. "Response: Deregulatory Takings and the Breach of the Regulatory Contract: Some Precautions." *New York University Law Review*. 71: 1007.

Wright, Ronald. 1996. "When Do We Want Incomplete Agreements: A Comment on Sunstein's Holmes Devise Lecture." *Wake Forest Law Review*. 31: 459.

Wyman, Bruce. 1903. "The Law of the Public Callings as a Solution of the Trust Problem." *Harvard Law Review.* 17: 156, 161.

Young, Ernest A. 1999. "Preemption at Sea." *George Washington Law Review*. 67: 273.

Yoo, John C. 1998. "Sounds of Sovereignty: Defining Federalism in the 1990s." *Indiana Law Review.* 32: 27.

Zajac, Edward E. 1995. *The Political Economy of Fairness*. Cambridge, Massachusetts: MIT Press.

Index of Primary Legal Authorities

CASES

CONSTITUTIONS, STATUTES, REGULATIONS AND OTHER MATERIALS

Subject Index